LOOK TO
THIS DAY

Books by Wilma Dykeman

LOOK TO
THIS DAY

By Wilma Dykeman

HOLT, RINEHART AND WINSTON

NEW YORK   CHICAGO   SAN FRANCISCO

Some of this material was first
published in the *News-Sentinel*
of Knoxville, Tennessee.

Designer: Vincent Torre
8684805
Printed in the United States of America

"Look to this day!
For it is life, the very life of life . . .
For yesterday is already a dream, and tomorrow
    is only a vision;
But today, well lived, makes every yesterday
A dream of happiness, and every tomorrow a
    vision of hope."

                         —From the Sanskrit

"Only that day dawns to which we are awake."

                         —HENRY THOREAU

LOOK TO
THIS DAY

When a visitor comes up our driveway between forsythia bushes and tamarack, mimosa trees and crepe myrtle, and stops his car under the broad limbs of an old elm tree, if he walks across the lawn and up three front steps, then pauses and turns, in the distance, facing south, he will see the entire range of the Great Smoky Mountains.

That is, if it is a clear day he will see the mountains. Then they may stand out sharply, a rugged spine marking the dividing line between North Carolina and Tennessee. Their green forested slopes and blue pinnacles may seem quite near and friendly.

At another time, if the day is misty with rain or hazy with Indian summer, the mountains may recede into the distance and merge at some inexact point with the gray sky itself.

Or, if there has been snow, the peaks may loom up like forbidding monarchs, each scooped-out hollow of their sides appearing as unapproachable as the craters of the moon.

When the first sun glints along their icy crests, and when the purple shadows of an early winter sunset creep up the steep inclines, the mountains are aloof, remote, and detached from any man-made world.

Our house is on the crest of a hill, with other homes nearby. But there are some four acres surrounding us: lawn and trees, vegetable garden and flower beds, and a wooded bluff which falls steeply down to a river at the foot of the hill. The river rises clear and bold in the high mountains of North Carolina and Tennessee, but by the time it comes to us its waters are brown and polluted and we have little joy of it.

Across the river is the town of Newport, forty miles east of Knoxville, Tennessee. Our house is in the town, and yet not so in many ways. This is home for my husband and me and our two sons.

We have another home, too. Sixty miles east, in North Carolina, near Asheville but five miles in the country, is the home where I lived as a child. My mother, our boys' grandmother and their stoutest advocate, a widow for more than thirty years, lives here, and we are often with her.

There are sixteen acres in this place: a rolling meadow edged by grapevines, an old apple orchard and steep wooded hillside. A bridge between thick rhododendron bushes and tall white pines crosses the stream in the front yard, and nearby is a pool fed by a spring at the base of a large old oak tree. The stone and concrete edges of the wide shallow pond have been softened by moss and vines that the years have brought to grow there. I can remember when that pool seemed as large as a sea to me and when its cycles of life— tadpoles and frogs, minnows and fish, dragonflies and lizards —held me fascinated for long hours during many seasons.

Dark green laurel bushes, wild azaleas that flame red and yellow in the spring, galax and trillium—all these and a variety of other shrubs, trees, plants flourish here.

These acres are surrounded by steep hills. And so, at one

home we are on a crest, looking out upon a long, sweeping prospect of distant mountain ranges. At the other home we are in a green wooded valley, with the sound of a rushing stream, in the midst of hidden pockets of beauty. We should hate to have to choose which of the two we prefer, for by their combination we come to a whole view: the near and the distant, the intimate and the panoramic, the spacious and the specific.

We look out upon them from a distance, and we view them from within at their very heart, these Great Smoky Mountains, this Blue Ridge country, which is the background for our own search for the whole life.

Frequently we go away. Fresh scenes, different modes of life, other people and their ideas, other countries and their past—all are of interest to us. So we go wandering down a mountain path, along a superhighway, across an ocean. Looking. Listening. Tasting. Smelling. Feeling. Not so intensely as we might; not so often as we would like. But often enough to keep both the staying and the going fresh.

For we always return. We have roots. In a time when rootlessness is not only a vogue but a way of life, we hope that our roots do not make us smaller, but larger human beings. We hope they make possible not a provincial but a universal vision.

This grows precariously lofty. The simple life, wary of needless complication, touched with sophistication and concern, makes no claim to Vision, only to squints here and there of the possibilities of our lives.

Contrary to popular belief, simplicity is neither easy, common, nor inexpensive. In dress, an annual report, or a style of life, its achievement is difficult, rare, and costly in effort and taste.

Its satisfactions are unique—personal and permanent at a moment and in a world where all seems to grow increasingly impersonal and impermanent.

The simple life begins in nature and ends in human nature and seeks an elemental experience of each. It rejects the gaudy "necessities" and the trivial ornamentations by which we separate ourselves from the earth, the wind, the woods, and water, which are still man's natural habitat, despite his proliferation of concrete city canyons and labyrinths of asphalt and miasmic smogs.

It renounces the dozens of elaborate deceptions by which we separate ourselves from one another. It seeks the essential rather than the sensational in our human relationships, despite a nationally intensified appetite for the gross, the obvious, the meaningless encounter.

The simple life breaks a fresh crust of bread—and finds nourishment for the spirit.

The simple life listens to an old man's reminiscence—and touches the continuity at the heart of our innermost hope.

The simple life discovers a clump of fragile green ferns flourishing in a winter woods—and acknowledges the wonder of all living things.

The simple life stirs the dust of strange city streets—and recognizes a familiar face; it glimpses chaos at the heart of self-sufficiency, and plucks a festering thorn from the flesh of fleeting beauty.

Its triumph is in personal discovery of the truth that life can be found only when it is lost, that the greatness of our adventure is achieved by awareness of the small landmarks which light our daily way.

And yet—is it perhaps already as extinct as the proud passenger pigeons that once inhabited our land? Or is it simply in retreat, vanishing down the frantic highroads of power and conflict, the comfortable aisles of luxury, the congested freeways of commerce and recreation and frustration?

To pause—and look. To wait—and listen. To laugh or despair, not by proxy but for one's self—to choose. That is the freedom of the simple life, its discipline and its release. It is a way of being and becoming.

It is a freedom from self to a larger field of vision, a discipline of ideas rather than an enslavement to things, a release into that innate simplicity which is twin to the infinite complexity of the universe.

A toast! To both the sophisticated and the innocent, the believers and the doubters: Look to this day!

An invitation, too, to share the turning of a year—beginning with one summer, at home and abroad in this country, ending with the following summer abroad and at home in Europe.

Walking out in the cool of the evening I was ambushed by the sweet, heavy, summer smell of honeysuckle. Yesterday that odor was not here. Tonight it drifts around me in a current of air heady with warmth and memory.

Along the back reaches of the lawn, between forsythia bushes, through the tall hedge and over one trellis, honeysuckle has twined its tough tentacles. Untended, unnoticed, unwanted, it has come; now it flourishes.

The odor of honeysuckle is one of the richest perfumes of nature. It suggests the leisure of long summer nights full of moonlight, the sounds of children running to catch fireflies on the lawn, friendly talk on patios and porches.

If our whiffs of honeysuckle were bottled by the dram and sold for dollars (named Vampire or Playgirl or Careless Love perhaps?), would we cherish it more?

For one perfect moment, suspended between the day's rush and the night's rest, between heat and dew, I was happy that none of the chemicals we had tried had completely withered the stubborn honeysuckle. In memory it will always remain green, its fragrance the essence of summer.

The chores of the season—how relentlessly they arrive. How faithfully they await our attention, or, more accurately, our time and muscle.

Only yesterday (I might concede it was last month, but surely not a half-year ago?) I finished getting the last all-wool garment thoroughly freed from the smell of last summer's mothballs and completely smoothed from the smash of last summer's storage. Only yesterday the porch and yard furniture was finally stacked away for shelter from rain and snow and storm. And I'm sure it was only yesterday that the whirr of the lawn mower was silenced and the charcoal broiler was stashed away for a rest.

Yet here we are today lugging all these things back to their proper posts for another season of sun. This time we are going to make it in one big push: no dallying about with a chair or two at a time, a sweater or suit or skirt packed away now and then. We will get all the winter storage stored, all the summer necessities unstored, and we'll get the show on the road.

The porch blossoms anew with wicker and chrome and cushions. The picnic area comes alive with redwood and metal. The outdoors suddenly becomes the third level of our house, without the limitations of walls, without the confinement (or protection—however you choose to view it) of ceilings.

And I glance at the comfortable lounges and chairs and wonder if there will be any time to sit in them—just sit. Will the summer scamper by as quickly as the winter, and leave me still planning to enjoy the lazy heat when frost is already threatening?

Closets become light and roomy now. Bulky overcoats and jackets, sprawling boots, scattered gloves and scarves and toboggan caps make room for thin materials, gauzy wisps of covering, brief swim suits, sandals created from strips and thongs and air. Madras bleeds on every hanger; and drip-dry fabrics dominate the contents of luggage for every projected vacation journey. Will I just be discovering what has been outgrown, worn out when summer whirls to an end—and I'm shaking out the wrinkles again?

I am meeting the chores of the season head on, confronting them with candor and determination. Maybe I'll have them finished by August this summer—and be ready for Decoration Day when Labor Day arrives!

Webster's Unabridged Dictionary defines filibuster: "A member of a legislative or deliberative body who, in opposition to the proposed action of the majority, obstructs or prevents action by the extreme use of dilatory tactics, such as speaking merely to consume time."

I know very little, except what I read in the papers, about legislative filibusters. But if a family may be called a "deliberative body," then I am an experienced hand at filibusters. For obstructing or preventing action of the majority, there is no expert in Washington who can outmaneuver a reluctant boy on Sunday morning.

Small voice from the next room: "Do I have to wear this white shirt?"

Parent (with all the decisiveness it is possible to muster): "Yes."

Long and decidedly audible sigh.

Parent (hurriedly, with preoccupation): "Go ahead and get dressed. We're late this morning." (What morning aren't we late?)

After a long silence: "This shirt has starch in it!"

"Of course." (Then, with the diversionary tactic of humor.) "What did you expect it to have? Tapioca?"

No laughter. "I hate starch."

"Put your shirt on." (The brisk, all-business approach.) "Finish dressing. We're already late."

A longer silence. "There's starch in the collar, too."

"Of course there's starch in the collar. Especially in the collar. Now will you please be good enough to DRESS?"

"It scratches my neck."

"You won't notice it as soon as we've left home." (The psychological approach.) "As soon as we're with other people, you'll forget all about your shirt and how you feel."

"You want to bet?"

(Parent doesn't like the odds on this, and ignores it as a rhetorical gambit.)

"This shirt isn't made right—"

"I bought that shirt two weeks ago; it's a very good shirt; I thought you'd be pleased. . . ." (The martyr approach. A last resort, but all is fair in this sort of love and war.)

"I'm not pleased with it. I hate it. It's too tight around the collar and it cuts off my breath. . . ." (Two can play at this martyr role.)

"See here! You get dressed this minute. . . ." (The descent to direct threat hovers in the atmosphere.)

"If I could wear another white shirt . . ."

Parent (sighing): "I thought you meant you wouldn't wear ANY white shirt. . . ."

Son: (Sighing) "I meant THIS old shirt. . . ."

"Well, then . . ."

And so, on a technicality, the contest is a draw. At least the parent thinks so—until she looks at the clock and realizes the time for attending services has long since passed.

The path wound between tall old trees, thick patches of rhododendron, and frequent tangles of dog hobble. Its twists and turns followed beside the headwaters of the Tuckaseigee River, deep in the mountains of western North Carolina.

We were on an overnight fishing trip to a camp set in the midst of twelve thousand acres of woods and silence. The fireplaces of the gray weathered hill cabin converted to a camp were stacked with green logs against the evening's chill.

The clear waters and deep pools of the river were stocked with wily trout. By day the sun was bright against a blue sky and by night the stars were as clear and close as crystal balls. Who could ask for more?

I followed the path that ran beside the river. All the others of our party had gone on ahead, searching for a pool to their liking where they could cast their flies; or they had fallen behind, trying their luck and skill at a certain ledge or sandy bit of beach.

They were intent on fishing for trout. I was doing another kind of fishing. The rod I carried in front of me was a deceptive banner. It made my wanderings in this fisherman's paradise legitimate. It gave me an understandable excuse for loitering in the woods at midmorning or late afternoon. But the fish in Tuckaseigee were never safer than when I ventured forth with line and bait.

The toe of my shoe broke a tiny toadstool in the rich dank humus. I stooped and picked it up and turned it over in my hand. Its vivid orange color glowed like a coal in a hot fire, and its texture was like velvet. The underside of the mushroom was crimped with countless pleats. Such perfection seemed impossible.

I ran my fingers along the little velvet ridges and studied the symmetry of stem and cap and the deep orange coloring. Then I looked at the lush profusion of growth, from smallest fern to towering spruce all around me, and I considered that each fraction of each growing thing held this same perfection and proportion.

I considered, too, how easily and carelessly the toe of my shoe had broken it.

That night, long after I had tossed the little orange mushroom aside, we stood out under the late-summer sky. The brilliance of the stars was at once near and far away. And marvelously as we were made, with the intricacy of heart and lung and blood and brain and senses, how small we stood beneath that starlit dome.

"Catch anything today?" one of our friends asked.

"Not a single fish," I answered.

Are you familiar with the Law of Mushrooming Returns? I suspect that you have encountered it in action, if not with its formal title. Let me explain.

I bought new curtains for one of the bedrooms at our house. "A simple enough undertaking," you say? It seemed so to me. I had planned to take down the old curtains, wash off window sills and rods, hang the new ones, and have the whole operation completed within twenty or thirty minutes.

Not so.

One pair of curtains (after an hour's skirmish with hooks and rods) finally hung by the bed. It seemed a shame for part of the material's design to be hidden, and it occurred to me that the bed might really look better against the opposite wall. I called for help and we made the change.

With the bed in a new place, the chair that had stood at its foot had to be moved, of course, and the desk sitting right beside the bed made this side of the room now seem top-heavy. We shifted the desk to another wall. This called for rearranging a chest of drawers.

These various moves revealed the inadequacy of the rug that had been used, so we brought one from the study into the bedroom.

The new and larger rug necessitated removing one book-case from the room. (By now it was lunchtime and we took a meal break, then went back to hanging our curtains.) The color of this new rug called for a different bedspread, and so I began to form plans for a new decorating scheme.

It finally seemed that the new curtains would not match well with these latest colors and I would have to shift the curtains, in a few days, to an altogether different part of the house.

Meanwhile, back at the study, we had to rearrange the furniture in that room to suit the smaller rug, which was switched in there. We shifted pictures and one mirror accordingly. We're shopping for another chair. In fact, my purchase of two pairs of curtains achieved a complete second-story renovation.

This experience has led me to ponder similar ones in many

areas of everyday life. What about that apparently innocent little blouse a woman buys, then discovers she is searching for a suit to match the blouse, and finally winds up with shoes and pocket book and gloves to complete the ensemble?

Or what about the man who has purchased what seems to be a nice self-contained piece of land, only to discover that he needed the adjoining couple of acres for an "approach" or "protection," and finally decided that the lot on the opposite side would also be nice for "rounding out" his property? (And if he has bought that big power mower for one stretch of grass, he might as well make it pay its way and mow a good healthy swath.)

These are examples of the Law of Mushrooming Returns —in contrast to the law of diminishing returns, that point beyond which any investment of money or labor will not yield a proportionate increase in production. My new law recognizes that point at which some simple investment or undertaking brings about activity out of all foreseeable proportion to the original intention.

Cleaning out desk drawers, calling up old school friends, or buying curtains—almost anything can set this law into action, for better or for worse.

A generous amount of conversation is devoted to our general inability to remember. Places, dates, especially people's names: "I don't know what's happening to me. I just can't seem to remember anything any more!"

There are courses available which promise an improvement in memory. After two weeks, or three weeks, or sometimes six weeks (for the upper-bracket executive course) of intensive study and work, you are assured of an ability to remember which will be second only to that of the full-grown African elephant. That is, if you can remember to get to the class on time each night.

What I propose, however, is the opposite of training in remembrance. I suggest a course in forgetfulness.

Think of all the excess baggage with which we encumber our minds and hearts and burden our todays and tomorrows.

There are the wrongs—real or imagined—inflicted on us by others. How vividly most of us can recollect these! I have heard people even boast of their own or a relative's tenacious memory concerning differences, quarrels, conflicts from the past. As though it were something to marvel at, or be proud of, this ability to nurse a grudge, to occupy the brief time of living with ancient bickerings! Forget it!

Then there is the heavy cargo of our own mistakes. Any human being more than six days old has accumulated a sizable list of errors he has made. Errors of judgment, of omission and commission, small and large. And the more a man or woman has tried to do, the more blunders—as well as triumphs—he or she will have achieved. Constant reminiscing over mistakes, once their lesson has been pinpointed, is so much excess freight. Forget them!

And what of the recollections of our illnesses, our moments of pain and despair? What of those people who can tell you nothing of the recollected warmth and sweetness of a spring night, the first strawberries of the season, the throb and anticipation of a new day beginning in the city, but who can recount in detail each pang and misery of an operation long since past? Forget it!

If memory is to be desired, forgetfulness has its uses, too. The choice is ours, if we will remember to exercise it.

Think of living in a world where there are no mornings! Then there would be no opalescent glow along the horizon as the first light begins to appear, no stirring of birds in country woods, no accelerating beat as the tempo of city life increases, no smell of dew on grass in summer or an unblemished snowfall that came during a winter night.

The Psalmist has said, "Weeping may endure for a night but joy cometh in the morning."

We may weep for all our yesterdays and their shortcomings during the night, but doesn't the morning bring hope for today and its potential?

The world shows a fresh face to those who travel early in the morning. Sometimes there is fog. The dense swirling curtain shrouds you in a world alone. Other infrequent vehicles pass like ghosts. Nothing is visible beyond the boundaries of the highway. Then the first rays of the sun begin to burn away the fog.

In some parts of the country you begin to pass farmers on their way to barn and field and you see the livestock waiting to greet them—cows, horses, chickens, pigs, guineas—all hungry. Once in a while smoke even curls from a kitchen chimney.

Or, in the West, in the great woods there are all sorts of animals to be encountered early in the morning—heavy-antlered elk, bear, deer, porcupine, even a moose. And in the desert there is the first shaft of sunrise tipping a sudden butte or mesa, the occasional movement of an animal or man dwarfed by the enormity of space.

And in the towns the first tradespeople open their doors, sweep sidewalks, exchange greetings with friends, gulp coffee at the all-night café. But wherever you observe early morning there hovers this sense of a fresh beginning.

It has been said, "Only that day dawns to which we are awake." Daylight can come over the hill or across the plain or above the skyline three hundred and sixty-five times, but unless we are aware of the meaning of the morning we shall have been dead for a year.

And somewhere on this planet morning is always just arriving. Always we are traveling to meet ourselves.

"He's suffering from shellout falter!"

Thus a friend described one of his business acquaintances with whom he had just had lunch. Don't you recognize the man immediately?

There is the fellow who always finds his wallet just a fraction of a second after someone else has paid the bill.

"Now see here, I wanted to get this one. . . . Well, maybe next time. . . ."

And you know that next time his effort will be just as lame.

There is the woman who is out with "the girls" and who always manages to reach for the check at precisely the moment someone else has picked it up.

"Oh, dear, I'm sure it's my turn. . . . Now next time, I insist. . . ."

And you know that next time will never come.

These are the petty annoyances, but don't all of us, sooner or later, experience shellout falter of perhaps a deeper kind?

There are those who are fumblers on opinions. They wait to be sure that they will never take an unpopular side before they take a stand on anything. And if we laugh and feel a momentary peeve at the person who never quite manages to pick up the bill, how much deeper is our disgust for the individual who will not assume his share of the burden for decision in our society?

There is the man who chronically criticizes local or national leadership. "I didn't vote for the rascal. That sort ought to be booted out of office." He never adds that he failed to vote at all. He feels great relief at being free of all responsibility for failure. Or so he thinks.

There is the woman who tears down every effort toward improvement on the part of her friends or even her family. "They're no better than the rest of us. Show-offs!" And she is too anemic of will, too jealous of her own comfort, to make any effort toward improving herself.

These people will not contribute in that most important arena, where we must run the risk of criticism, brave the possibility of laughter, and endure the likelihood that we may be wrong. But only as we take these risks ourselves do we earn the right to criticize others who are now paying the bills, bearing criticism and laughter and the responsibility for error.

Perhaps we are too fully informed about fallout shelters to protect us from enemy attack without. It is time to devote a little thought to the inner shellout falters, which betray the enemy within each of us, stinginess of self and shallow lack of faith.

Knee-deep in June I have made a discovery. If, during this month of weddings and roses, chiggers and campfires, there is anyone more superfluous than the father of the bride, it is the mother of the camper.

The opening day of summer camp arrives—and so do little family groups in well-packed station wagons and four-door sedans. Parents and boys and curious little sisters peer out of each window with a mixture of eagerness and apprehension, high hope and low suspicion.

Their eyes search for those tennis courts and swimming pools pictured in such lavish splendor in the well-thumbed catalogue. They look for stalwart sun-tanned counselors whose muscled vigor adorned the brochures. They nudge into the parking lot amidst a turmoil of duffel bags and foot lockers, tennis rackets, baseball gloves, ponchos, packets, and promptly add their mite to the collective confusion.

Suddenly, before she can say here's-the-poison-ivy-lotion or don't-forget-to-brush-your-teeth, the mother of the camper beholds a transfiguration.

Her little boy shakes hands with the camp director; he meets cabinmates; he is assigned to the Pimas or the Algonquins or another tribal group; and suddenly he is a total stranger.

Behind her stretch days of sewing on seemingly endless yards of name tags; behind her lie hours of sorting last year's shorts and T shirts, matching socks into pairs, making last-minute runs for stamps, flashlight batteries, a shoe brush. And it was all for this stranger.

He turns his shoulder, as indifferent and casual as a sturdy little boy's shoulder can be, and pretends that the woman in the shirtwaist dress behind him is some unknown wanderer who hitchhiked a ride in the family car or perhaps some unfamiliar employee of the camp. The mother of the camper prepares to hie herself home.

After appropriate handshakes all around—with counselors and director and other superfluous parents—father and son take a brief, brisk farewell.

Then the Algonquin, the Pima, the new member of the tribe turns to his mother and she gets the smoke signal from the flash of his eyes.

They shake hands.

It is no time for instructions, no place for endearments. The mother of the camper retrieves that familiar hand for one more shake. She squeezes it a bit too hard perhaps.

Then she climbs into the car and asks the father of the camper to drive away from there—very fast.

Are you a double-checker?

A checker is a perfectly bearable person—oh, a trifle fussy and occasionally annoying, but nevertheless bearable.

He checks his tires each morning to be sure that one hasn't gone flat during the night. Before he leaves home he pats his pocket to be sure that his billfold is where it always is; he glances at his watch when the correct time is announced on the newscast; when children are riding in the car, he tries each door to make sure the locks are working. When eating out, he checks the bill the waiter brings; and when a memo for "lawn care and tree repairs" arrives, he tries to balance the items listed against the invisible landscape improvements.

Female checkers always take a last look at themselves in the mirror; they are certain before they leave home that they do not have two left gloves but exactly one for each hand. They test the children's bath water *every* time, and they always taste the casserole to be sure the seasoning is right. They check the pantry and the freezer before they go to the supermarket and they never forget their grocery lists, which they check off carefully, item by item. Come to think of it, they are a pretty unnerving bunch, and just barely bearable.

What then of the *double*-checkers? The ones who lick every stamp twice, read the address on the envelope and then reread it before they yield it up to the post-office slot? The ones who lock a door Houdini couldn't have opened and then run back to shake it and test it and rattle the handle before they rest assured that it is really fast?

Double-checkers are the daily garden-variety skeptics among us. They cannot accept on faith the satisfactory functioning of any switch, lever, lid, handle, guard, machine, or mortal. They do not give any credit to the first glance, the over-all survey, the single look. They check and double-check the functions of everything around them and the reassurances of those among whom they live, and they do not trust easily the information of their senses.

I divide them into two classes. There are the utilities-checkers and the people-checkers. The first group includes those who go back to look again and be sure (a) the lights have been turned out, (b) the stove has been turned off, (c) the thermostat has been turned down. The second group includes those who (a) call twice to confirm the time of any date you make, (b) ask you to repeat three times your ZIP-code number, (c) send birthday greetings two days early so that you won't receive them late.

Now I must close—and double-check my punctuation.

The handsome, powerfully built man sat in his street-front office on one of the main thoroughfares of a town in the Deep South's so-called Black Belt. As we talked he pulled open the middle drawer of his desk. "You see that pistol?" he asked.

We nodded. It lay handy to his reach on top of a pile of papers.

"I could take it, walk out that door, and shoot the first Negro who came down the street. I'd never worry a minute about punishment. Token, if any at all."

There was a silence.

I wondered then, and I have wondered in the dozen years since, how it would be to find myself one of the Negroes walking along on the pavement outside his office, breathing, moving, having my being in an atmosphere where my very life was held in such contempt, where my value as a person was less than random dust. In such a poisoned atmosphere how could the spirit of black men or white men grow?

Is all conscience dead? Is all compassion festering? I sometimes wonder. And then I hear of those few who are acting out the conscience and compassion stirring in many. Sometimes they are dismissed as "idealistic dreamers" or berated as "hopeful do-gooders." Looking at the record, we might conclude that realistic do-badders have swaggered in power long enough. Only dreamers would have had the courage to set the experiment of democracy to work in a raw new land; perhaps only do-gooders can make this experiment successful in an old and shrunken world.

Locust blooms are so heavy this year that it seems as if half the trees along our roadsides and fence rows have suddenly come out of hiding and announced themselves as locusts.

Clusters of creamy white flowers cascade from every limb in rich profusion. They resemble wisteria blooms. Their chief characteristic, however, is their heavy odor. Carried on the warm breeze, it is almost tangible in its heady sweetness. It hangs in the hot stillness of noon over field and highway, pungent and inescapable.

Several times during the past few days I have been caught in mid-passage by this fragrance. And as I have looked up from a strip of hot asphalt or concrete, turned aside a moment from the glare of neon or metal or glass, I have felt refreshed by the sight of the trees draped with their harvest of blossoms.

If no bee ever made honey again from its essence, if no fence were ever built again from its sturdy trunk, we should still have to be thankful for the locust, whose perfume banishes for an interval the stench of exhaust pipes and gasoline and acrid smoke.

Are other families afflicted with maladies that beset our household? These everyday disorders are not listed in doctors' manuals, but I have found names for some of them. They include Early Morning Blindness, Before Meal Deafness, Nightly Hydrophobia, and Galloping Amnesia.

The Early Morning Blindness is especially noticeable on Sundays and manifests itself by a shrill cry of exasperated impatience in need of immediate relief: "Where are my new gray socks?" The new gray socks are where they were put, of course, in the left side of the second drawer with all the other socks. Only a person of badly failing eyesight could miss them. This same blindness also applies to neckties, cuff links, and other trinkets of civilization. Baseballs, ping-pong paddles, and the most minute parts of model airplanes are blessed with instant visibility.

Before Meal Deafness is peculiarly irritating—not to those who experience it so much as to those who live with the afflicted ones. Men of all ages are peculiarly susceptible. The symptoms are easily recognized: Those who can hear their names whispered three rooms away or who can detect the slightest flaw in an engine's purr or a musician's beat are suddenly, at the loud clear call of "Breakfast," struck with total deafness. Oddest manifestation of all, the patient may even mumble some response ("Just a minute" or "In a little while") to a call he later claims never to have heard at all.

As for Nightly Hydrophobia, this is almost solely a little boys' and girls' indisposition. Those children who have spent half an afternoon reveling in a pool of thousands of gallons of water are all at once repelled at the thought of a small tub of the stuff—coupled with a bar of soap. They resist all encounters with water that is not filled with ice cubes, fish, or other people. There is no known cure for this non-fatal hydrophobia, except the acquiring of years.

Of our four maladies, Galloping Amnesia is the most difficult to describe. Its symptoms vary with each household. It is, of course, a form of forgetfulness, but highly specialized. For instance, someone who can retain an astounding number of figures in his memory cannot recall, even after patient coaxing, the common names of dahlias, nasturtiums, and lobelia. This is Galloping Amnesia. A boy who can hold in mind a lengthy sequence of plays during a chess game does not always manage to get to town and back with total recall of the three items he was to buy. There are men, so I have heard, who forget wedding anniversaries and wives' birthdays, but never disremember a single golf engagement. This is Galloping Amnesia in its most pernicious form.

Perhaps everyone at your house has 20-20 vision for handkerchiefs and tie clips, hears the first call to dinner, loves to stop a game or argument to take a bath, and remembers dates, appointments, and grocery lists. If so, don't tell your neighbors—or me.

Is there any taste more delicious than that of the season's first corn? Rich, sweet, delicate, the milk of the kernels is succulent beyond description, the essence of summer's harvest.

No food loses its freshness quite as rapidly as corn. Its flavor exists in exact proportion to the number of hours since it has been picked. A couple of hours off the stalk and its quality begins to deteriorate. A couple of days off the stalk and it's fit only for cattle or pigs. That is why the wealthiest large-city dweller can never know the exquisiteness of corn at its best as long as he stays in his apartment-hive, while the simplest farmer can enjoy an eating experience of gourmets if he grows and picks and cooks his own sweet corn at just the right moment.

It is good, on a summer morning, to go out into the quiet, dew-fresh garden and walk down the dark green rows of corn. The ears to select must have changed their tassels from pale gold silk to dry brown bristles. And when the husk is peeled back from the ear to the innermost layer of whitish leaf, the kernels are exposed—moist and delicate, full but not hard.

The difficult decision is whether to savor such freshness on the cob, dripping with butter and salt, or to have corn stewed, the top edge of the kernels sliced off and the milk scraped down to the cob, all cooked quickly with cream until it is tender, and not a moment longer.

I do not recall ever having met a person who did not like corn.

Certainly it has been a mainstay of many civilizations. Recently, in the Mexican state of Puebla, archaeologists reported finding remains of mankind's first domesticated corn. It was estimated that the corn had been used sometime between 5040 B.C. and 3300 B.C. In the same cave were chipped spear points, flint choppers, fragments of woven blankets, and string nets. From a rootless nomad, primitive man was settling down, at least for periods of time long enough to cultivate a crude crop.

It is intriguing, as the steam rises from a pot of corn boiling in our electric kitchens or on our well-lighted patios, to think of those primitive men and women in their smoky caves and scratchy blankets enjoying, even as we do, the summoning fragrance and nutlike flavor of a corn not unlike ours today.

Even then summer must have seemed a rich season with this golden gift of the earth to relish to the fullest.

A friend has a nervous breakdown; adolescents in a sleek suburb are discovered to be drug addicts; a respected national leader is revealed to be a petty thief.

"We live in an age of anxiety," apologists say. "Threat of human extinction hangs heavy over our heads. No wonder little individuals and big countries are nervous and subject to breakdowns."

Is this an accurate diagnosis? Is the root of our insecurity a fear that the bomb may fall tomorrow; or is it a worry that the ax may fall today? Is it the possibility of annihilation of the human race that destroys our peace of mind; or is it the probability of our exclusion from some club, some promotion, some society that demolishes our tranquility?

Perhaps the Big Bang that may lie just around the corner for civilization doesn't jangle at our nerves nearly as much as the wham and whimper of traffic and household and business that assaults us daily. It isn't the race for survival that is creating the stress which tortures many of us; it is the race for status.

Our minds can build bomb shelters more rigid than anything our civil-defense planners design; we will not, perhaps cannot, confess to ourselves the potential for death we now possess.

But the daily small demands drumming at our consciousness are less susceptible to our indifference. Minor irritations are supposed to be manageable; when we fail to absorb or reject them, the breakdown is immediate and obvious.

A clinical psychologist of national reputation recently observed: "Clear-cut neuroses and phobias are on the decline and what we see more and more of are what I would call character complaints." (Isn't that a thought-provoking phrase, "character complaints"?) "I don't think the threat of the bomb exists for people—people deny it, in a sense—it's not real to them. The things that are real are the close and personal things."

And he defines those with character complaints as people "dissatisfied with themselves, or their work; they have mild or chronic depression; they have feelings of being isolated from people; they lose spontaneity and lack enthusiasm."

There has been a medicine on the market which claimed to cure "tired blood." Can someone manufacture a pick-me-up for "tired character"?

We are depleted and defeated by the little problems, while the great challenge of our age and our humanity lurks out there—waiting.

The nights are alive with a new voice. It announces that spring has long since passed, that summer is at its crest, and that autumn lies just beyond the next flick of the calendar. It is the cry of the katydid. Dry, insistent, distinctive—it fills the forepart of the night with a sound as old as time, as new as each recurring summer.

Katydids came early this year. By my own informal methods of reckoning the first warning chirrups usually break forth on a warm night in mid-July, during the second or third week of that month.

I heard my first one this year on July third. At first I thought that I was imagining the noise. I listened attentively, for this is one of the sounds of the seasons that is my very favorite.

Sure enough, there it came again—that single, quick, rasping call from somewhere out among the trees and shrubs. Within a few nights a whole chorus had joined in, and now the early darkness is filled with multitudinous cries. Katydids are in full swing, and doesn't folklore say they're a harbinger of frost just six weeks away?

Strange little creatures, these green-and-gold insects, at least by comparison with human creatures. Their ears are not on their heads and their throats are not the sources of the sounds they make. Actually, katydids hear with their front legs, for that is where they catch the calls being made to them.

They "speak" by rubbing the tough parts of their front wings together. One of these wings is characterized by a file-like rough texture and the other has a resonant edge, so that each fellow has his own built-in fiddle-and-bow. And it must be noted that only the males have this apparatus. In the katydid kingdom females are voiceless.

Neither the physical peculiarities nor the fragile beauties of the kaytdid interest me as much, however, as that seemingly haphazard yet subtle symphony of sound that fills the summer night.

As I walk across the lawn after an evening out, or sit on our porch as we finish a leisurely supper, or lie awake while the rest of the household is asleep, I hear the many-winged katydids fulfilling the patterns of their lives. And I know that I am only one of many creatures given the fullness of this earth for an interval of awareness.

Free of an ironclad itinerary; unfettered by advance reservations for rooms along the way; footloose from appointments, telephones, routines—we set forth to know some of our country.

Our path, transcribed onto a map by one of our fellow travelers, was that of a drunken sailor in a storm—zigzagging, swerving, veering far off course at the most unlikely moments. Such seeming lack of purpose, such apparent dictation of whim rather than necessity was deceptive, however. Our goal was intangible. Our destination was not a place on a chart but an arrival at understanding.

The question we had asked ourselves, not formally, of course, not in so many words, but casually, implicitly, was this: What is it, from sea to shining sea—this America of which we study in school and sing in groups and for which we pledge our lives in military and peaceful services?

We wanted to meet it in its diverse moods: the abundance of Kansas, Iowa, Indiana; the fertile valleys of Oregon and California and Texas, or the desolation of Death Valley's depths; the exhilaration of Mt. Washington's heights above

New Hampshire; the gentleness of Wisconsin's Dells, Pennsylvania's Amish farmlands; a breeze stirring the Spanish moss along a Louisiana bayou, or the wildness of ocean breaking at Cape Hatteras; jagged lava beds of Lassen, and Arizona's Shiprock.

We wanted to find the numerous Americas: of the Navahos in the West and the Seminoles in Florida; of the Scotch-Irish in Appalachia, the Spanish in New Mexico, and the French in Louisiana; of the Germans in St. Louis, the Polish in Chicago, the Dutch along the Hudson, the Scandinavians in Minnesota, and of the English, Jews, and Negroes stretched from Jamestown to Houston, from Savannah to San Diego.

Monticello, the handsome residence of the multi-faceted Thomas Jefferson, and San Simeon, the monument to the great acquisitor, William Randolph Hearst; Hoover Dam, a giant sweep of concrete impounding waters for a thirsty countryside, and the levees on the Delta at Greenville, Mississippi, to hold the waters back; snow lingering in the crevices of the Northwest's Glacier Park and giant saguaros thrusting up their spiny arms in the Southwest's burning desert; Plymouth Rock, the Mohawk Trail, Cumberland Gap, Lewis and Clark's route, the Pueblo at Taos, the mission at Carmel, the Alamo; and Oak Ridge, at our own back door. Could each provide some special glimpse that would be part of the whole visage of our country? Each did.

When we left for our summer of meandering across the country, we hoped to blend excitement with education, leaven history with imagination, expose ourselves to the physical variety and wonders of this land. All three purposes were more or less achieved—the last one most fully.

When we came home, we carried in our memories the noble sawtooth Teton Mountains at dawn, the blue of Crater Lake at noon, the pink-and-reddish stone forest of Bryce Canyon at evening. We brought the white blooms of bear grass, blue lupine, brilliant paintbrush, and sounds of Rocky Mountain jay birds, Indian ceremonial songs, rain on the Olympic Peninsula, and the voice of a Negro singer in Memphis. We kept the smells of fishing wharves along the coasts of the Pacific and the Gulf of Mexico, of apple orchards in Oregon and ripening melons in Colorado and the pungence of greasewood brushes under summer sun.

We were part of much that we had met, and it had become part of us. We were no longer strangers in our own land. We could be more complete human beings because we had approached a more complete acquaintance with our native grounds.

And along the way it had been great fun.

There are several towns of the U.S.A. I have especially enjoyed visiting more than twice: Williamsburg and Taos; Carmel, California, and St. Augustine, Florida.

Several cities I might add to that list: Charleston, Denver, San Antonio, Chattanooga, and Portland, Oregon.

There are four which remain my favorites, however: San Francisco, New Orleans, Boston, and Santa Fe.

Each has its drawbacks, its warts on the official portrait. But each also has a character of its own. Each came out of a unique history. All are part of the drama that made and welded America into a unity, and yet each has had a distinctive role to play.

The hills and sea are part of San Francisco's lure. It is the sense of her past, the sometimes gaudy, sometimes tragic yesterday which exists alongside the modern beat of today that sets her apart from other merely scenic cities. It is the exotic blending of an individualistic national minority, the Chinese, which adds to this special atmosphere.

And nowhere in America is the French influence as distinguishable as in New Orleans. Spanish moss and bayous and warm winds off the Gulf contribute to New Orleans' characteristic quality, but it is in awareness of her past that the present grows more fascinating.

As for Boston, its Copley Square and Charles River, its Bunker Hill and Old North Church, its spacious Commons, impregnable Beacon Hill, and time-crusted cemeteries—all link the past of our nation with its present and future. It is a city with no "show" and so much to show.

Separated by centuries and philosophies, Santa Fe and Boston are memorable precisely because they are so different. Adobe, Spanish in design and dream and heritage, Santa Fe symbolizes for me the desert Southwest. The sun is baked into its bricks; its tempo is its own; its past colors today.

Why, I wonder, can't other American cities discover and project their uniqueness?

A curious city, our nation's capital; a living contradiction and paradox, a city of the ephemeral and the eternal, compounded of cynicism as old as man's greed and faith as strong as man's love of self-government.

Summer is the season when lines of camera-bedecked sightseers spring up anew like mushrooms each morning on the White House lawn, when hordes of small boys change their life's ambition as they troop through the FBI offices, when thousands of panting climbers stand atop the Washington Monument and gaze toward a wide horizon or stand silent for a moment before the Lincoln Memorial and search inward depths.

How many of us, as visitors, are torn between two strong and conflicting emotions as we become even a tiny part of the pulse beat of our capital? There is the reverence that stirs within free people when they encounter their shrines of freedom; and there is the revulsion that rises in honest men when they find evidences of corruption large or small within those bulwarks of freedom.

This, then, is the living paradox of Washington—that our freedom to be responsible leaves us also free to be irresponsible, our freedom to be wise leaves us also free to be wanton, our freedom under law leaves us also free to try to evade the law.

We are a human breed and our government is administered by human flaw as well as Divine guidance. Part of the genius of our Founding Fathers lay in their recognition of just this fact—that error would arise and sometimes would prevail—and in the system of checks and balances they devised, which provided that error, though it come, need not be perpetuated.

Thus, although the current news from one day or year to the next may seem a tarnish on our citadels of democracy, our hope is re-enforced by those four eloquent panels on the walls of the Jefferson Memorial. Their wisdom is summarized in the simple words that link and lift us all together: "I have sworn upon the altar of God eternal hostility against every form of tyranny over the mind of man."

What would you nominate as the most valuable asset our country will possess during the last decades of this century?

Our vast oil resources, which can be used to run the wheels of a complex industrial society? Our reserves of coal, which also yield power for a mechanized civilization? Our bountiful reservoirs of water impounded for man's use? Or the mineral wealth we can adapt to our needs? Perhaps the sophisticated computers we are developing to reshape our concept of work and drudgery?

I believe that the asset we will search out most diligently and treasure most dearly during decades to come will be a green, growing, uncontaminated portion of the earth. An area we need to give man a sense of momentary peace and impart to him a sense of the larger order and design of life.

My conviction about the future is so positive because we have just experienced its truth in the present. Driving the length of the megalopolis of the Northeast, we hurtled down turnpikes and interstates and thruways. Alongside us streams of cars, trucks, buses, and vans rushed, roared, ramrodded their ways to some distant destination.

The stench of gasoline and oil assaulted our eyes and noses and throats. Constant noise dinned in our ears. The humid air, reflected from concrete and metal, blew against us, but did not refresh.

A day of such driving, a glimpse of the crowded warrens strung together in one urban sprawl, and suddenly a woods —a refuge of trees and stream—seems the most precious thing a person could encounter. An untamed piece of earth where the grass is spongy underfoot and the leaves are shady overhead and where there is quiet—yes! above all, a moment's quiet—becomes something of inestimable value.

Those who tell us that we will one day soon esteem our green havens above gold reserves and revere the earth's wild places more than the gadgets of man's power are not idle dreamers. They are tough realists in the vanguard of a new awareness of man's needs.

For the preservation of man's very sanity we shall find it

essential to preserve also the woods and waters and grass, and the clean air and sweet silence they produce. Our most valuable asset is diminishing daily. And so is our sense of man's place and meaning in the world. To save the one may help to restore the other.

Cities, like their people, do have an individuality of their own, and although it seems that many of the towns across the country are growing more and more homogenized, looking more and more like one another with the same standardized stores, schools, churches, suburbs, there are still the differences that make our older, larger cities distinctive and interesting.

For my taste there are few conglomerations of people, buildings, and machines anywhere in the world that can be called beautiful. Men thrust up soaring skyscrapers into the light and blind themselves to the cancerous slums in the shadows. Achievements of honest business and industry and artistry are diminished by a honeycomb of corruption in high places and squalor in the depths.

Pre-eminence in size also makes New York and Chicago pre-eminent over our other cities in their contrasts of character. The contrasts exist both within themselves—and between the two. The popular image of New York as glamorous, brilliant, and exciting, while Chicago is burly, sprawling, and unattractive seems to me quite out of focus.

Despite its Tribune Tower and Wrigley Building and Marina Towers apartment-house-in-the-round, Chicago does not reach up as New York does. The broad sweep of Michigan Avenue seems to set the tone for Chicago, with the shops, hotels, backbone of the city, on one side, and the curve of Lake Michigan's waters lapping the nearby shore. And the stale breath of the city is swept away in a moment when the fresh watery wind blows in from the lake. To stay in touch with trees, sun, water, wind seems somehow easier in Chicago than in New York.

Contact with people seems more natural, too. There are fewer women with lacquered hair and fewer men with the lacquered pleasantries of professional courtesy. Chicago saleswomen don't call a customer "Miss" or "Madam" as curtly as in New York; waiters seem less bored with your presence in their dining rooms; and everyone seems less afraid or weary of being a simple, warm human being.

And to stand above Chicago at night, at the top of the shiny Prudential Building, and view the strands and loops of lights strung along the shores and inland from the edges of Lake Michigan is to catch the reflected prophecy of the manswarm of a city. Chicago then seems one broad meadow laced with millions of fireflies moving in flashing patterns of light and shadow; and underneath, a tough and vibrant race.

New York is a challenge. It demands your wit for survival; and if you ask for success, too, it requires your soul. It is a place where nothing is improbable and the variety of its possibilities breeds both energy and frustration.

Each time I return to New York, I claim it anew for myself: its dangers and delight, its treasuries of art and drama and music, its horrendous subways and dingy side streets, the exciting variety of its restaurants and stores and religions to nourish body and spirit, and above all the diversity of its people, from the desperation of Harlem to the dream of the U.N.

New York and Chicago: the hub of two worlds but each distinctively American—one of the East, one facing the West.

We were in Badlands National Monument in South Dakota.

"Titanothere Skull" was the label under a great skeleton of the powerful jaws and head and teeth of a prehistoric creature of the Badlands. The explanation read: "Titanotheres were giants of their time. This one, Brontops, was only medium-sized. One stood eight feet high at the shoulder and weighed as much as a hippopotamus. Despite his bulk, his brain was small—about the size of an orange."

Nearby were the delicate bones of a mouse. The sign under these remains said: "Mouse bones are abundant in the Badlands rock. Unlike titanotheres, these little mammals were 'successful,' for they have not changed in 40,000,000 years."

When my family looked at the exhibits, one of them remarked, "Well, you know Walt Disney didn't immortalize Danny Dinosaur but Mickey Mouse!"

And he was right. It's the quick, clever, meek, indefatigable, adaptable little mouse that usually wins, apparently not only in cartoon strips but in life as well—for about forty million years, to be exact.

Perhaps size itself has little to do with survival or importance in any product or creature. It is the dependence on size alone that is dangerous. From his heights the titanothere must have looked down on the minute mouse with scorn or, even more dangerous, perhaps unconcern. When we believe quantity can substitute for quality, we tempt disaster.

All day long we have driven through the high, lonely, haunting, sagebrush country of northwestern Colorado, northeastern Utah, and southwestern Wyoming.

Yesterday and today—through Rabbit Ears Pass across the Continental Divide and down the western slope of the Rockies, across the prairies to Dinosaur National Monument in Utah and the site of the most extensive prehistoric dinosaur remains in the world, and up into Wyoming and the Rockies again—we have ridden through a sea of sage.

And all my life, since my first visit West at the age of seven, the sight and smell of sagebrush has possessed me, as surely and permanently as it ever possessed any native riders of its purple lands.

From small spears to large snarled bushes, its range of size is equaled by its range of color—soft gray shading into green at midday, and in the evening under a brilliant sunset or the shadows of night the gray-green blending into a lavender of the subtlest hue.

It is not the sight of sagebrush that stamps itself so indelibly in the memory, however. It is the smell of sagebrush, especially after rain or under a hot noon sun. Then the pungent, spicy odor surrounds a traveler and grips him with invisible force.

No matter whether we have ever lived here or not, the West is part of our national experience. Its legends are part of our myth; its spirit is part of our mystique; its past is part of our present. And nothing can bring this more alive and render it more personal than the scent of sagebrush.

In the vast expanses of sage-covered desert, in the sharp upthrust of rugged mountains and barren cliffs and deep canyons, the men who explored and settled and cherished this country found something they could not describe and could not forget. And we understand, under the sun at mid-day or when long shadows stretch across the austere hills and deserts at evening, why, once they had breathed fully the sharp fragrance of sagebrush, they could never again leave the West for good.

I know I shall return. In other hills that are my home, in another region that is my native ground, I shall still grow homesick for this high, lonely, haunting country. I shall come back—to see, to smell the sagebrush.

We have spent several days in British Columbia's Van-couver and Victoria. Both cities, on Canada's westernmost coast, offer a variety of parks and gardens for public enjoy-ment, complete with tearooms for a bit of leisure. There is an area labeled "Horse Shoe Pitch"; there are zoos and na-ture trails and picnic tables and corners for concerts and chess.

The most interesting fact about the beauty of these thor-oughly British cities is that this is a beauty scattered throughout the metropolis. You find it in the residential areas and in the commercial centers. Small homes that would be insignificant in many towns are transformed here into the background for exquisite flowering showcases. And all this is achieved by imaginative use of the most common varieties of blossoms.

On steep hillsides overlooking Vancouver are pocket-size yards and terraces fit for a prince's enjoyment. Yet they are cultivated by average citizens with above-average care and patient labor.

Snapdragons, delphinium, asters, and roses are large and

prolific. The everyday mainstays of color, however, are the marigolds, zinnias, nasturtiums, and alyssum. Their brilliance and profusion make them look like living realization of my December daydreams of gardening.

In Victoria the lampposts are abloom with hanging baskets of petunias, begonias, geraniums, and showers of blue lobelia that cascade down on all sides. The cost of these baskets to the city each year is estimated at thirty dollars apiece.

Are they worth such an investment?

Are the little individual gardens scattered over these cities worth the many hours of sweat and the many dollars for seed, and the imagination that has gone into their creation?

Who can say?

Kahlil Gibran, the Indian poet, may have suggested one reply:

> *The philosopher's soul dwells in his head,*
> *The poet's soul is in his heart;*
> *The singer's soul dwells in his throat . . .*
> *But the soul of man who lives among flowers*
> *walks hand in hand with eternity.*

Who would dream that begonias and lobelia could be closer to eternity than steel and concrete and chrome?

Today the country around Carmel, California, is not lonely. Once, not very long ago, it was. Roads of sand and gravel wound between gnarled cypresses and blue ocean; now there are paved highways.

But occasionally a hawk still hangs in the sky above the

steep mountains or a storm breaks wild waves against the rocks and promontories, and then we feel in familiar country again.

We came to know the Big Sur through Robinson Jeffers' poetry. He is not in vogue just now, but neither are the birds and ledges, the stars and stallions, and certainly not the stoicism of which he wrote. He celebrated the harsh magnificence of life at the continent's end.

Years ago we drove along the coast of California on that stretch known as the Big Sur. The barren mountains rose sharply on one hand and on the other the sea broke with rhythmic thunder. The scene seemed almost as familiar as our more friendly hills at home because of Jeffers' powerful poems. No one could read that man without sharing a sense of place as strong as that in any ancient saga.

We searched out the hidden little road where Jeffers lived. And suddenly—there he was! A lonely figure down by the ocean gathered driftwood. He came along the beach and up toward his house, and he paused and spoke to us. We talked a few moments and then he invited us up to his home.

Tor House, it was called, and he had built it by himself with rocks shaped by the ocean. It lay low and snug against the landscape. Nearby stood the rocky upthrust of Hawk Tower, his study; it was a jagged observatory between land and sky, sea and mountains, where, as I had read in one of his poems, he might gaze at the "boundaries of granite and spray."

Jeffers' countenance was like his home and his poetry: austere, deeply grained, attuned more to the ruggedness of nature than the refinements of men. His eyes might have been blended of sea water, so clear yet unfathomable was their blue and green. The planes of his high forehead, prominent cheekbones, strong chin might have been chiseled from the crags and boulders he so respected.

Doves cooed under the eaves of Tor House all afternoon

as we talked, and it was the sound of time itself around us. He spoke of his two sons, and their portraits were in the room. One was a muscular, athletic specimen of youth, and the other had the features and bearing of a Spanish grandee. As we visited, Mrs. Jeffers returned from a trip to the village, and her reaction to us was cordial, spontaneous. Her mobile face and Irish eyes were a perfect contrast to her husband's stern features.

As the afternoon faded, we made ready to leave. And then Jeffers granted us the ultimate gesture of his friendship: He invited us into the sanctuary of Hawk Tower. As we climbed and stood with him looking over sea and mountains we felt that we, too, merged with the landscape—even as he and his work had become one with these rocks and sky.

His spirit still lingers at Big Sur today.

We came upon the great Sherman tree late in the afternoon.

We had driven through groves of the towering sequoias in two other parks—in Yosemite, where the Grizzly Giant, with foreshortened limbs and twisted foliage thrusting out from its heavy trunk and making its name particularly apt, ruled over the Mariposa Grove; and in King's Canyon, where a small but majestic four-square-mile area is all that remains of what was once the most extensive of all giant-sequoia forests. And each time we had come to another stand of these trees we had been filled with a real sense of wonder.

But when we went into Sequoia National Park, in the falling part of the afternoon, and wound our way through the still woods, approaching at last that monarch of trees, our wonder turned to awe.

We recognized it immediately. It stood there in a large forest of fellow giants, yet it was easily pre-eminent. It was not lonely, yet it was alone in its size, its grandeur, its sheer endurance, and slow growth through centuries of time.

In the presence of this largest living thing on earth, as well as one of the oldest, we were silent with a sense of the glory of creation.

That glory cannot be communicated in the statistics compiled about the Sherman Sequoia. It is approximately 272 feet tall, and 101 feet in circumference. Its trunk contains an estimated 600,000 board feet of wood.

A little of the wonder may be realized from the age of this tree, somewhere between thirty-five hundred and four thousand years. Most of man's recorded history on earth has taken place since the tiny seed (so small that three thousand weigh but a single ounce) took root and began to grow in this friendly soil.

Civilizations have flourished and perished; certain species of animals and plants have dominated a portion of the earth and disappeared; man has struggled from the cave toward the moon—and this tree has been growing, weathering storms, resisting blight and insects and the onslaughts of fire. Healing its injuries, growing new tissue over the scars of time, it has stood fast.

As we paused in the light slanting down through its web of limbs, this tree became the embodiment of every memorable tree we had known: the majestic evergreens and tulip poplars in the Great Smokies, the wide-limbed oaks and maples of our childhood, the joy of Christmas trees.

This sequoia bears serenity in its gnarled knuckles of roots and its noble crown; it becomes a gift and a promise that life, which seems so tentative and fleeting, is also tough and long. It is a green witness to the continuity of life.

We have visited the ruins of two distinctive cliff-dwelling cultures in America. One flourished about A.D. 1250 in the canyon-mountain country around Mesa Verde in the southwestern corner of Colorado.

Today this "green table" area is preserved for us to visit and read the unraveling puzzle of how these Indian peoples walled up their apartmentlike dwellings under the wide ledges abounding in the region; how they improved their way of life with pottery for cooking, domesticated flocks of turkeys, and evolved a complex religious belief and ceremony in many ways similar to that of the Hindu and other Eastern religions.

From the remains they left when they mysteriously fled (a long drought? marauding enemies?), archaeologists have pieced together a picture of their daily life. It is a fascinating study in antiquity. In fact, of all our national parks, this is the only one set aside to conserve the works of man rather than the wonders of nature.

The other cliff-dwelling site we visited was in the contemporary village of Bel Air, one of the more exclusive residential areas of Hollywood and Los Angeles.

It is characterized by steep hills, barren except for brush cover and a few gnarled trees, and steep canyon drives. Not long ago numerous inhabitants of this unfriendly though dramatic terrain were forced to flee their luxurious dwellings as fire swept through the brush and devoured a number of homes.

It is interesting, though depressing, to view the remains of some of these houses in the way archaeologists examine such sites as Mesa Verde.

Here and there, looming against the sky on the ridgetop

or clinging to the side of a steep canyon, stands a chimney—some large and decorated, others with built-in stainless-steel ovens still intact—revealing how these people prepared their food. Still other chimneys, near blackened patios of brick, with elaborate hearths and spits for broiling, attest to outdoor eating habits.

Dry swimming pools of many shapes and sizes remain near the piles of rubble where the houses once sat. Knowing the desperate infighting which engaged many of these inhabitants while they secured such homes, we are struck by the single most startling feature of these ruins: their smallness. The tottering chimneys and cracked pools seem like playthings, and the lots where the costly houses stood appear to be postage-stamp size.

In the Mesa Verde museum is a skull labeled simply "Frieda, young female." Imbedded in the front bones is a sharp arrowhead, aimed by "person or persons unknown."

One wonders, among the cliff dwellers of Hollywood, how many Freidas might be found today, with deadly weapons buried in their quivering backs if not in their skulls.

And if the inhabitants of Los Angeles ever flee their terrain in one mass migration, it will be no mystery. Smog—that eye-smarting, throat-choking mixture of fog, smoke, and exhaust fumes—will have driven them away. Then the archaeologists of future centuries can come and compare the cliff-dwelling cultures of Western America.

Las Vegas is a desert. I do not mean that it is a city set in a desert. I do not mean that in a desert country there exists this oasis. My words say precisely what I mean: Las Vegas itself is the desert. The land surrounding it burgeons with secret life—animal, vegetable, and mineral. But the territory within, the human landscape, is a desolate wasteland of withering life.

Has there ever been a city so dedicated to pleasure where so few people looked pleasant? Has there ever been a way of life dedicated to the pursuit of happiness with such grim intensity?

In its slot-machine emporiums, raucous with the noise of free floor shows few bother to watch, there is the steady clang of levers pulled by hundreds of arms drained of all awareness except the nervous energy that drives them on remorselessly. In its lavish night clubs big stars labor desperately to camouflage their little talents; and in the carpeted gaming rooms only the risk of paper fortunes can momentarily quicken the atrophied pulses of a jaded species. The smell of death hovers in the air.

The desert of Las Vagas is air-conditioned, stuffed with food and drink. But it is possible to die here of a hunger and a thirst that make the scorched and barren earth around it seem a green haven of delight.

By all the rules of a systematically scheduled trip, we should have arrived at the north rim of the Grand Canyon about five o'clock in the afternoon, along with the daily influx of tourists. We should have settled in our quarters, viewed the canyon, eaten dinner—in short, followed the established pattern. But we did not, and as often happens in traveling, thereby hangs the tale of an unforgettable experience.

Full darkness had fallen by the time we came into northern Arizona and the Kaibab National Forest. The air was as refreshing as a chilled drink. The smell of grasslands and woods carried message of the rain that had come that afternoon.

A coyote loped across the road in front of us. The tall ears of a Western jack rabbit disappeared into the bushes. Clean white clumps of aspen grew more frequent among the forests of evergreens on either side of the road. By the time we came to the entrance of the park itself and began the twenty-mile drive to the rim of the Canyon, we were wrapped in a mood, rarefied, solitary, as near a moment of perfection as night and nature could combine to create.

And then, over a dark hilltop of pine and fir, a white three-quarter August moon swam into view. All that had seemed merely pleasant and beautiful was thereby touched with magic. Clumps of pyramid-shaped spruce gleamed like silver-tipped sentinels interlaced with the tall stems and quaking leaves of the aspen under moonlight.

The forests were broken by sweeps of rolling meadow. A doe and her fawn raised startled heads beside the road. We passed herds of deer grazing in the grass under the pale light, which was less than day, more than night, suspended in some rare and momentary limbo.

A buck broke across the highway and clambered up an embankment into the woods. All around us the secret life of nature fed, stirred, freed during the night of man's intrusions.

We came to the end of the highway, found our lodging, then walked along a narrow path to the edge of the Canyon.

It lay in immense shadow under the white light of the moon. There was no measuring its depth or silence. Tops of pinnacles were visible far below us, rising from recesses of fathomless dark. We knew why it was called grand.

We also knew that, in another sense, the evening we had

just shared, climaxed by this moment of immaculate encounter, had been no less unique and inevitable than the Grand Canyon itself.

The names of America's streets and roads and alleys are part of the music and meaning of this country. Milk and Water streets in Boston, Beacon Hill's Joy Street, and narrow little School Street. How different their names and atmosphere from Richmond's Three Chopt Road, its Clay and Marshall streets commemorating leaders of the Old Dominion and this country, and Williamsburg Road. And in Tennessee's capital city of Nashville there is Granny White Turnpike, incorporated in 1850.

The earliest American towns had various patterns and systems for naming their streets. The one adopted by most cities followed the Philadelphia plan. This was for streets to be called by numbers—First, Second, Third Street—in one direction; and names, most often of trees, in the other direction. William Penn, in calling the streets of his city after various trees, was careful to use only those "that spontaneously grow in the country."

As the popularity of his system of naming spread, however, many City Fathers were not so careful to have only native trees, so that it became possible to have a Sycamore Street or a Cypress Avenue in regions where no sycamore or cypress ever took root. Perhaps the most common addresses in our country today, then, combine numbers and botany: Second and Elm, Seventeenth and Walnut.

Until the city of Washington was laid out, no American city had an avenue on its map. The word "avenue" came from the French and was used to designate the tree-bordered approach to a country house. After its use in the plans of Washington, it became popular with many other cities. And certainly the name of Pennsylvania Avenue has a special meaning for citizens of the United States.

It is these emotional overtones that make the street names memorable, of course. The influences of Beale Street and Wall Street, Sunset Boulevard and Broadway touch different segments of our lives, but each brings its own distinct picture and reaction in our minds.

How varied, too, are the names of old Charleston—Meeting Street, King and Queen streets, Cabbage Row. And old Santa Fe—Camino Perros, Cerrillos Road, and Agua Fria. How much romantic legend is conjured up at mention of New Orleans' Bourbon and Bienville and Rampart streets, and San Francisco's Sutter and Market streets, Nob Hill and Old Chinatown Lane.

Of all the street names in America, however, the one with the deepest meaning to many people is still Main Street.

I am distressed, angry, outraged. There is an indifference pervading our national character and a destructiveness perverting our national purpose which should be evident to anyone whose eyes are open, anyone who still nourishes a flicker of concern for this country.

After journeying more than eighteen thousand miles on America's highways and bypaths during one long swing, I am distressed by the dumps along our thoroughfares and the litter along our trails. I am angered by the wanton nationwide destruction of our national heritage, and I am outraged by the national attitude this waste and defilement reveals.

From ocean to ocean it stretches, this country of ours, a

wonderland of fertile fields, boiling geysers, majestic woods, lonely plains, towering mountains, and plunging canyons. Its variety staggers the imagination. Its bigness and boldness capture us. Its shifting subtleties call us back to West and East, North and South, again and again.

Yet on each new visit we see a little more, or a great deal more, of the nibbling ugliness, the rampaging despoilation.

They are the blind who can wander all day in the Olympic rain forest and never glimpse the fragile ferns they trample, the flowers they break; who can stand on the green heights of the Blue Ridge and uproot a purple rhododendron or flame azalea for themselves.

They are the greedy who strew the rocky shores of Acadia Park in Maine, the clear boiling pools of Yellowstone, the trails of Carlsbad Cavern, the snowy heights of Mt. Rainier with their mementos of appreciation: wastepaper, beer cans, chewing gum, cigar stubs.

They are the functional illiterates who are apparently unable to read signs and leaflets pleading for consideration of the parks which belong to all of us, for respect of our common earth.

They are the moral illiterates who simply do not care.

The sequoia monarchs in several Western parks are being literally trampled to death. Sequoia trees have no tap root; their shallow root system is remarkably vulnerable. Thousands of footsteps annually packing the ground, scarring visible parts of the roots, ignoring "no trespass" barriers can eventually destroy a living thing that has withstood centuries of lightning, fire, and insects.

Arizona's Petrified Forest, one of our unique primeval heritages, is literally disappearing. It is being carted away, particle by particle, by souvenir thieves.

In Wind Cave, North Dakota, some of the fragile honeycomb formations distinctive to that underground park are gone forever, destroyed by those who had to touch or break anything of beauty or of value.

What will become of America, the land and the people, if we do not realize we are destroying ourselves? We are obliterating beauty we cannot replace; we are burying ourselves in our own garbage. We fear cataclysmic catastrophes that may occur tomorrow. What of the daily disasters all around us, testimony to human sloth, selfishness, and indifference?

It is easy to identify the region of the country where you are driving by the kinds of animals you find smashed on the highways.

Driving along a four-lane ribbon of concrete in South Carolina a few mornings ago, we passed the crushed body of a red fox. Its bushy plume and pointed face seemed strange indeed on this hustling thoroughfare. We had never before seen the quick red fox overtaken by an automobile.

In the mountains of the South there are frequent possums that have had their nightly prowls interrupted by the crashing advance of a car. Along the Blue Ridge Parkway there are sometimes woodchucks (or groundhogs) whose remains testify that they were not quite agile anough in their waddling efforts to cross the road. In New England there are skunks, killed as they scurry from stone walls and old meadows on their necessary foraging. Out West, of course, there are the jack rabbits; and along some of the straight, long stretches through the desert or plains country there are often so many carcasses of these large-eared creatures that a traveler must wonder if Western highways are not paved with three parts asphalt and one part rabbit.

And everywhere, knowing no bounds of region, no rural or urban limitations, are strewn the bodies of our own pets

—cats and dogs with cherished names and their own special niche in someone's life.

These are just the small victims of progress. Insignificant? Perhaps. Yet one New England newspaper has pointed out that the skunks and some other small animals helpful to man are being slaughtered wholesale by automobiles, while certain rodents and other pests they helped control are flourishing.

Thus, in yet another unexpected way, we manage to upset the balance of nature. And we defy all rules of sportsmanship, throwing a monster of steel and glass and terrible speed at a small animal blinded by headlights, terrified by noise.

And I suppose there isn't anything we can do as we crush the bits of bone and fur and blood and obliterate them into the concrete—except echo those lines written by James Stephens many years ago:

> *Little things, that run, and quail,*
> *And die, in silence and despair!*
> *Forgive us all our trespasses,*
> *Little creatures, everywhere.*

Queen Anne's lace is in full bloom. By the roads, in overgrown pastures, across abandoned fields, the white blossoms are spreading a filmy cobweb. This is a flower of late summer.

Actually a member of the carrot family, Queen Anne's lace is a vegetable as well as a wild flower. It is an immigrant American plant, whose beginnings were on the European continent. So adaptable was the wild carrot, however, that it soon became common throughout most of the United States. Indeed, it is strange to think of the time when Queen Anne's lace was not part of the native scene of this land.

Domestication of the carrot itself goes back to prehistoric times. The historian Pliny says that the finest specimens of the plant were brought back to Rome from Candia. During the reign of Queen Elizabeth I the carrot is supposed to have been taken to England by the Dutch. There are records which tell of halls and banquets at which the ladies wore carrot leaves instead of feathers in their hair.

As one who used to pick armfuls of Queen Anne's lace when a child, I can state unequivocally that at anyone's court I would rather have worn the green fronds of the wild carrots in my hair than the heavy plumes of feathers from dead birds. Indeed, sometimes playmates and I used to weave long necklaces and boas from our gatherings of Queen Anne's lace. The stems are rather tough and lend themselves to knots and splicings. The blossoms made a coronet or mantle worthy of the proudest play-queen or lady in waiting.

The plant is known by different names in different parts of the country. Among its aliases are bird's-nest, laceflower, devil's-plague, and rantipole. None of these do it justice, not even laceflower, which suggests the delicacy but not the stateliness of the plant. And isn't it pleasing to have such a common specimen—such a weed, if you will—bear the specific regality of "Queen Anne's" name?

Its tiny white petals on an intricate network of stems, bound together like the most exquisite threads of silk or linen, the wild carrot blooms profusely. And at its very center is one dark drop, like a cushioned jewel or a bit of luxurious purple velvet; just the beauty patch this pale flower needs.

Let those who will profane it by calling it devil's-plague. For my taste, it is Queen Anne's lace, royalty of the roadside.

A large part of summer seems to be used up in arrivals and departures. There are the big arrivals: relatives on their annual visits, that couple you met on a trip two years ago and with whom you exchanged Christmas cards, children's roommates. There are the large departures: on a cross-country safari, a month at some special resort, a visit to one of your relatives or the couple you met two years ago or an old roommate.

There are also the small arrivals: weary return from the grocery store with a small commissary supply; happy return from swimming pool or tennis court or simply a firefly-catching expedition on the lawn; welcome return from a long day in office, field, factory, or studio. Or, on second thought, is there any such thing as a *small departure* in a family consisting of more than two? Having spent the better part of a summer in perpetrating these ordeals, these crimes against all human patience and good will, I venture to suggest that departures are among the most stringent of man's trials.

Of course we expect the large leave-takings to drain time, energy and emotion. (After all, Cousin Veronica is eighty-seven and a half years old and may not be able to make the trip from Colorado again! Or we do expect to be away from home for eight long weeks and why shouldn't we take leave twice of dripping faucets, stove switches, and fuse boxes, and close the blinds a bit tighter?)

It's the everyday embarkation that really saps our strength, however. For example, on a quiet, apparently peaceful morning you announce that you must "run downtown" for some simple item: a loaf of bread, a spool of chartreuse silk thread, a roll of film for the camera that has been acting strangely.

Suddenly voices materialize as abruptly as the three witches in *Macbeth*:

"Say, could you pick up those shoes I left to be mended at the shop?"

"If you're going to town, could you bring back a good supply of cold drinks?" (What is a "good" supply and why must they be cold when they come from town?)

"Will you be near the post office? We need some stamps."

"And what about that new chair for my room?"

(Now wait a minute. Wait *just* a *minute!* This is a quick trip to the shopping center, not a furniture expedition.)

A full morning's work grows out of that spool of thread, or loaf of bread, or roll of film.

And what about those picnic, fishing-trip, golf-game departures? Too lengthy, repetitive, and harrowing to consider. ("Did anyone remember to put in paper napkins?" "Someone has been tampering with my best rod." "Where are my shag balls—I left them right here.")

Isn't there some way just to say—"Good-by"?

Several times over a long period of years my husband—at first by himself and later the two of us together—visited Robert Frost on his New England farm. During the early visits Frost was still something of a private figure, although a famous poet of course. But finally he seemed to pass into public domain, like a magnificent natural treasure—the Grand Tetons, the Great Smokies, or a national monument such as Monticello or Mount Vernon.

Our last visit with him was during an afternoon and evening in August. The place, near the village of Ripton, Vermont, was a little hillside cabin where he spent many writing hours, and a farmhouse just below, where he ate and slept, where we took supper with him at his impromptu invitation.

Deliberate, soft-spoken, with the strength and stillness of mountains in him, he was no more to be taken for granted in his responses or his gifts than are the mountains. He had a quick instinct for the incongruous. Deep wrinkles around his lively eyes recorded both the laughter and the irony of years.

Three things I especially recall discussing that day. First, apples and poems. The fact that we two had grown apples in the southern Appalachian hills, and that we also tried to grow poems, had first made Frost accessible to us. Frost, of course, had been a heaping measure more successful than we at poem-making, but it was the problems and pleasures of apple-growing to which he steered the conversation. The names of tart, twisted, old-fashioned varieties of our mountain orchards fascinated him: Milam, Sourjohn, Sheepnose, Limbertwig, Maidenblush, Belle-o'-Buncombe. These were some of the unique, cherished apples grafted on lonely little farms by men who valued flavor above productivity.

Second, Frost spoke a parable especially for us. A well-known writer friend of Frost's had a first wife who was also a successful writer. Their marriage had failed, not from lack of love but from the clashes of two careers. The separation of these two people had wounded Frost, because he cherished both of them and he believed they belonged together. His shrewd, friendly eyes watched us closely. My husband and I were touched by his concern for our personal relationship.

Third, the white-haired poet thoroughly enjoyed learning that in the Southern mountains Federal officers are sometimes called the Big Law.

"The Big Law." He nodded slowly. "Who's the Little Law?"

We answered those were the local officials.

He grinned boyishly, as though planning mischief, as though planning a poem. "The Big Law," he murmured, "it's after us all."

The last soggy swimming suit has been hung on the line to dry. The last smoke-cured blanket and mud-caked sleeping bag has been cleaned. The last finger burned over a campfire and bruised by a hatchet has healed. The campers (millions of them) are back from the woods and the hikers are home from the hills.

America's passion for the outdoors seems to be increasing each year. May we assume then that the call of nature is becoming clearer above the roar of the subway and the rush of the thruway? Should we believe that the desire to be alone with tall trees, uncluttered earth, quiet streams has moved these millions to pitch their tents across our land?

One U.S. Forest Service official has said that each year more campers have their own tent-trailers, gasoline stoves, folding tables and chairs, "and everything necessary to make them feel as though they had never left their own back yards." He failed to mention that many also took along their own radios, so that no quiet could shatter the illusion of being at home.

"In general the American public is very social, quite gregarious, and likes crowds," the Forestry official observed. "Campers tell us they go camping to meet people."

I thought a person went camping to meet himself. Or at

most his family. Himself (and his family) in relation to a wholly new world—a world of bugs, birds, fog, leaf mold, hot sun, sudden showers, minor discomforts and major satisfactions, and self-reliance.

No wonder some of our campsites are becoming little more than rural slums. We have subverted their natural purposes, their gifts of solitude and health.

One day not long ago we chanced to drive along the highway for some distance behind two boys on motorcycles. The machines they rode were heavy, powerful things, throbbing with the thrust of fuel that fed the engines. Their chrome trim and painted parts glistened in the sun. They hurtled along the highway, massive and strong as ancient mastodons roving the face of the earth.

And perched atop each machine, without protection—without even helmets in this case—was a marvelous pattern of such intricacy that few can even grasp its wonder.

Surely the human body is the most perfect, the most delicate, the tenderest and toughest machine that has yet been invented, but how often we expose it to destruction by the cruder, man-made motors and propellers of mechanized life.

Isn't it peculiar that we can marvel at the precision of a camera lens and yet take for granted each day the functioning of our eyes? Or that we should find so incredible the working of vast computers and yet never realize the complexities, the terror and awe contained in that little bone box we call our heads?

To reflect for a moment upon the ceaseless labors of the

heart, the finite workings of the circulatory system, the design of flesh, blood, bone, muscle, which makes a human being is to be confounded before the miracle of life itself.

There they rode, however, weaving daringly along the pavement which could snap their bones as easily as brittle twigs, astride the motors which could smash their bodies in a moment's everlasting destruction.

That solemn and ancient proclamation that we are fearfully and wonderfully made surged through my mind. Perhaps the most wonderful aspect of our body's perfection is our casual acceptance of its daily presence, and the most fearful aspect is the disregard with which we can submit it to purposeless danger, wanton wreckage.

How beautiful were those two leaning bodies on the swift-roaring motorcycles. Their grace and intricacy made the assembly-line products of our industrial empires seem gross by comparison. They split the air, and the wind that moved behind them seemed to whisper, "Fearfully and wonderfully made." But we are often deaf to whispers and the racing of motors drowned out this one as the young cyclists disappeared around a distant curve.

"I am no politician and still less a prophet. But I am, if I may be allowed the term, a 'geo-biologist,' and I have looked hard and long at the face of Mother Earth. I feel and I am convinced of one thing: That nothing is more dangerous for the future of the world, nothing moreover less warranted in Nature, than the affected resignation and false realism with which in these days a great number of people, hunching their shoulders and drawing in their heads, predict (and in so doing tend to provoke) a further catastrophe in the near future. More than all the remnants of hatred lingering between nations, this terror of inevitable war, which sees no cure for warfare except in even greater terror, is responsible for poisoning the air we breathe. That is why, humbly and devoutly echoing a divine utterance, I feel the need to cry to those around me, 'What do ye fear, O men of little faith? Let me beg you to rise for a moment above the dust and smoke obscuring the horizon and gaze with me at the course of the world.'"

These are the words of one of the great men of our age, Pierre Teilhard de Chardin, who delved deeply into a knowledge of science and soared steeply into rarefied heights in his vision of religion.

Born in France in 1881, he died in New York in 1955; but collections of his works have appeared at intervals during the years since his death and his thoughts have remained very much alive, vigorous and growing.

Teilhard's books fill a void; they combine dedicated intelligence and realistic faith to examine the scientific and religious nature of man. Teilhard himself was a member of the Society of Jesus and a professor of geology. He played a major role in the discovery of Peking man, an anthropological landmark. His thoughts on the phenomenon and the future of man may play a major role in rediscovery of ourselves.

To read his works is to eat of the bread of life. They are not soft and sweet as teacakes. They are not synthetic globs of some jellied concoction devised to resemble a basic food. They are ground out of the whole grain, and they provide nourishment.

If you are looking for a quick and easy snack to satisfy your mental lethargy or spiritual anemia, do not look into Teilhard de Chardin's books.

But if you want substance from which to draw strength

for survival, partake of the thoughts of this man of science and religion.

"We are told," he says in *The Future of Man*, "that drunk with its own power, mankind is rushing to self-destruction, that it will be consumed in the fire it has so rashly lit. To me it seems that thanks to the atom bomb it is war, not mankind, that is destined to be eliminated. . . . The atomic age is not the age of destruction but of union in research."

What this noble thinker challenges us to undertake is nothing less than the adventure of research into knowledge of man and God and our relationship with each.

Weeds and wild flowers flourish everywhere and suddenly it is again the season of pollen, dust, burrs, and stickers.

Neglected meadows glow with the royal hues of goldenrod and purple ironweed, soapwort called—in the poetry of mountain vernacular—farewell-summer. The tall rosy lavender of joe-pye weed appears in swamps and fence corners, its muted hues and heavy-headed blossoms seeming to contain the very essence of autumn.

Wild asters are abundant. Along roadsides, across the fields they spread a blue carpet with their small, fringed blooms, and where they mingle with the goldenrod their colors would call up the Van Gogh in any painter. Like Van Gogh, who splashed the brilliant mustard fields of southern France onto canvas and left us therewith immortal summers that will not fade, we feel we would squeeze the very blues and yellows directly from their tubes to capture the purity and vividness of a patch of asters and goldenrod.

Abandoned vegetable gardens now take on disturbing resemblance to the ruins of deserted Aztec villages long since reverted to nature. Vines entwine each shriveled stalk or stem, overrun every fading plant, obliterate every row until the orderly neatness of spring's planting and summer's cultivation is only a dim memory.

In the first early sunlight, morning glories transform this wilderness into a momentary carnival of color. Draped over corn and okra stalks, the deep blues and pinks and milky whites of the trumpet-shaped flowers bring the dying garden briefly back to life.

Less welcome fall arrivals abound, too: ragweed and Spanish needles and that clutching, clinging pest known by the name of beggar's-lice. It is difficult to walk anywhere in the country and not have pollen, dust, burrs, stickers fasten to our clothing. It is not difficult at this turn in the year to remember that all living things eventually return to dust; perhaps it is just as well that we grow familiar with the smell and feel of it.

We have come through an unsettling equinox in our family life, moving from one season of growth to another season of maturing. We took our older son from the mountains of Tennessee, where the sourwood and poplar and hickory trees are just beginning to turn their color and Grimes Golden and Stark's Delicious and Stayman Winesap apples are ripening, to the hills of Massachusetts, where birch and maple trees are in brilliant dress and Baldwin and McIntosh are thick on the ground.

We went from the last lazy afternoons of Southern summer heat to the first crisp mornings of New England autumn. And he went from the easy familiarity of relatively simple surroundings to the challenge of new teachers, fresh subjects, and unknown classmates in a highly competitive prep school. One hand pushed him forward while the other yearned to hold him back.

Words are such slippery little bridges of communication at moments like this. He has worked for weeks toward this day of entrance. You have worked for years toward this minute of parting.

You look at each other. Words say nothing.

"Have a good year."

"I will."

"Write us when you can."

"Sure."

The distance from Tennessee to Massachusetts is not as far as the distance between you now. You are tight with pride and sadness.

"Good-by."

The stone walls of New England—sturdy and useful and beautiful. Weathered through long winters of drifting snow and ice and the thaws of springtime and the mellow sun of summers and autumns coming all too soon, these walls are almost always similar in color. Whether in upstate New York, in Massachusetts, Connecticut, Vermont, or New Hampshire, they have the patina of warm gray, like old pewter, with the high lights and shimmer of that metal. It is a living color, with depth and texture. It was acquired only by time and exposure to the blasts or the blessings of the elements.

Seen from a hilltop, these stone walls make patterns over the landscape. They define field and pasture, separate orchard from meadow; they encompass a little homestead; they encircle an old cemetery; they disappear into the edges of woods where trees are taking over hay lots once laboriously cleared by some hopeful farmer.

They follow the contours of the land, rising and falling with the waves of the terrain, hugging the slopes as steadfastly as if there were roots binding them to the earth. And, then, as you walk beside one of these walls, you take notice of the intricate and careful beauty of its construction.

Dry walls, most of them are called, because they are laid without any cement or clay. Only the skill of the builder and the shape and solidity of the stones holds them in place through decades and generations. They have stood long and well. Woodchucks and skunks and other small animals have made homes in them. Ferns and field flowers have sprung up beside them and softened their angular lines.

At this season of the year, Virginia creeper and sumac are blazing red along the old walls. I paused a few days ago beside one of them and wondered about the men who laid these stones, one upon the other, one beside the other. There were veritable boulders along some of the stretches of that wall. Square, granitelike giants among stones only a little less impressive in size. What mighty wrenches of someone's crowbar, what masterful straining of someone's muscles must have been involved in getting those stones into the places where they have settled and stood firm these many generations.

A sense of time hangs over these walls, the time yesterday when men cleared their fields by their own labor and in the process built something necessary and handsome, the tempo of today when we do well to take time to walk across a meadow bounded by these landmarks.

The stone walls of New England—I hope they will never

disappear. Something there is that *does* love a wall, when that wall is both art and testament.

What influence is it that brings to certain locales at certain times a ferment of intellectual activity, a flowering of artistic or political genius?

Virginia had its period of providing presidential leaders to our country in times of crisis as well as peace. Other states and regions have had similar moments of greatness. The Chicago area had its literary renaissance with Dreiser, Sandburg, Masters, and Ring Lardner. The Southern quickening included Ellen Glasgow, Wolfe, Faulkner, and Robert Penn Warren. Certainly no single village in America, however, has had a more important or interesting manifestation of this ferment and flowering than the quiet, tree-shaded town of Concord, Massachusetts.

To a Southern visitor Concord is the epitome of all that New England villages are supposed to be. Here is the square, with elm-fringed streets leading out to green surrounding countryside. Here is a replica of the first parish meeting house, serene and simple, white frame gleaming from many coats of paint. (To anyone surfeited with the standardized brick churches springing up in every suburb from coast to coast one of the loveliest features of New England's towns is the cherished frame church, sturdy with the care of generations, set amidst grass and trees, dignified in its poverty of ostentation and richness of tradition.)

Also here in Concord, on one householder's independent acres, was developed the famous Concord grape. I wager that our family, member for member, has consumed more juice, ounce for ounce and gallon for gallon, of the Concord grape than any other "average" family—and so we had to pay respects to this site. The tablet which marks it for such stray visitors as we says that the fruit came into being "after three generations of work and wisdom."

It is not the countryside, or the occasional claim to fame such as comes to most towns, which draws Americans to Concord, however. The lure is a desire to know more intimately on their native grounds two distinctive Americans, Emerson and Thoreau.

The spacious white home of Emerson still accepts callers. The cabin of Thoreau has long ago crumbled and disappeared. But along that part of Walden Pond where the destructive paws of "Progress" have not yet reached, the spirit of the recluse philosopher seems remarkably present. Henry Thoreau was one of the cockleburs we need from time to time to prick our conscience and keep us from sliding into comfortable conformity.

As his Concord neighbor, Ralph Waldo, warned, "My life is not an apology, but a life. It is for itself and not for a spectacle."

And again, "What I must do is all that concerns me, not what people think."

Walking beside Walden, I realize that I spend a part of my life I can ill afford to lose in apologizing for that of which I should be most proud. Thus is our backbone weakened, our time wasted, and our spirit dampened down when it should be set ablaze.

There are occasions when nature takes over the schedules, routes, plans, and scenery—and presents an unexpected bonus. All that is required of us is that we accept the gift and know what it is we have been given.

We were just this fortunate when we visited the coast of Maine. We came to Bar Harbor late in the afternoon and decided to explore Acadia National Park, even though darkness was fast approaching.

We drove along the park entrance road and up Cadillac Mountain, between bare rock ledges and wind-whipped evergreens. We came near the summit and there, with sudden boldness, appeared the rim of the world: land and water and sky sharply defined.

At the top of the mountain we left our car and climbed on the highest granite outcropping with a full 360-degree view. On the horizon to our west streaks of red and pink flamed across the darkening sky. The sun, which had shone so gently all day on Maine villages and farms, spacious homes and snug barns, coast and sea and marshland and hills, was disappearing.

On the horizon to the east, stretching a path like crinkled tinfoil across the undulating water of the ocean, was the full moon just risen.

All else lay in shadow, quiet, suspended between the day's departure and the night's awakening.

We stood braced against the wind which blew across the mountaintop, not cold but brisk and clean as if it were newborn that instant. The sun's flush faded. The moon rode higher in the sky.

We drove down the mountain and around the coastal road which bounds the park. A sign and the voice of the old Atlantic told us when we came to a spot I had never forgotten from a former visit: Thunder Hole. We walked through the pale clear moonlight down steps carved in the boulders along the ocean's edge to a deep indentation between two massive walls of stone.

Into this deep but narrow passage, with rhythmic constancy, drawn by some invisible current, pushed by some powerful thrust of the tides, rushes a wall of water. The force with which it breaks against the surrounding rock walls and surges back through crevices and caves beneath the ledges reverberates like the sound of thunder indeed.

It is an awesome sound and sight. As the wave recedes, the water pours back out, draining from all the bowls and curves worn smooth by this constant abrasion.

Then it comes again—the rush, the mad roaring break against the containing ledges, and the echo of Thunder Hole bellows in the moonlight. A concentrated glimpse of nature's power and beauty was our gift that night.

We grasped it in full measure.

Grand Pré, Nova Scotia.

The Acadians would have been the last to believe that words written on a bit of paper could prove more real than the marshy land they dyked and tilled along the Nova Scotian coast more than two centuries ago.

They would have been the first to doubt that verses could commemorate their daily labors long after the stout oxen they worked were dead and the fruit trees they tended were rotted and gone.

They were a simple, earth-loving people, those Acadians who had come from France to the easternmost provinces of Canada, but they live in the history and imagination of the English-speaking world because of a poem.

Evangeline was written by Henry Wadsworth Longfellow, who was an American and who never even saw this land or its people he described so accurately and vividly.

Poor *Evangeline*, the poem, has long since been left behind in the advances of esoteric modern versification, as quaint as the kirtle its subject wore, too readily understood to require twentieth-century poetic or psychiatric analysis. But Evangeline, the heroine, somehow seems to survive.

Readers still discover those opening lines:

This is the forest primeval.
The murmuring pines and the hemlocks,
Bearded with moss, and in garments green, indistinct in the
twilight . . .

And they go on to follow Evangeline and her Gabriel through their long sad journey's search. And so the poem, the Acadians, and a dark chapter of this continent's history live on.

There is a National Historical Park at Grand Pré, where Canada has preserved the memory of the Acadians who were deported from their homes more than two centuries ago. It is a gem of a park, centered around a stone memorial chapel of mid-eighteenth-century architecture, with bright dahlias, snapdragons, petunias, argeratum, sweet alyssum, coxcomb, geraniums, and other old-fashioned flowers clustered in thick beds. The lawns are soft green carpets.

In front of the church-museum is a statue of Evangeline, and nearby is a little apple orchard, similar to the ones her people tended.

Why were the Acadians forced from their land? They were caught in the struggle between two massive powers. France and England each sought dominion over the new world, and after the Treaty of Utrecht in 1713 gave the entire French colony of Acadia to Great Britain, these farmers still refused to take an oath of allegiance to the King of England. They clung tenaciously to their religious and national traditions.

From 1713 to 1755, British governors sought to obtain their allegiance. But farmers are by nature a conservative lot; the ways of the land have taught them patience and persistence; they do not switch their fealty easily or because of some meeting in a distant place. At last the local authorities, fearing the weakness of their own hold on this area, decided to deal with the recalcitrants.

On September 5, 1755, all the men and boys of Grand Pré were assembled in the local Catholic church. Colonel Winslow informed them that they were the King's prisoners. Guards surrounded them and they were told to board ships in the harbor, where their families could bring food and join them in removal out of the country.

During the rest of that year 6,500 Acadians were transported into exile to some eight of the now United States. Only in Louisiana did they form a permanent settlement, and the people called "Cajuns" there today receive their name from these exiled Acadians.

The earth they tilled remains, the land—and a poem recording their love of that land and their removal from it—here in Grand Pré.

"Weather rules the island. Here the wind is king!"

We could believe what the big, sturdy man in the heavy jacket said. We were in those eastern corners of Canada where sky and sea and rocks are more plentiful than people.

Turning inland from the rugged shore line of Cape Breton Island, we had followed a dirt lane over a hill to the end of its passage and the place where this cordial recluse and his wife lived. Over a bridge, across the clear, cold stream that plunged toward the nearby ocean, was his snug farmhouse and a big barn and a yard crammed with bric-a-brac.

There were lobster traps, jugs, and jardinieres of assorted shapes and sizes, a sleigh of ancient vintage and a buggy, and flutter wheels of a dozen colors, heights, designs. The busy little yard seemed to stand as a barricade against the loneliness of the surrounding countryside.

The wind was blowing gustily, exercising the fragile flutter wheels to the limits of their capacity, and the frantic whisper of their rotations contrasted with the controlled power which buffeted them.

Cape Breton has been called "the highland heart of Nova Scotia." Part of it has been settled by French people, part of it by Scots—and each has made adjustment to the dominating reality of sea and hills.

"It's been a hard fishing season," our new friend said. "The fishermen here have just had two days of fishing during the past week. Cod and mackerel they're after now, in September. In June and July it was lobster. Come now into the house and see our things."

He had been a career officer in the United States Army until a few years ago. Upon retirement he had come to this remote corner of Cape Breton Island, drawn back perhaps by memories of his mother who had been reared here. He and his wife had lived in many parts of the world, and they had spent a large sum of their life collecting certain objects. Bells—ranging from those worn by cows on Swiss mountain slopes to those adorning Eastern religious temples. Veils— varying degrees of gossamer beauty woven of rare silks, silver, and gold. Glass and jewelry and clocks; shillelaghs and paintings and carvings. Here were the inner lines of their defense against loneliness.

He was a robust man, full of humor and hospitality. His wife was a small, shy woman. But it was she who had climbed the Matterhorn, and it was she who made us coffee to drink in the cozy kitchen at the heart of the house.

And each time we made ready to leave, they thought of another rare item they must show us. We went to the barn and talked with the horse, who awaited his lump of sugar from our host's pocket as imperiously as if he understood that he was a necessary part of this household.

At last we shook hands. As our car turned back across the brook, we saw them standing there amidst the lobster traps and flutter wheels, and behind them the house stuffed with mementos of another world. . . .

There was also the plump little woman in the fishing village of Peggy's Cove. During its brief summer season Peggy's Cove may be an artist's paradise, but in autumn and winter the scattered houses perch like deserted gulls' nests among the boulders. The sea is rough here. This woman's home was one of the few habitations still warm with human life in this rocky, watery niche of coast.

We spent the night at her house. Deep feather beds swallowed us in comfort as we listened to the wild waves breaking on the ledges relentlessly.

The following morning, with mist and fog outside and the gulls crying around the lighthouse, she made us a huge, delicious breakfast on her roaring wood range. We ate in her kitchen, surrounded by rows of lovely English china plates which decorated the walls. Her heat-flushed cheeks wrinkled in a smile. "Yes, my china is company for me when I'm alone here on winter days and nights."

How frail the citadels we build to endure our solitude! Yet I cannot pity those who meet their loneliness in the clean bite of the wind and the majestic assaults of the oceans. Save pity for less noble encounters.

Gossip begets gossip; money begets money; ideas beget ideas. The investments we make of our talents and time determine the dividends we receive from life. Sometimes those dividends enrich other men's lives as well.

At the entrance to a handsome modern building of glass and stone and redwood in the town of Baddeck, Nova Scotia, are these words: "The inventor is a man who looks around upon the world and is not contented with things as they are. He wants to improve whatever he sees; he wants to benefit the world; he is haunted by an idea, the spirit of invention possesses him, seeking materialization."

The tribute is to Alexander Graham Bell, and this is his museum. We are familiar with his role in the development of the telephone, of course. But it is the wide range of scientific interests which claimed his attention, the humanitarian principles which guided his research that are the core of this museum erected in his adopted homeland.

Scotland was the place of Bell's birth in 1847. When he was quite young he came to Canada and later to the United States, where he became a citizen and pursued his career as a teacher and scientist.

While he was teaching in Boston, he became a friend of Gardiner Greene Hubbard, a wealthy lawyer who sought Bell's advice on the education of his daughter, Mabel. The girl had been left deaf by a childhood attack of scarlet fever.

Bell married Mabel Hubbard and she and her family were a lifelong source of encouragement in his work. With his father-in-law, Bell helped found the National Geographic Society in 1888. A few years later, while he was president of the society, he engaged his son-in-law, Dr. Gilbert H.

Grosvenor, as editor of the group's publication. Grosvenor developed the *National Geographic* into one of the world's distinguished magazines.

Perhaps Bell had a lifelong interest in the affliction of deafness because his mother had begun to lose her hearing when the boy was only twelve. At that time unenlightened public opinion set great barriers between deaf-mutes and unafflicted people. Bell devoted much of his talent to finding ways by which the deaf child might be integrated into society. His extraordinary training in the science of speech and sound eventually contributed to the invention of the telephone. Thus his concern for the afflictions of one small group led to the improvement of all men's lives.

And his ideas spawned other ideas, as he made significant contributions (illustrated in this comprehensive little museum) in aeronautical research, use of radium in the treatment of deep-seated cancer, development of the iron lung, and marine research. He was seventy-five years old when he died, still haunted by ideas, still possessed by the spirit of invention which from this cranny had reached around the world.

I don't know what's happening to the clocks at my house. Come to think of it, I'm having trouble with the calendars, too. The hours don't seem to have their usual sixty minutes any more. I know the days aren't twenty-four hours long. And I cannot believe that the weeks are fulfilling their appointed seven days either.

Sometimes it seems that I have only finished Monday

morning, with the whole week stretching ahead of me, and suddenly it's Saturday night.

Some days have the same collapsible tendency. I'm sure I've just finished my morning coffee when it's already time for after-dinner coffee.

I feel somewhat comforted, however, since I've come across some comments of sharp old Dr. Samuel Johnson, about inroads on our time. "Life," he said, "is continually ravaged by invaders; one steals away an hour, and another a day; one conceals the robbery by hurrying us into business, another by lulling us with amusement; the depredation is continued through a thousand vicissitudes of tumult and tranquility, till, having lost all, we can lose no more. . . .

"If we will have the kindness of others, we must endure their follies. He who cannot persuade himself to withdraw from society, must be content to pay a tribute of his time to a multitude of tyrants; to the loiterer, who makes appointments which he never keeps; to the consulter, who asks advice which he never takes; to the boaster, who blusters only to be praised; to the complainer, who whines only to be pitied; to the projector, whose happiness is to entertain his friends with expectations which all but himself know to be vain. . . .

"To put every man in possession of his own time, and rescue the day from this succession of usurpers, is beyond my power, and beyond my hope. Yet, perhaps, some stop might be put to this unmerciful persecution, if all would seriously reflect that whoever pays a visit that is not desired, or talks longer than the hearer is willing to attend, is guilty of an injury which he cannot repair, and takes away that which he cannot give."

But what about the assaults I have made on the time of others? Perhaps their calendars turn even more swiftly than mine. Thieves, all of us, needing only to unite against the common enemy.

The man of the house brought me in a bright but somewhat stunted little gladiolus bloom a few days ago. I was delighted. Then, as I arranged it with some greenery in a decorative vase, I smiled to think how I would have spurned this flower a few short weeks ago.

In midsummer the gladioli were in full bloom, so heavy that they bent on the sturdy stalks, and as each blossom opened, the color climbed the spearlike stem to its uppermost tip. They were large blossoms with velvety petals, shades ranging from a white so pure it seemed like morning snow in winter to red so deep it seemed like clotted blood. Wide bowls and tall containers were required to display the bounty of their loveliness.

But now it is autumn; the foliage of the flowers we picked earlier is turning brown and dry. When a sudden bonus appears and a flower shows up among this dying, withering process, we feel especially appreciative. So I welcome the bloom I would have cast aside in another season.

The same in true of our vegetables. When tomatoes were at their peak, we sliced only the largest, ripest, most perfect specimens for our table. And Golden Bantam corn had to be at just the right moment of ripeness, fullness, milkiness for us to pick it. Now we handle knobby little tomatoes with care and lay them on the kitchen window sill to grow a little redder. Nubbins of corn we would have overlooked on an earlier day are welcome tidbits, a last link with summer's abundance.

As we scavenge for the last fruits of summer and enjoy some of the final remnants as much as—perhaps more than —we did the first harvest, I wonder if we do this in our living, too. In the wealth of time which surrounds us when we are children we can be prodigal with hours and days. Then, as the years begin to shorten, we grow more aware of the briefness of our days and we begin to savor the seconds and the minutes. Weeks we once might have dribbled away to little purpose now seem as precious as a month did then. Nubbins of time are suddenly sweeter than the full grain of seasons once taken for granted.

I look at my last glad blossom of the year and I enjoy it because it was unexpected. I relish the sweetness of the last sun-ripened tomato because it was a volunteer. Who knows what may flower in what corner in what season—if we look to each day's gift?

A startling series of deaths due to botulism occurred in our state and then across the country several years ago. Botulism is a form of food poisoning. It is especially sinister because the food it affects neither smells, looks, nor tastes different from good food. Thus, the victim takes into his digestive system something which he hopes may nourish him, and instead it becomes his killer.

Not long after those deaths I received in the mails an ordinary-looking four-page news sheet. Its print and paper neither smelled nor looked different from that of many normal publications. I began to read. And as I absorbed into my consciousness, my thought system, the hidden hate and vilification and half-truths and whole lies that were set forth on those printed sheets, it occurred to me: "This is botulism of the brain!"

Isn't it odd how carefully we nurture our children's

bodies when they are growing from infancy to childhood to maturity, and how carelessly we often neglect their mind's nourishment? How many quarts of citrus juice and how many dozens of vitamin pills and how many pounds of tested and approved meat do we dole out in the course of one child's lifetime? And how many hours and days and years do we overlook the violence administered on television, in books and papers, a teaspoonful at a time, or the sadistic and tawdry "entertainments" doled out a dose at a time?

Botulism of the mind is so much subtler and slower a killer than the botulism that affects the body. But it is no less sure.

The physical self, battling to throw off the wretched poison of contaminated food, often dies in the struggle. The spiritual self, seeking to rid itself of the malignant poison of contaminated thoughts and brutal ideas, often destroys itself in the effort.

A man runs amok and cruelly kills an innocent person; a nation becomes spiritually bankrupt and systematically slaughters thousands, millions, of human beings. It is deadly all right, this putrefying of the mind. It can be cured, or prevented, only by daily and wise concern.

Every town needs a "Miss May." She was in essence a lady; she was in influence a leader. Any city or community can ill afford to lose the likes of her.

I suppose there were those who thought Miss May was indestructible because she had given herself to so many succeeding generations. Her strength was not only physical.

She gave with her hands, the lowliest manual labor—and with her head and her heart as well. And wherever she gave, it was to build.

I can see her now as she stood in the neat, attractive stone house she acquired in her later years (even helped construct, in part). Gracious and hospitable, yet surrounded by a certain sad reserve, she welcomed a guest to share her chicken and rice, or her needlework, or the ceramics she adopted as a hobby.

I can remember her as she stood before the handful in the graduating class of her school—head tilted slightly to one side, cheekbones high and prominent beneath the large brown eyes that searched each pupil's face for a spark of ambition, a flicker of the hope she had tried to kindle there.

I can visualize her before the congregation in her church—tall, erect, exemplifying reverence and dignity in a world that had too little of each, pleading for the pennies or dollars that would finally install a new heating plant, bring new benches, buy a new piano in this bare wooden room.

I can realize the unusual balance of pride and humility that gave Miss May her special grace, set her character apart. She stood upright with the strength of an oak when strength was needed, and she bent with grace and the ease of a willow when her help was needed.

Miss May never knew idleness. The fact that she was a Negro was incidental to her essential worth, but it was central to the limitations set on her by an indifferent, sometimes hostile, world. She knew hard work all her life. Who can estimate the costs, in extra labor, wounded pride, disappointed trusts, that she paid because of a fact of her birth? I cannot begin to make such an estimate.

She saw men die violently and needlessly. She saw young people waste their talents and fling away their lives as carelessly as cigarette stubs. She saw the leaders on whom she must depend for survival gouge and wrench and squeeze to make pennies out of another's sweat and dollars out of another's need. She saw it clearly and recorded it in memory. But she did not yield to the luxury of cynicism or to the ease of hate. She persisted. Occasionally she prevailed.

Her father died when she was small; her mother was left with nothing but a family of young children and the will to work. Work they did—on neighboring farms, in the fields and households, growing their own crops and securing their own survival from a few unproductive acres.

And with it all, Miss May was determined to educate herself. She did, and then she was determined to educate others. She did this, too, for forty-five years. From one-room country schools to a consolidated brick building in the county seat, she taught class after class.

She married, but had no children of her own. So she took whatever surplus of food anyone would give her and she canned thousands of jars of fruits and vegetables so that her schoolchildren might have nourishing lunches in the winter, whether they could pay or not. She found shoes for some of the bare feet that came to her door. She provided discipline for those who had known only wayward abandon all the years of their childhood. Her searching eyes looked upon them with tenderness and mercy—and measured them for the size of jackets they might need and the size of ideas they might grasp.

Many of those Miss May taught are teachers now themselves. Many of those for whom she fought on one battleground have long since fought for her, and all of us, on farther battlefields. Many of those with whom she worked failed her and themselves. Others succeeded. None will forget her.

In her own way Miss May taught us all. The whole community was her pupil. We can ill afford to lose her instruction.

Our high-powered twentieth-century life has its menacing features. There is fallout from above earth and the equally gloomy prospect of sardinelike survival below earth. There are auto crashes and muggings and possible slow poisonings from polluted water and air.

But there is one area of danger I have never seen publicly discussed. In fact, this foe is so diabolically clever that it has insinuated itself into our lives under the guise of convenience.

For sheer demoralization of human character, for constancy of purpose and relentlessness in waging warfare on man's fragile nerves, for a gradual chipping away of confidence, equilibrium, and general well-being no device can quite equal the automatic elevator.

To those of us still clutching the skirts of progress, hanging on with an occasional backward look as well as a forward shove, the automatic elevator is a symbol of our despair.

To those trying to hold a narrow beachhead of simplicity in the midst of mushrooming complexity, the automatic elevator is surely the omen of approaching defeat.

For this is not merely a mechanical invention to lighten man's labors. It is a contrivance of bizarre wit and infinite resourcefulness. Its strategy of conquest is the oldest in the world—surprise. Its attacks are models of the unexpected.

For instance, during recent months, in hotels, stores, hospitals, and apartment houses, I have seen stout men assaulted and all but overcome by the abrupt thrust of an automatic elevator door in process of closing itself. These doors are supposed to remain open as long as anyone is entering the elevator; and while a crowd is jamming itself through the portals, all is well. But when the stream turns into a trickle, the magic eye becomes the evil eye.

Part of the shrewd scheme of nerve warfare seems to be to pick off individuals one by one (the shopper laden with toppling bundles, the harried mother grasping twins by their reluctant hands, a pompous executive jealous of his dignity). If possible, the coup is carried out in full sight of a crowd of interested spectators.

My own first scars of battle were received when I was following a bellboy into a hotel elevator. He and my bags entered with perfect safety. Only a half-step behind, I started across the threshold, too. But the noiseless beast was lying in wait. Suddenly it lunged, caught me full on the arm, then retreated, as if overcome by remorse. I knew it wasn't remorseful, however, because it caught the man behind me with exactly the same strategy.

It isn't actual physical contact with these sly doors that I resent as much as the battle shock they leave behind. Your sense of confidence is shattered; your belief in invincibility wanes. If you can't trust its doors to admit you peaceably to its interior, how can you count on an automatic elevator to deliver you, sound in mind and limb, to your destination?

And it is no comfort to look up, as you soar past the twentieth, thirtieth, fortieth floor and see that big button marked "Emergency," or a neatly printed notice instructing what you must do in case of a stop between floors in mid-air.

It's a cruel choice—walk or submit to this battle of nerves. To the cold, calculating automatic elevators, wherever they lurk, waiting, I throw down the gauntlet: "I have just begun to fight."

Rain is one of the miracles by which we live. And yet, until we have experienced the withering misery of its absence we seldom welcome the forecast of its presence. Sunshine and clear skies are considered "good" weather—until we experience a drought.

In Yucatan, Mexico's southernmost peninsula, there are the astonishing remains of the cities of the ancient Maya Indians. Many believe that the chief reason for the decline of their civilization was insufficient rainfall.

Today their great stone images of the Rain God—reclining so that he may hold moisture in the hollow of his chest and stomach—reign silently over a lifeless domain of tremendous pyramids, stone temples and dwellings, chiseled designs and decorations, even an astronomical observatory—all covered now by the patina of time and surrounded by jungle. Indeed, in the jungle are vine-covered relics of this Mayan past which still await discovery.

Several years ago I stood beside the steep stone walls of the Sacred Well of Chichen Itza. It was dusk. The cries and calls of birds and animals came from the tangled wilderness just beyond the well. Otherwise there was silence. The milky green water was still and deep.

I could almost believe that the old fierce priests of the Mayan empire might reappear in their brilliant ceremonial regalia, dragging sacrificial maidens to be thrown into this pool. Such deaths were supposed to appease the Rain God. And it was he who held power of life and death over all the land and its people. The bones and jewelry of many human offerings have been dredged from the bottom of this well.

The size of the Mayans' pyramids was impressive; the

structure and ornamentation of their buildings was amazing; the vitality of their curiosity and imagination was recorded in these stone monuments—yet these people did not solve the problem of prolonged drought which plagued them, and their civilization perished before Columbus and Cortez ever reached American shores. Since our visit to the strange and fascinating ruins of Yucatan, I have been prompted to change a sigh to a smile when I see rain clouds darkening the horizon. I know they bring one of the miracles by which we survive.

When a person chooses his work, he is making the most important decision of his life. (Of course, some people never choose their work. They drift from one form of money-making to another, but these are surely the ones—be they wealthy or destitute—of whom it could be said that they are "barely keeping body and soul together.")

A person's choice of work may be more decisive than his selection of a wife or husband. Indeed, it may be the reason behind that selection.

I know this from personal experience. My husband, long before we ever met, had intended to spend his life in business, as had his father. But somewhere along the way he became interested in literature and writing—and Thomas Wolfe's mother and sister brought us together. Only through our mutual interest in working with words could we have met and married and lived happily ever after.

Several years ago William Faulkner said that a man's work is the only thing to which he can devote all his time and energy and talent during all his life. Neither recreation nor love nor war nor anything else can fill his days completely, but man can always carry on his work. In fact, in most cases he must carry it on.

It is not only a person's profit to pursue work for which he is fitted; it is also his privilege, and should be his passion. And it doesn't matter so much what that work is—designing a dress or a strategy of battle, plowing a field or formulating a new scientific theory, lending money across a bank counter or washing dishes or tightening screws on an assembly line—the job is less important than his attitude toward it. If he can come to it with enthusiasm and purpose, he is a successful person. But if he drags to desk or plow, factory or easel, despising the means and fruits of his labor, he is surely the unhappiest of all creatures.

We hear a great deal about machines and computers taking over man's work. Then we must extend and deepen our definition of what work is. We may find that the real challenges of human effort lie in the realm of mind and spirit more than we have willingly admitted in the past.

Surely, today, work worthy of the human endeavor stands in need of us; and we, each of us, stand in need of our work.

A do-it-yourself article recently pointed the way to Instant Immortality.

"If you have a dull, routine job and lack drive, ambition and competitive spirit, chances are you'll live longer."

Now the question is: Are you living longer, but enjoying it less?

We tend to mourn for those who have lived short lives, rather than for those who have lived empty lives.

Remember for a moment a man who lived only thirty-one

years. Much of that time he was poor. He was forced to do work he detested in order to survive and accomplish the work he loved. His body was finally broken with illness.

But who can mourn for Franz Schubert, whose inner ear heard melodies never heard before, whose genius poured forth music never conceived before? Mourn rather for the many who have lived in the centuries since and have never been touched by the spark of his beauty, the outpouring of his creativeness.

Of Schubert one acquaintance said, "He was a very little man, but he was a giant."

Of his life we might say, "It was very short, but it has never ended."

Who can yield to the dramatic power of his C Major Symphony and not know that this composer lives this very moment? Schubert's C Major—his long and powerful Seventh—is one of the most popular of all great symphonies. And what of that familiar melody from the Unfinished Symphony, written when he was only twenty-five years old?

During his thirty-one years Schubert composed over 600 songs, 18 operas, 9 or 10 symphonies, 16 string quartets, a large body of church music, 12 sonatas for the piano and 4 for the violin, and numerous smaller pieces.

When he lay on his deathbed, half insane with pain for three days, he said to his brother, "Don't leave me in this corner under the earth. Do I not deserve a place in the sunlight?"

His place was not only in—it was of—the sunlight. His radiance spills into our lives today if we accept the gift. Not the number of our years, but their quality. Not the length of our days, but their depth. There may be no Instant Immortality, but Schubert at thirty-one was eternal.

The eyes brim with hot, bright tears; the cheeks flush, and the rigid little body trembles.

"But it isn't right!" the outraged child cries. "It isn't fair!"

How many times have we adults experienced such a moment with our own or others' children? And heard the angriest, ugliest accusation which they can hurl at us and our overgrown world, "It isn't fair"?

There is nothing more devastating than injustice. From injustice springs tyranny—of a loved one or a nation. From injustice flows disorder—in an individual family or in the larger community.

A priest with a rather unorthodox way of expressing himself on quite orthodox problems was recently quoted as saying, "Children can stand vast amounts of sternness. They rather expect to be wrong and are quite used to being punished. It is injustice, inequity, and inconsistency that kill them."

Discipline is not only a matter of regulation concerning a more-or-less-arbitrary system of rules; it is a matter of fair play, not only to one person but to all concerned. It is a method of consistency, in which the values and actions that were honorable today are also honorable tomorrow, and the courtesy and concern due one person is also due all persons.

Thomas Jefferson once observed, "I believe that justice is instinct and innate, that the moral sense is as much a part of our constitution as that of feeling, seeing, or hearing."

Anyone who has seen the passionate conviction of a child in his rebellion against injustice, to himself or to a teammate, must tend to agree with Jefferson. Anyone who has seen a friend give up security and forgo comfort to help secure justice for a fellow human being must feel compelled to subscribe to Jefferson's belief.

Perhaps it is this sense of indignation, this hunger for a more perfect equation between our beliefs and our actions, our creeds and our realities, this rejection of bland indifference and deadly hypocrisy that stirs some of our youth today. If it is "injustice, inequity, and inconsistency that kill them," perhaps that is also what kills us.

Now arrives the dry season. Mist may come in the night or heavy dew in the morning, but this is an outer moisture. It does not seem to penetrate to those roots that are wasting away, those leaves and fruits that are withering from within. Each thing that grows seems to be shriveling from its innermost core to its outermost shell.

The sights, sounds, smells of dryness are everywhere.

Leaves rustle in the wind and begin to fall in the first fresh covering of color along mountain paths and city drives. Prickly chestnut burs plop to the ground in the quiet stretches of night. Sapless thorns and stickers and Spanish needles plague the walker in meadow or at the roadside.

Tobacco hangs drying in barns and sheds, the aroma of its broad, veined leaves as rich as its tawny color. Apples dry where they have fallen in wasteful abundance on the ground.

The big, bold blooms of zinnias now fade to brown seed pods on their sturdy stems. Tomato and potato vines are withered and tough in the garden.

The rattle and snap of dryness fills the abrupt mornings

and the long heat of late afternoons. Crickets click like Halloween snappers in the dying grass. Tall weeds bristle and break sharply. Acorns pelt the ground like rain, and the sound of a jarfly at midday is the essence of all parched things.

Creeks and rivers slow their pace. Rocks long hidden become visible once more in the dwindling streams. Ponds shrink to muddy puddles.

Yes, it is the season of dryness: smell of smoke and sound of grasshoppers, time of Ecclesiastes, who said, "Then shall the dust return to the earth as it was . . ."

Perhaps the day will soon arrive when sons can be brought into the world and reared without mothers. This seems to be a consummation devoutly to be wished by many writers, most psychiatrists, and all successful Broadway playwrights.

From material gathered in my limited examination of the subject, I deduce that it will be all right for daughters to continue to have mothers for a while. (Although this possibility is rapidly giving rise to an abolitionist school of thought, too.) But the real damage to human personality and stable civilization comes when mothers have sons—and then have the effrontery to try to rear them.

There seems to be no way for a mother to win in this cause. If she has sons and shows them affection—an occasional hug, a peck-on-the-cheek when no one of the peer group is watching—she is smothering them with mother love. (And every curbstone psychiatrist knows that that is a malady which is closely akin to an old-fashioned garroting.)

On the other hand, if she restrains all evidences of affection (and who has that much will power?) she will bring the lads up to be coldhearted woman-haters. (And every first-night theatergoer knows what that condition can lead to.)

And whatever is wrong with the boys when they become adults (overlooking the minor point that no human of either sex is perfect), it will be directly traceable to the mother's influence.

When Napoleon was in exile on St. Helena, he dredged up just such an excuse for his failure and exile. "My opinion," he said, "is that the future good or bad conduct of a child entirely depends upon the mother." I suppose he blamed Waterloo on his mother. (I wonder if Wellington gave *his* mother credit for the same encounter?)

Even Ralph Waldo Emerson, who prided himself some-what on being an original, echoed the sentiment. "Men are what their mothers made them," he pronounced.

Perhaps it is time some latter-day saint countered with the theory that "women are what their fathers made them." Or can it be that daughters simply are not adept at finding scapegoats for their shortcomings?

Sometimes I shudder with dismay when I stop to consider that I have had the temerity to bear two sons, and that even now they are storing up all manner of quirks and foibles directly traceable to my character (or lack of it), my sched-ules (or disdain of them), my affection (or absence of it).

The only thought that comforts me is knowledge that any uncertainty in this situation is directly traceable to—to whom?—to my mother?

"He's a good man with the know-how, but he'll never be able to provide the know-why."

Perhaps that diagnosis applies to the most obsolete man of our century.

If we cannot any longer concentrate simply on know-how subjects, realizing that a mechanism of steel or plastic may soon render all we learn useless, should we not begin to accelerate study in those areas where man's mind cannot be replaced? A machine can know how; it can never know why.

A French philosopher has said that the release of atomic energy gave us the power to be gods before we were ready to be men. It is this power that poses the ultimate question and presses the ultimate dilemma today between know-how and know-why.

What might happen if we could find the formula to release man's intellectual potential, his moral imagination? These are the raw materials we shall need for our new age of reason and renaissance.

Even the most sophisticated machines eventually become obsolete. Are we also moving toward obsolescence of human beings? If not, perhaps the reason is that we have found the importance of know-why.

Why not orchids in the kitchen?

Quite often, when I am a guest or speaker at a meeting, or club, or convention, the thoughtful host or hostess will present me with an orchid.

Once upon a time orchids were so frail that it seemed to me they wilted after only a few hours' exposure to the common air. Now, however, they have become a hardier breed and even after a hard day's or evening's wear they may still be fresh and beautiful. Who can bear to throw away a lovely, exotic flower? Certainly not I. And so I store it in the refrigerator.

Since orchids, like diamonds, are inappropriate to all of the week-day errands and simple functions we attend, the days a corsage lies in cold storage simply prolong its death instead of its life.

A few weeks ago I found myself with three orchid bouquets on hand at the same time. One was perfect white, another was that pale green bordering on chartreuse, and the third was traditional lavender edging into purple. Since I felt that anyone to whom I offered these corsages might be insulted at secondhand posies, and since shelf space for more mundane articles such as milk and bread and grapefruit was growing scarce, I wondered how I could manage to use and enjoy the beauty that was uselessly stored away.

So I took out my green orchid and pinned it to the kitchen curtains, which are of a heavy brown material. It was a harmonious color combination. It brought glamour to my cooking and household chores!

For three days I enjoyed my blossom and its fancy ribbons from the moment I drew water for breakfast coffee to the hour I switched off the light at night. Then I brought out the other two flowers and they served their turn for my pleasure and visitors' amusement.

As I looked at the orchids on my kitchen curtains, I thought of the rare talents in people which are often wasted through hoarding them too carefully.

I thought of the glamorous little things many of us would like to do, for our family, our friends, ourselves, and yet we hold back because we think an unusual occasion is necessary for our gesture, our compliment, our generosity.

Don't you know people who work so hard to preserve everything they have and everything they are that they, like flowers in the refrigerator, seem to be prolonging only their dying and not their living?

Why not orchids in the kitchen? Why not beauty on Monday morning as well as Saturday night? Why not laughter in field or office or shop or school or factory? Why not life to the hilt wherever we find it?

One of America's gravest problems springs from one of our greatest blessings: abundance. From the fertility of our earth comes food in such plenty that the storing and sharing of it develops into a major undertaking. From the throbbing production lines of our factories stream goods of such variety and quantity that we must initiate a psychology of "I want I need" to consume them.

Now it develops that we have serious overproduction at a completely different level, too. The supply of written words in this country far exceeds the demand.

The lush growth of corn in our midlands appears as trifling poverty when compared with the luxuriant growth of that corn which flows from typewriters, pencils, inkwells. To add to the difficulty, the number of creative writing courses and summer writers' conferences is increasing around the nation.

The result is more and more manuscripts. And this at a time when many old familiar magazines and newspapers are disappearing, merging, shrinking the market for deathless prose and hack reporting alike.

The result is that writers are more insecure than farmers and do not have the effective unions that exist in the manufacturing world. Amateur or professional, they are the forgotten segment of our proud production-minded economy.

But there is a solution. Why shouldn't a manuscript or writer's parity plan be initiated? The government could set a word minimum on works it would purchase, and any un-sold manuscripts would be bought as surplus goods and stored in literary "elevators" or warehouses. Futures for these works might not be brisk on the open market, but construction of the storehouses themselves would be a major boost to the economy.

Further, why not create a word bank? In this plan, produc-tion would be controlled at the source. Writers would be paid not to write. Their imaginations could lie fallow for a while.

Amounts paid for unwritten stories, articles, and memoirs would be determined by past sales in the author's career. Likewise, the number of unwritten pieces for which he would be paid could be calculated by the average produc-tion of past years. And since writers are noted for their lack of thrift, the money paid into the word bank would obvi-ously soon re-enter the mainstream of our economy.

Best of all, from the Washington standpoint, a whole new bureau could be set up. Perhaps it should be called Depart-ment of the Non-Producing Arts. Or what about Bureau of Artistic Conservation, with a subdivision, Word Bank Con-trol Program?

A patch of our driveway is covered with black walnuts. As the tires of our car, and those of visitors, crunch over them, they are getting a free and effortless husking. The green outer shell that smelled so pungent during late sum-mer is now black, dry, withered on the outside, wet and spongy inside next to the nut itself.

The leaves of the tree, so distinctive and lacy, that made a shade from the westering sun all through the summer, have long since fallen.

The limbs, bare and twisted, stand boldly out against the winter sky. Their rough bark is tight and strong.

The black walnut is one of my favorite trees. Perhaps that is because it is associated with such pleasant personal memories. When my father moved to these Southern mountains after half a lifetime spent in the country just outside New York City, he fell in love with the woods of the region. And one of his hobbies became woodworking. (That was in the days before it was fashionable to be a do-it-yourself hobbyist, a craftsman, but then my father was never very much concerned about fashions. He seemed to have that innate sense of security, that confidence in his own taste and style which assured him that if he would not conform to fashion's whims, she would eventually, in all likelihood, be won to his inclinations.)

In his neat and spacious woodworking shop, which adjoined our garage, I often lingered, watching my father's hands transform a length of dull dark lumber into a glowing object of unique beauty. Under his patient polishing the richness of the grain gradually emerged. No wood that he used was more satisfying than the black walnut. None yielded a grain more lustrous and varied.

Later, I learned that the Cherokee Indians and the early settlers of this region used walnut juices for one of their best dyes. I saw some of the hand-woven materials dipped into deep dye-pots and transformed into a rich, dark brown. Many of the mountain baskets, too, are laced with white-oak strips stained brown by walnut brew. They are my favorites.

Botanists agree that black walnuts probably were not in our original hardwood forests of the South. Perhaps they, like my father, came and found a pleasant compatibility

with the hills and woods and life here. I'm glad they came—
and stayed.

The telephone rings.

You reach for it desultorily. Your mind is far away, on
tomorrow's engagements, on plans for next week, full of
trivia and Important Matters all jumbled together.

"I have a collect call for anyone at this number. . ."

Your mind leaps into place. Your ears strain for every
word spoken by that brisk impersonal voice.

"Will you accept the charges?"

"I certainly will."

It is one of your sons calling. You most certainly will
accept the charges. It has been a long time. . .

"Hello?"

"Hello." It's his voice all right, here in the room with you,
a little deeper than you remember it when he left. "I thought
I'd better call to let you know I'm not dead—or anything."

You had decided that some official would call you if he
were dead. It's the "or anything" (a broken arm from
soccer, zero on a vital test, some doom even your most
pessimistic moments could not foresee) that troubles you.
"Well, we're so glad you called! How are you?"

"I'm all right."

"How's everything at your dormitory? How is your
roommate?"

"He's all right."

"It's been rainy here. How is the weather there?"

"O.K."

"What about calculus? And history? And those French
verbs? Are you surviving?"

"All right, I guess."

There is a momentary pause. Then a burst of information. "One of the clubs had a dance last weekend."

"Did you have a good time?"

"It was all right."

Another pause for a breath. "How is everything at home?"

"All right." You've slipped into the pattern. You search your memory for some local news of interest to him. "I saw some of your friends the other day. They asked about you."

"O.K."

"Do you need anything? Can I send you anything?"

"I guess not. But thanks anyway."

"We miss you. We think about you. The holidays are not too far away."

"No. Well, I'd better go now. It was good to talk with you. Back to the salt mines!"

"Call again soon!"

You hang up. Reassured by such lengthy detailed conversation? No, it was just the sound of his health, his assurance, his respect that was good.

A few days ago the man who shares my life and I walked over an old apple orchard we once owned. Planted at the turn of the century, many of the huge old trees were nonetheless sturdy and productive when we came to own them. Some of the finest, most flavorsome fruit grew on their high, twisted limbs.

Almost a hundred acres were in that orchard, some of it steep along a hillside. And at various places special varieties of fruit grew especially well. The mountain men who worked in the orchard named these various places, and we all knew the precise spots as clearly as if there had been a full-scale map on paper—Stayman Winesap Cove and Stark's Delicious Ridge, York Imperial Hillside and Golden Delicious Flat, Virginia Beauty Plateau and Black Twig Knoll.

Now all is changed.

Our apple shed, a frame building with tall old rock-and-cement storage cellar, has been remodeled into a dwelling. Where apples once bounced red and yellow and green along a grading table and into crates, someone now enjoys a snug sitting room. Downstairs, where the apples waiting for winter's demands once gave off a sweet and spicy aroma, there is now a basement, perhaps a garage.

The sprawling house of rustic logs with wide veranda has been refashioned into a compact cottage. And at the rear, the old stone springhouse, covered with moss and vines—as beautiful as it is obsolete—is crumbling away.

Much of the orchard itself has disappeared. Some of the trees have fallen under the power saw. Some have been enveloped by a creeping wilderness of sprouts and saplings, growth so dense that in certain places there are already stands of fern usually grown only in deep woods. The acres have been divided and subdivided.

A few of the apple trees are being reclaimed by one old-timer who tends them with spray and fertilizer and loving care. In this little oasis it is possible to come out of the second-growth woods and find a tree hanging heavy with ripening red Winesaps. It is possible to walk along a path and find large, clear Golden Delicious rolled into your footway.

Yet the orchard we knew is no more. Only the blue sky above and the surrounding hills and the droning bees underfoot, sucking the sweet juice of the bruised windfalls, are familiar. So quickly is our handiwork refashioned by man's impatience or reclaimed by nature's patience.

An uncle of mine used to tell about an acquaintance who calculated—through genealogy, his own history of illnesses, and a battery of other statistics—his life expectancy. Then he totaled up his assets, quit work, and allotted himself a certain annual income until he was seventy-three years old.

"The trouble came," my uncle concluded, "when he lived to be eighty."

And of course came the inevitable question, "How did the old fellow make out after he was seventy-three?"

"Well, he had some lean years!"

Most of us try to anticipate those lean years, storing away various sorts of security for the time when we will be less able to make our own way, in every sense of the word.

Yet whenever I hear the fable of the ants and the grasshopper, I cannot help wishing that the ants had enjoyed the summer a little more, even though I acknowledge the fact that the grasshopper could not enjoy winter at all because of his wasteful frivolity.

How difficult to achieve that delicate balance between the gay and the grim, the spendthrift and the miser, the one who cannot live fully today because he is anticipating tomorrow and the one who will not be able to savor tomorrow because he has frittered away today.

I know a woman who has a major investment of time and money in a rich collection of linens. Tablecloths, banquet spreads, napkins, exquisite place mats from many parts of the world are among her treasures. Yet the sole enjoyment this lady has of her linens is in looking at them occasionally. She keeps them carefully packed away, while she and her family eat on plastic place mats. She is saving her beautiful linens—for what?

I have a friend who rarely uses the pretty pieces of lingerie she owns. She is hoarding them for some future moment. She does not realize that using something special may transform a routine day into an occasion.

It is in such little ways that we make today a pleasant memory for tomorrow. Rare and valuable objects can't be used indiscriminately (or wherein would lie the thrill of their rarity?), but they must be used sometime, enjoyed at some point, or wherein lies their value?

Remembering my friend, and my uncle's story, and my own growing sense of the livableness of life, I put one of my best cut-work linens on our table last night. I don't know whether my husband and sons noticed it or not. I did. And that was sufficient.

Now it is November.

The romantic decor of spring has been peeled away, the lavish baroque of summer and autumn has faded. Winter establishes a classic beauty in our landscape. Trees strip down to their essential forms of trunk and limb and twig.

Cleared of the veil of summer's foliage, in the sharp light of cold mornings and chilly afternoons, the character of the land becomes apparent. Contours of empty fields and hillsides lie as visible as ribs and vertebrae of some great skeleton. Mountains loom sharp with snow or shrouded in clouds against the near horizon.

Streams that have been hidden under the leafy limbs of

low-hanging willows and sycamores and sprawling spice-wood bushes are visible again. Their clear, swift waters glint in the chilly sunlight as they thread down the sides of steep hills and through narrow ravines to the broader sweep of rivers in the lowlands.

Across many mountain slopes, networks of paths are revealed. From sheltered farm and scattered homes they lead up the hillsides, wind around the contours, following with leisurely grace the route of least resistance on their climb.

And in the naked woodlands, gashes of old wagon roads and sled trails become distinct once more. Like the lines on a human countenance that has had deep experience of life—its demands, its growth, its grim necessities and unexpected joy —these traceries across the face of nature lend meaning and character to the countryside.

There are those who speak of November's bleakness. They find it a harsh month in the mountains. Yet to me it has always seemed one of our subtlest, strongest seasons.

True, the colors are muted grays and greens and earth-browns now. True, we are peeling down to the unyielding granite backbone of ridge and valley. True, existence takes on a sharper awareness of the fundamentals—cold, warmth, waning light, welcome food.

But all of these are the essence of living: red clay, rock ledge, woods mulch, roaring hearth. It is good, in November, to stand away from the green cover of springtime past and the white blanket of winter to come, and discover the earth in all its silent strength.

Our dog is a good companion for a walk. By nature he is a walker, rather than a hiker. So am I.

My definition of the two is strictly personal. A hiker has a definite destination, determined well in advance and frequently demanding in its attainment. A walker, on the other hand, may or may not have a prearranged goal. Often his decision to walk comes on the spur of the moment. And his effort may be strenuous or lax, as his mood dictates; but almost always it is exploratory.

Our dog starts each new walk with enthusiasm. How else should any successful venture begin? Head up, eyes and ears on the alert, he trots to the fork in the road and looks down each of the ways we may follow while he awaits the choice of which we shall take today.

Once I have set my foot along the road to the woods, he bounds ahead. Circling, pausing, he sniffs at a mound of leaves and then at some nearby underbrush and returns to the leaves again. Curiosity satisfied, he looks at me and returns to my side, re-establishing our relationship.

He stops. His tail is at full mast; his ears are pricked straight up. The sound he hears does not reach me, but together we stand quietly a moment beneath the trees. Small noises, of wind and dry, dead branches and hidden insect movements are around us when we listen.

Then there is a purposeful lope forward, looking on either side to make sure that nothing which should be seen escapes attention. An unidentified hole calls for exploration. My little companion gives it his full and thorough concentration. When he is content that it holds no secrets he must dig out, he comes on his way once more.

Getting far ahead of me, then falling behind, pushing under fallen logs, through tangles of briars, peering up and down, and smelling each current of air and patch of terrain with a methodical sort of abandon, our dog possesses the woods completely during the little while that we are there.

Nothing is too small for his examination, nothing too unimportant for his concern. He has time to pause if he wishes and to turn aside if it is necessary. His goal is simply the walk itself.

Our dog and I are walkers.

A lady said to me, a note of desperation creeping into her voice, "Who speaks for the middle-aged? I know enough about growing up intelligently and growing old gracefully. What I want is someone who will tell me how to grow middle-aged confidently."

What are the years of middle age anyway? They have a way of changing as a person's perspective changes. When you're sixteen, anyone from twenty-one to thirty is already middle-aged. At thirty, the deadline shifts to include anyone between forty and fifty. Who, eventually reaching those prime years, will accept that lumpish category? None of us then is middle-aged.

But what of the very attractive lady who told me she wanted to grow into those years confidently?

She may have concluded that this is the forgotten time of life. The pressures of youth and the problems of old age attract the attention of national committees and important foundations. If you are under seventeen or over seventy, you are pretty sure to be remembered on your birthday, pampered when you're not feeling well, and deferred to in your eccentricities. If you have an anxiety or a need, there will be some study explaining it, some agency exploring it, or some expert exaggerating it.

But if you're caught in those windward years (the wind has abated, but the sails are still high), you win little enough attention, little enough rearmament. You are at that in-between age—between early grandchildren and late grand-parents, between nostalgic reminiscences of college and nudging reminders of retirement, between the defiance of teenagers and the dogmatism of octogenarians. Your prob-lems and anxieties are your own.

You are too young to be exalting and too old to be ex-hilarating. You can hold your job, vote, pay taxes, try to understand the international situation and the annual deficit, attempt to overlook advertisements about retirement ha-vens, and avoid tranquilizers as long as possible. Between widely spaced pinnacles of goals achieved, you tread in val-leys of quiet desperation.

And yet—these may be the richest years of life. If you can give yourself to the very young and escape being de-voured by them, if you can give yourself to the very old and avoid being smothered by them—somewhere between there is the possibility of discovering yourself. Yesterday is still clinging, and tomorrow is coming up fast, but you are the sovereign today. Who could confidently ask for more?

A friend once sent Albert Einstein a novel by one of the world's acclaimed contemporary writers. A little later Ein-stein returned the book to his friend and confessed that he had not finished reading it. "Life is not that complicated," was his reported comment.

Perhaps one of the world's great minds probing complex-ities at the heart and periphery of the universe, found the language of mathematics more simple and clear than that of

Once upon a time she had been one of the best-known writers in this country. In the early decades of this century some of the largest publishing houses had brought out well-received volumes of her poetry and verse dramas. A little later she had written novels and these, too, achieved distinction, if only modest fortune.

She had come to the mountains of western North Carolina to live many years ago, and from her experiences on a picturesque hillside farm she had forged a memorable volume of sketches and stories.

Slowly, during the past quarter-century, her production and her reputation had begun to diminish. Another volume of poems, a last collection of short stories—the intervals between publication grew longer; the reading public's memory grew shorter.

I found the remodeled residence that had been turned into a "rest home." A friend, who had learned I would be passing through this town, had told me that this was where our writer of yesteryear, now aged and feeble, was sheltered. There are many such places scattered across the country on little side streets, in slowly decaying parts of town where big old Victorian mansions have been abandoned for suburban split-levels. The need for these rest homes, by whatever name they may be called, seems to remain constant and acute, so that no matter how grimy the porch is, no matter how flaked the outside paint or how patched the roof, the rooms inside are crowded to capacity.

As I went into the lobby, an elderly woman sitting primly on a plastic upholstered sofa greeted me. I inquired where I might find my friend. "Down there." She nodded in the direction of a hall. "Are you a relative? Have you known her for a long time? Where are you from? Is it chilly outside this morning?"

I was overwhelmed by the strange little woman's questions, but I knew from the lost and eager expression on her face that she did not crave answers as much as companionship.

A nurse arrived, and as we walked down the linoleum-floored hall the smells of disinfectant and cleansers and medicines seemed to reinforce the sense of loneliness that hung over the place.

I turned into the small square room where my friend sat. Strapped into a rocking chair so that she would not, in her feebleness, fall, she seemed as frail as a frightened bird. Her white hair was like a spun halo around her face and her wide blue eyes glistened with the effort to remember who I was. Her bird-claw hands clutched mine. Her thin sweet voice thanked me over and over for coming to see her.

I told her about all the books she had written in the past, and she struggled to remember, seemed overwhelmed that I should have remembered. I saw her spirit fluttering feebly in a cage, caught between a yesterday that had been quick with creativity and accomplishment and a tomorrow that was bleak with inertia.

It took some effort to break her grip on my hand as I made ready to depart.

"Don't leave me." Her eyes were wide and round, desperate in their emptiness. "Don't leave me."

I went back through the lobby, but the green plastic sofa was empty this time. Only the sound of shufflings and quiet sniffles in the long hall and the permeating smell of disinfectants accompanied me through the door and down the steps.

There are so many like my friend. Hidden away, entombed from our consciousness or our conscience. Forgive us, frightened, forgetful, lonely ones everywhere.

There are numerous ways to sight-see. I discovered that one of the happiest is to go with a thirteen-year old guide who happens to be your son and is your superior in experience of the city you explore together. He can show you short cuts and side streets and dole out tidbits of fact that bring the place alive.

It was a gray day in Boston with occasional gusts of November wind. There was not enough chill to call forth mittens, not enough to command turned-up coat collars. Tall, limby elms, long since stripped of leaves, stood as though scrawled in black ink against the wintry sky. It was a good day to walk, to make acquaintance with new information and new faces. When you're with a thirteen-year-old, you're likely to meet both.

In Boston Common I was made aware of the fact that these forty-eight famous acres in the heart of the city had been sold by John Winthrop for $150. Today they're worth at least a million dollars an acre. But the trees and pond, the walks and benches remain an oasis of nature and leisure in the center of commerce.

I met the frolicsome squirrels who make a fat living by panhandling the birdwatchers and animal lovers who abound hereabouts. I met the frozen statue which stands on the rise in the center of the Common, commemorating the ordeals of our Union.

Also I met Mary Dyer, 1660, who was hanged on Boston Common for being a Quaker. It invigorated us, my schoolboy and me, to appreciate that the tolerance written into America's founding documents did not come to flower fullblown, but was nurtured by the blood of individual sacrifices.

On Beacon Hill we sauntered along the narrow alleys and streets with familiar names, but this was unlike previous visits I had made in the vicinity because now I had a guide who could arouse the flippant friendliness of the French poodle being walked at the corner, who could inform me that glass had once been nonexistent in this country and windows therefore a luxury, who could share surmise about the deceptively plain-looking woman who walked ahead of us for several blocks before she turned into a deceptively plain-looking house.

When you take a thirteen-year-old for guide, you learn the best places to find the tenderest charcoaled hamburgers for the least cash outlay; you meet strangers who are ready to be friendly; and you acquire a miscellany of knowledge. Almost none of it is useless.

When we speak of thankfulness, we tread a threadbare tightrope between pomposity and indifference. For fear of repeating hollow clichés we remain silent.

Yet to render praise is a good and useful thing. In humility and pride let us celebrate five constant gifts—five simple gifts they are that attend most of us at birth and go with us to death; in the interval between we make of them a curse or a blessing. Given into almost everyone's possession, no one can possess them for another.

I give you the five commonplace and marvelous reasons for our gratitude today and forever: sight, hearing, smell, touch, taste!

Our sight! To see morning fog lifting off of mountains and the sea rolling in from its distant deeps; to behold the pattern of a butterfly's wing and the grace of a hawk's savage flight and the strength of a healthy child's body; to view a pyramid or temple of antiquity layered with time's veneer; to find spring's first trillium blooming in the woods and summer's last morning glory trailing up an abandoned cornstalk. . . . To see, this is to be alive.

Our hearing! To hear the first drops of rain on the roof after a long drought, and the first words your baby ever forms with his small clean lips; to hear a hoot owl in the night; to listen to the majesty of Bach and the perfection of Mozart and the melancholy of the Banjo song; to recognize a voice you love calling your name. . . . To hear, this is to be alive.

Our smell! To smell freshly laundered clothes that have dried in the wind and the sun; to smell the ink and paper of a new book opened for the first time; to smell leaf smoke and bread baking and marigolds and mint. . . . To smell, this is to be alive.

Our touch! To touch the hard coolness of marble and the soft warmth of lamb's wool; to feel the moist tender flesh of baby arms that have just learned to hold your neck; to feel the luxurious relaxation of a hot bath, the sharp bite of a winter wind, the caress of sun on your skin. . . . To touch, this is to be alive.

Our taste! To taste the absolute goodness of water when we are thirsty; to bite a vine-ripened tomato and a tree-ripened peach with their dripping juices; to savor fresh buttermilk with flakes of butter, and dill pickles with a hint of garlic, and fresh rolls with a golden crust; to taste the wind when we first go out in the morning and the snow as it falls in winter. . . . To taste, this is to be alive.

Our senses are our reality and our civilization. Risk triteness or enthusiasm, but never indifference. Walk the tightrope and give thanks for the five great gifts. Live!

Men are not equal in heritage or environment, bestowed talent or acquired wealth. But one commodity we all possess in common: Today.

Twenty-four hours of sixty minutes each. Sixty minutes of sixty seconds each. Today the same for all of us in its quantity, as fixed as the pattern of stars or the path light will follow or the direction of the sun. But its quality as variable as a baby's moods, as a cloud's shape, as the wind itself. Time's quality we make for ourselves.

For today, I am thankful. For the ingredients of today: morning's awakening, night's sleep, coffee's fragrance, water's taste, laughter's pleasure, the anticipation of wings carrying us to strange terminals and wheels returning us to familiar places; music, food, weather, books, affections, surprises—the fevers and fires of today.

For yesterday, too, I am thankful. For the events that went before: seas' forming and mountains' settling; Socrates drinking the hemlock and lying down in dignity; Jesus tasting the vinegar and dying in love; Shelley singing an "Ode to the West Wind" and Lincoln scrawling his Gettysburg Address; our ancestors' fortitude—their graces, their mistakes, their endurance. "Today is the pupil of yesterday."

For tomorrow, too, I am thankful. Tomorrow is dreams; doubt overruled by faith, vision. Tomorrow is new fire struck from today's sparks. Where we stumble today, we may run tomorrow. Where we experiment now, we may exult next time. Tomorrow is the stars, and the challenge beyond. For tomorrow's hope, ever green and tender, tough and living, we give thanks.

Yesterday, today, and tomorrow—the time and trinity of our lives.

New England in winter boasts one distinctive treasure: its white birch trees.

I had enjoyed the birches in summer when their oval leaves cast a cool green shade on tended lawns or wild woodlands, and in autumn when their brilliant color transformed the landscape into a glow of polished brass and gold. But now I have encountered winter birches, and their beauty is dazzling.

The slim white trunks bring light to the darkened woods, grace to the stripped forests, and freshness to the stark and dusky season. They bend before the wind and beneath the snow, small and supple and strong.

Their bark is pale as the chalked skin of exotic ceremonial dancers, with black beauty patches placed at casual intervals. Clustered along ice-fringed brooks, thrusting through a drift of snow, the universal appeal of winter birches' beauty attracts every practitioner of hackneyed art (including prose). But it is the encounter with the tree itself—hidden root, glistening bark, barren limb, resilient grace—and the dark and chill surrounding it, which is the art, the essential experience.

There is much head-shaking and hand-wringing and sighing over the younger generation. At mention of teenagers, adults are thrown into the Slough of Despond, the Bog of Misunderstanding, the Quicksand of Futility.

One teacher has told us: "Our youth now love luxury. They have bad manners, contempt for authority. They show disrespect for elders and love chatter in place of exercise. Children are now tyrants, not the servants of their households. They no longer rise when elders enter the room. They contradict their parents, chatter before company, gobble up their food, and tyrannize their teachers."

Do you recognize the symptoms? They were described—and deplored—by Socrates in the fifth century, B.C. Which only proves the truth of the French proverb that the more things change the more they remain the same.

Tensions between parent and child, authority and experimentation, status quo and change, age and youth have always existed. Now there are more people to be tense; rebellion can come quicker and louder and in a greater variety of ways than has been possible before.

The more I struggle in the labyrinths of understanding, however, the more convinced I become that it is not authority, so much as the hypocrisy of many of our authorities, that our young ones reject. There are enough commandments and too little commitment. It is not our strength they lament, but our weakness. It is not our discipline of them that they contradict but our lack of self-discipline. The eyes of youth are clear—and sometimes hard. If we do not like what we see reflected in them, perhaps we'd better look in the mirror.

If nominations were being taken for the poorest excuse in the English language, my candidate would be: "It's too much trouble."

A parent is asked by his child to participate in some game or project that may seem trivial or profound, but he replies, "Not now. It's too much trouble."

A woman on a weary treadmill of small friendships and petty conversations says, "I've always wanted to take a trip to some distant place, meet different people. But it just seems like too much trouble."

A young person talented in music or painting, tennis or machine work is encouraged to give a little something extra in attention and practice, and shrugs: "It's too much trouble."

What we are saying when we offer this shabby excuse is simply, "I'm too anemic mentally and too flabby physically to make that extra effort which can add some fresh dimension to my life."

Genius had been defined as the ability to take infinite pains. Nothing is too much trouble when the goal is important.

Some time ago I visited a laboratory at Oak Ridge where scientists were conducting research in genetics by studying mice. Thousands of mice were housed in specially built cages and carefully constructed rooms. The life history of each rodent was catalogued in great detail. If an emergency arose, or a new development came, these scientists thought nothing of spending extra hours in their laboratories.

The master French writer, Gustave Flaubert, is said to have rewritten his classic *Madame Bovary* so many times that he was the despair of his publishers, who received carefully detailed alterations even after the book had gone to press. And Tolstoy was changing, improving *War and Peace* even as it was being printed.

One of the most pleasant homes I know is not one of the largest or most elaborate. It is a house in which the windows sparkle and the lights glow, where each piece of furniture seems to have been polished with tender care and each little piece of bric-a-brac has special meaning for the place it adorns. And in the kitchen no one seems to find it bothersome to brew a cup of tea on a chilly afternoon or whip up a sour-cream chocolate cake.

All of these—scientist, writer, homemaker—know the rewards of taking the trouble to do their work well. None of us can accomplish all we might wish. But in those realms where we play for keeps, we must find a better reason for our non-participation than that weary excuse, "It's too much trouble."

When winter comes and the first frigid winds sweep in out of the west, I think again of the wide, lonely, desert country where the Navahos and other of the Indian tribes live.

I wonder what it is like in those hogans that hover so close to the earth, providing shelter in summer from the blazing heat and refuge in winter from the relentless cold.

I wonder about the small sheepherders, with their tangled hair and wide dark eyes that look out so gravely and stoically on the world around them, and I remember statistics about tuberculosis and pneumonia and other illnesses that are related to economic and social conditions. I think of the strange yet admirable tenacity embodied in the statement, "Most Indians prefer their old tribal ways and traditions."

When Columbus discovered America, there were approximately 845,000 Indians living in what is now the United States. (Judging by Western movies and television shows, it often seems that more than that many Indians were involved in any single action against a wagon train or Army outpost.)

With the diseases and wars our civilization brought them, this number was reduced to 240,000 by the end of the nineteenth century. The present figures put the population at roughly 525,000. For that half-million, life is very rough indeed.

The average Indian family on a reservation has a yearly income of $1,500. That's half the $3,000 set as a poverty line. Unemployment on reservations is eight times the national average. Education ends at eight years of schooling for many of the children, and nine out of ten of the dwellings are considered substandard.

The American Indian hasn't vanished. He's just been abolished. Abolished from our consciences and our conformities. We inflict a high price on those who do not go along readily with our "way of life." We forget them.

And still the winter winds blow across the desert country. They are not half so cold as the chill that freezes the human heart.

Snow!

The excitement of the season's first snow does not seem to diminish with the years. Those first flakes wandering earthward arouse anticipation and lure me from whatever chore or pleasure I may be engaged in. I watch the few flakes multiply to many and become a surging whirl of white, cutting off mountains, town, the sky above, and the horizon beyond.

The magic of snow's beginning, the mystery of its patterns is sheer delight. I do not need any scientific explanation of its formation—although it increases my wonder to be told that no two flakes are alike. The marvel of immense diversity in such a unity of white! What I do need most of all to welcome the snow again is the unclouded eyesight of a child.

Snow is a sculptor that brings new forms to old familiar objects, creates fresh visions from worn and cluttered scenes.

A tall brown blade of weed becomes an etching with its frosted tracery of white on seed pod and stem.

The most obscure corner of the garden is transformed into a theater where unknown actors leave crisscrossing tracks.

The majestic mountains in the distance are visible in contours which were unseen before. Valleys are scooped white with drifts of snow, while ridges thrust up like bones blown bare and brittle in the wind.

Nothing is too small, too ugly, too broken or too abandoned to be touched by the snow and transfigured into something beautiful. Nothing seems too large, too awesome to be swept by the snow and revealed in a fresh sublimity, one hidden from our sight or knowing in another season.

Snow!

The excitement of it rustles through the schoolroom and renders study dull and irrelevant. The joy of it lifts us again into the fullness of winter and makes us look once more at the world around us, and see it for a brief moment, at least, new-minted, untrampled, the way it might have been at some long-ago Beginning.

Trying to comprehend the percentiles, quotients, ratings, curves, and other paraphernalia measuring, testing, and pigeonholing our children today, my imagination sometimes runs wild. (Since I can't even understand what the words involved are trying to say, the figures are totally beyond my grasp, and I have to resort to imagination. Or run wild myself.)

I imagine a boy named Shelley, Percy Bysshe. P. B. Shelley, seated before a long sheet headed Vocabulary—Word Use, has twenty minutes by the stop watch to make his multiple choices and mark the precise meaning of each word. But gradually he begins to think about the words—skylark? . . . cloud?—and he pauses to consider how two words might rhyme. He has subverted the test. The stop watch has swallowed him. Result: "Needs more vocabulary drill."

Or I think of a boy named Newton, Isaac. He has been rounded up for his I.Q. rating. The result is dreary: "Needs more group identification. Dangerous tendency to sit idly under apple trees."

An internationally known chemist, Dr. Joel H. Hildebrand, made some interesting observations on I.Q. tests a while back. He called them a great disservice to creativity in education. He felt that they failed to measure (because some things are beyond measurement?) those qualities that contribute to creative achievement. These include motivation, curiosity, drive, persistence, and industry.

Dr. Hildebrand said, "The first task of a child entering school is to learn to read and write and to understand numbers and to resist with all his strength any efforts to meddle with his personality." He went on to point out that it was fortunate for civilization "that Beethoven, Michelangelo, Galileo, and Faraday were not required by law to attend schools where their 'total personalities' would have been operated upon to make them learn acceptable ways of participating as members of 'the group.' "

Individuality, personality, originality—how are these "measured"? How are these "developed"?

A school administrator from a large Midwestern city told

me of a child whose Intelligence Quotient was on the record as being 54. For two years she was placed in the slower section of her class. When she didn't study and when her grades fell behind, teachers and others merely shrugged and pointed to her low I.Q.

Then it was discovered that the figure on her card was not an I.Q. rating at all. Through some incomprehensible mistake the number was that of her coatroom locker!

A search unearthed her real I.Q.—around 100—but for a crucial period no one had recognized that child as she was. She had become a reflection of some rating card rather than the other way around. She was a victim of techniques that may be useful—if they are kept in proper perspective and if they are judged as means, not ends.

Each season of gift-giving we hear over and over again the lament for the person "who has everything." Here is a list compiled exclusively for the man or woman who does not have everything.

For the person you know who does not have self-confidence, who lacks his share of the outrageous egotism so often necessary for success today, our gift suggestion is—a compliment. Give the big giant-size compliment that comes packed in adjectives and contains the extra ingredient of appreciation. The only cost of this inexpensive item is a little insight and a lot of imagination. And it's a gift you can give over and over again.

For the person you know who doesn't have companionship, give a visit. The carefree, unexpected, do-it-yourself brand of visit, prompted by no organization, boxed in good news and wrapped in happy reminiscence. This particular present costs a small amount of time and a large amount of concern for others. You can shape it to any length and size you like.

For the individual on your list who does not have joy, our catalogue proposes a gift of laughter. This is a very costly item. It comes wrapped in the tinsel of self-forgetfulness, tied with bright ribbons of awareness. The more of this precious commodity you give away, the more you have left. Laughter costs selfishness and pomposity, and to keep it you must share it.

For the friend who no longer has hope, give faith. This does not come in an economy pack; only the king size counts. Even then you cannot give any part of it away until you have accepted it yourself. The genuine article comes wrapped in flesh and blood and the down payment is your life. If you have this wealth to share with others, it's the shining gift to hang at the top of the tree.

And for every acquaintance remember the debonair Maurice Chevalier's credo: "I smile at all the girls. If they're pretty, it makes me feel good! If they're not pretty, it makes them feel good!"

No one has everything. There is something only you can give.

For weeks we have been covered with a concern for things, physical objects. Our bodies have ached in accumulating and distributing them. Our minds have grown weary selecting them. According to each of our fancies and finances we have been dealing in rocking horses or rare books, rag dolls or diamonds, tricycles, neckties, minks or marbles.

Then there were trees and ornaments, cards and turkeys —innumerable things, things to be bought, made, given, received, wrapped, and unwrapped.

And now the day is here! Suddenly things are the least part of its joy. For Christmas is a season of people, love between human beings, of the love between God and man.

Each of us lays hold of this love in his own special way and thereby claims his own unique gift which this day can give—new insight into its message and happiness. This happiness is different and deeper for me this year than ever before, because we have had a son away from home and now he is home again.

This day celebrates the birth of a child. And due to the wonderful purpose and mystery of that child's life, this day celebrates the birth of every child.

He came—all innocence and purity and hope and perfection—into a world where ignorance and indifference, hate and fear could bring Him down as surely as the slashing persistent fangs of wolves brought down new lambs on His native hills. He came in poverty with incomparable riches: the currency of wisdom in His pockets, love His legacy, knowledge of God and man in His savings account. He had nothing—and He had everything.

What child born under the fatherhood of God into the brotherhood of man on an earth of unspeakable beauty and cruelty inherits less? Or more? Random winds, shining stars, the brevity of life, and the infinity of space are inheritances of every human babe—if he will but lay claim to them before the hungers of his mortal flesh dim the splendor of his spirit waiting to be released.

It was the glorious, total, deathless victory of that child born in the Judean hills that He never lost innocence and hope and perfection in an old and corrupt world. For the rest of us, these birthrights fall away from our lives like garments shed at night, as we grow shrewd in the ways of men, careful for needs of the body, careless of needs of mind and spirit. Seeing in ourselves the enormity of his failure, we find renewal in the largeness of our Creator's wisdom and in the hope of our children's new beginnings. Could we but give our son or daughter armor against the assailants of this world—the failures that diminish confidence, the greeds that tarnish joy, the prejudices that reject personality, the cynicisms that poison the wellsprings of creation—we would rush to provide them such protection.

How, then, this Christmas day can we observe one child's birth appropriately and make every child's birthday close to His? Can we do more, or less, than purge ourselves of the ignorance and indifference, the hate and fear that killed Him, that, in the end, slowly or swiftly, secretly or openly kills us all?

Vignettes glimpsed in the winter landscape stick in the memory like last summer's cockleburs:

Cattle, scrawny and muddy with matted hair, turned into a field of brown cornstalks. The ears of corn long since gathered, the cattle tug at the last dry leaves clinging to the stalks and find stray nubbins where they have fallen during harvest time. It is a scene in browns and beiges and dun earth colors.

Crows perched on an ancient rail fence at the edge of a field, rising with shrill cries of alarm at the approach of a stranger, flapping into the dark pine forest behind them. Their solid jet wings and heads appear like punctuation marks against the lead-colored sky as they circle and disappear in the woods. It is a scene in blacks and grays and the dark greens of the pines.

Water running coldly iridescent over stones rounded and smoothed by centuries of wear, and between jagged boulders on moss-covered banks. The water's metallic shine reflects in the ice that fringes the stream's edges, delaying, covering, but never completely containing the water's fall. It is a scene of shimmering lights and darks, shadows and sparkles.

Junk—junk and litter clogging stream beds for miles through majestic and scenic countryside. Trash by the ton spilling down hillsides and into ravines, choking brooks and plants, scarring the face of nature. This is man's signature of his presence. It is a scene of rusted, twisted metal, chipped and broken porcelain, cast-off plastic and paper and tin, spattered glass and rotted cloth. It is the hideous mark of man revealed by winter's harsh, cold light.

The time has come to choose between my African violets and my family. Three men of assorted sizes and demands are outnumbered by dozens of violets even more assorted and exacting.

I was hooked into the African violet habit by that ancient gimmick of a free sample from a confirmed addict. Knowing my fondness for wood violets and the color purple, this friend-in-gardener's-clothing gave me an African violet. Thereby I became fit prey for manufacturers of special soil (everything but earth), plant foods, sprays, pots.

Then I was told to divide my plants. So I had two, an equal number with my children. I was still in control of the situation.

Someone showed me how to root a leaf and I had three plants. My family and violets were equal.

But while the family growth rate remained static, those violets multiplied. They overflowed kitchen window sills, dining room, living room, finally corners of the guest rooms. When a cousin revealed that her husband was shaving in the basement lavatory because his bathroom with fluorescent lights and northern exposure had proved perfect for her violet greenhouse, I inaugurated a plant-control program. I accepted no more gift rootings. I disciplined myself to stick broken leaves in a wastebasket rather than a pot.

But what of the plants already flourishing? A baby sitter can look after children for a while, but who ever heard of a violet sitter? You cannot just abandon plants your own hands brought into bloom.

The problem may appear simple to the noninitiated. "Plants are obviously less care than children," they protest. "You can set them in one place and they'll stay put. A little water is all they need. And they can't talk back."

Such innocence! Such infuriating naïveté!

You can set an African violet in one place—but it's usually the wrong place. Too much sun, they yellow and wither. Too little sun, they yellow and wither. Now, whatever dosage of sun a child gets, he won't wither! And if he wants a drink, he'll get it, something that the "stay-put" violet won't do.

And, a little water is all they need indeed! That brings up the controversy between the watering-from-above school and the watering-from-below school. (Partisans of each method are only slightly less fierce than the guerrillas in the war between the sexes.) But with a child you know just where to put the water! Even Spock and Gesell can't confuse you on that.

African violets can't talk back? What about those brown blotches that appear on the leaves when they're fed too rich a diet? What about those stems that snap when they're too roughly handled? They talk back all right—in their own language.

Everything considered, two boys and a husband are much less trouble. I'm ready to kick the habit and help hook someone else. Anyone for an African violet?

One of the simplest elements of our life; also the most complex substance of our being: love. A four-letter word, easy to pronounce, perplexing to define. It falls glibly from the tongue, yet twines its innermost meanings intricately through mind and heart. Its spelling comes readily; its rhyme falls handily; no word is more commonplace. But there is no reality more rare in achievement.

In love's paradox is its power. Another aspect of its ecstasy is its torment; another countenance of its endurance is its fickleness; another side of its tenderness is its toughness. There is an elixir of life which only love can brew, and a draught of death which only love can drain.

Of all love's mysteries none is more baffling than its birth and death. Love leaps into being like a light struck from a match; it dies as abruptly. It glows to life as gradually as a fire breathed into careful warmth; it lingers as long as the flame of life.

Perhaps the saddest truth of all is the carelessness by which we may let love slip away. Love between man and woman, parent and child, friend and friend may melt to ashes and lie as forever dead because we forgot, or never knew, or misunderstood the nature of the most compelling force in our lives.

If we lose the capacity to love, though we gain the whole world, we have lost our best self.

Sometimes we look upon winter as the season of death, of bleakness, of despair. Because the earth is locked in the grip of freeze and no green things grow and even the flow of water is silenced under crusts of ice, we consider this a time of extinction, an abandonment of life.

But life is not annihilated; it is merely hidden beneath the earth. Instead of flourishing in leaf and flower up in the sparkling air, it moves underground, nourishing roots and filaments of growth for a time to come. This is the season of quiet and hidden renewal.

Unlike the natural world around us, we human beings do not often observe a season of renewal. We expect each day to be a pinnacle of achievement. We want every week to be packed with a maximum of activity. We consider lost those hours that are not crowded into some prearranged schedule. Yet we do not always have to be in full flower to prove that we are alive. Sometimes we need to be putting down roots.

People, no less than plants, need a dormant period so that their sap can rise afresh and strong for a time of growth. Rejuvenation is not a matter of years or the age of a tree or a man. I know teenagers who need rejuvenating because they have lost that juice which brings zest to the daily encounters of living. I know octogenarians who have never lost their child's sense of wonder and adventure, because they have tapped some source of renewal for spirit as well as body.

A quiet season, a time when roots can search out deeper holdings and tap fresh reserves of nourishment, is to be cherished. Without it the flowering which we await is shallow, paltry, frantic, and soon withering on the stem. With it no miracle of growth is impossible.

There is a killer loose among us.

He, or she, may fit many names by which we characterize our horrible murderers—the Speedy Strangler, the Mad Mutilator, the Bloody Slasher.

He practices these, and a dozen other forms of murder, by savage blows on head or body, cruel twists and hurtlings of his victims, sudden crushing or suffocation, and sometimes incineration. With infinite cunning and variety this killer makes certain that each death is different from all the others he has dealt. Every corpse he leaves carries a distinctive set of bruises, scars, and breaks.

The killer is swift. In the space of a moment he strikes— and an eager young girl, an important elder statesman, a devoted mother or father, a bright college boy is turned into a lifeless mass of flesh, bones, skin, and blood.

Unlike the psychopathic murderer, he does not choose victims of a certain sex or class or degree of beauty. Unlike the mugger and armed robber, he does not lie in wait only for those who are wealthy and can yield him some return. Unlike certain mortal diseases, he does not attack chiefly those who belong to a special age group or ancestral strain, or who are indifferent to certain habits of health. Indeed, this killer is democratic. He slaughters the innocent as well as the guilty, the careful along with the careless, the thoughtful and brave beside the stupid and reckless.

Above all, this killer ranges wide. He stalks not a limited section of one large city, not the lonely byways of one rural locality but every road and alley, every street and freeway in every corner of our country. You may have encountered his grisly countenance lurking in your own driveway or along a sweeping turnpike, as you measured the miles across some part of America.

This killer is here. We know his power, his range, his brutality. Why don't we catch him and shear him of his strength? His name is Death-on-the-Highway. And we, each of us, are his potential representative and his potential victim. The Mad All-American Killer who has slaughtered more of our citizens than died in all past wars—he is you and I behind the wheel of a high-powered car when we grow, for one moment, careless, lawless, self-important. Will you, will I be one of his statistics this year; and on which side of the ledger, killer or killed?

We have had two days of snow which were precisely right for sledding. These are rare enough in our region to create considerable excitement in younger circles.

There is a slope of lawn to the west of our house which opens into a small level spot at the bottom where a home-made wire barricade has served as a backstop for baseballs in balmier weather. This hill is bounded by tall white pines whose limbs bend under their heavy white burden. Down this slope and under these trees the sleds have flourished for two days.

The sounds of shouting, screaming, laughter, excitement filled the clean cold air. Tall boys, small boys, thin girls, plump girls, numerous neighbors, a few strangers—they rode the snow-packed swiftness of the descent on an assortment of sleds with dazzling variations of posture. They rode sitting, lying, standing; like riders of the surf in tropical waters, they balanced themselves on waves of the earth's contour and were momentary conquerors of all they surveyed. Their energy seemed boundless. Their enthusiasm was as invigorating as the air itself.

I concocted errands that would take me outside so that I might tramp through the yard or along the driveway and become, at least by remote control, part of their rapture. I rediscovered the fascination of making footprints in deep, crunchy snow; I found fresh wonder on old paths.

The snow on the slope is melting. The pine limbs reach up once more. The children are back in school. But those two days are frozen in our memories.

Do you know the sharpest epithet a political or economic leader can level at an opponent today? Do you know the vilest name by which a community can label one of its leaders? No, it's not unprintable; it's just unthinkable. The term is Do-Gooder. Or Bleeding Heart.

To call a person or an organization Do-Gooder is to tag it as idealistic, ineffectual, and slightly comic. The cure presumably is a quickie divorce from efforts to do good. Become a Do-Badder. Dry up those bleeding hearts and transform them into calcified shells. Come out of the twilight world of gentleness and understanding and hope, and emerge into the bright, tough, new world, which isn't new at all, of course, just the jungle with neon lights.

It isn't hard to stop being a Do-Gooder. Discard concern for anyone outside your own narrow circle of well-being. Cultivate total and undiluted selfishness. (That doesn't come very hard to most of us.) Approach every family situation from the viewpoint of your own ego. In the community vote on every issue as it affects your own pocketbook right this minute. In national and international decisions reduce every issue to Bad Guys (Them) and Good Guys (Us) and denounce anything that interferes with your own comfort, pleasure, or daily afternoon nap.

With constant vigilance you can avoid ever being called a Do-Gooder or Bleeding Heart. You will have squeezed the warm, rich blood right out of your veins, and you can be assured that you have a tough, wizened remnant of an organ prematurely pumping embalming fluid through your body. When this happens, of course, you begin to write your own epitaph.

As we were driving along a crowded street, I noticed that the muffler on the car just ahead of us was dragging the ground. As a rule I am not what you might call a muffler watcher.

Of course, I knew the bare essentials: A muffler is some-where under and to the rear of a car and has something to do with the noise or lack of noise made by the motor. When something happened to our muffler, however, and we en-dured a roar roughly equivalent to a new eruption of Mt. Vesuvius and had to buy a new muffler, I suddenly became quite aware of them.

This is a homespun example of the phenomenon I have labeled my Law of Natural Observance.

Stated in its simplest form this law maintains that we see what we want to see. Most of us for most of the time do not see most of the world around us. Its grandest beauty and most degrading ugliness escape us because we are not look-ing. We see not only with our eyes but with our own special interests, our own tiny frames of reference.

To go back to the case of the commonplace muffler—or to progress from the example of the muffler—have you ever noticed that, as soon as you have some rather extensive dental work done, you become acutely aware of everyone else's teeth? Whenever you have to invest in a new roof for the house or a reseeding for the lawn you are suddenly examining the roofs in your neighborhood and the lawns around you? You are following the Law of Natural Observance.

Probably the most recent manifestation of this occurs in the realm of women's hair. With more and more investment in wigs, hairpieces, bleaches, and dyes, it is inevitable that women's attention should be riveted with increasing concentration on each other's hair. Which proves with a beautiful precision the exact ratio between our investment (of time or money or concern) and the functioning of the Law of Natural Observance.

The law also applies to travel. You may read about a distant state or region in our country or about a city in another part of the world, and feel only the most casual interest in any disaster or notable event that occurs there. But make one visit to that place, spend a few days in that region or city, and you will read the next headlines about it with the most intense concern.

As with many laws, the Law of Natural Observance is flexible. It may be stretched to include worlds we never knew existed—until we began to look.

Walking in the country not long ago we came to a hillside that had been cleared in years past. No one had tended it since; wind and rain had had their way with it, but gradually it was putting forth a new growth. Sassafras sprouts were everywhere.

I broke a twig to smell the spicy fragrance. Knowing how tenaciously the roots cling, I was reminded that a person could look at sassafras, as at most other things in life, from different points of view.

To a farmer these bushes would mean long days of drudgery, digging them out so that grass or more profitable trees could be planted. To old-timers who had a taste for herbs, however, sassafras would be a rich bed of roots and twigs from which to brew tea. To a mere roamer of the hillside, the shrubbery was a wild growth to be trampled through on a makeshift path.

Yet as I smelled the sassafras and thought of how some of its mitten-shaped leaves would look in a short while, after they had unrolled from winter's grip into full growth, I remembered that there were interesting facts and folklore connected with sassafras.

It has been credited (by unofficial historians) with aiding in the discovery of America. The theory is advanced that its strong fragrance, borne on the wind, caused Columbus to believe he was near land and seek a harbor in the New World.

In 1622, an expedition was sent from England to Massachusetts to produce sassafras for shipment back to the mother country. Accounts of its medicinal virtues had been so glowing that even officials of the British Government in Virginia were instructed to bring it home on return voyages.

Among many of the mountain people sassafras has been a tabu wood for burning in stove or fireplace. It is supposed to bring bad luck, if so used. Perhaps this belief goes back to Cherokee Indian lore, for the Cherokees also refused to use the sassafras for fuel. Perhaps there is more practicality than superstition to this belief, however, when we consider that sassafras, like chestnut, is very apt to pop out of the fireplace, and a live ember can set a log cabin or a frame house on fire. Bad luck indeed!

I have also heard that the early pioneers often used sassafras twigs, pulverized at one end, for toothbrushes. I wonder if those who used sassafras had 40 per cent fewer cavities than those who used another kind of toothbrush?

Results of a recent health survey proved that . . .

But wait! Some background data is necessary before these results are divulged.

The survey was conducted by this reporter and is, as they say in pro circles, an examination-in-depth of one of the pressing problems of our time. The problem is death—and how we can bolster our health to avoid the problem.

News dispatches, articles, symposia, polls—all flood us with information about fresh knowledge in the realm of health. They should help lengthen the days of our lives—and they surely have made us more self-conscious during those days—and nights.

For instance, there is milk. We learned not long ago that milk and cream promote cholesterol. And cholesterol causes heart attacks. One of the staples of our diet was tumbled from its eminent position as our "most perfect food." To avoid the lurking dangers of whole milk and cream I turned to tea with lemon at lunch and dinner, with black coffee for breakfast.

Then I read that cadmium causes high blood pressure. Tea and coffee contain cadmium. The cups rattled from my trembling hand and joined the milk glasses in a crash upon the floor.

But thirst is a human condition. What shall we drink? Fruit juices? Fruit juices contain sugar, and sugar is fattening, and as everyone who can spell the word calorie knows, it is excessive weight that aggravates high blood pressure and heart ailments. No relief there.

Where are we to turn then? To simple water? Wait! If we choose water, it will be either fluoridated or unfluoridated. In the first case, opponents of fluoridation warn us we'll be imbibing poison; and in the latter instance, supporters tell us we'll be suffering neglect of teeth, bones, etc.

Milk is out. Tea and coffee are out. Fruit juices and water are out.

Before dehydration sets in, let me quickly announce the results of my survey as mentioned above.

One out of every one person is going to die. No one can dispute this conclusion.

Why not relax a little and go in peace and some bit of comfort? At least we can avoid spending all our days in fretful anxiety over cholesterol and cadmium.

Isn't it fine that a lovely, lacy day celebrating romance should come right in the middle of February?

There are three different martyrs named Valentine whose feast day is on February fourteenth. But historians do not grant them much connection with the day as we know it.

One of these was a Roman priest and doctor who was beheaded. Another was a bishop. He, too, was beheaded. The third was a martyr, but the precise manner of his death has gone unrecorded.

The only fact I see in common between these men named

Valentine and the day named after them, but rejoicing in romantic love, is that each involves to a greater or lesser degree losing one's head.

> *"Will you be my Valentine?*
> *I'll be yours if you'll be mine."*

A simple couplet of barter, at first glance, but masking a complex state of mind and various difficulties of digestion. It conjures up all the red roses and violets, all the ribbons and laces, and all the honey-sweet words that have decorated valentines through palpitating generations.

It invites the simple heartache and happiness of "falling in love." Such a strange term, "falling in love," suggestive of catapulting down a deep dark well, toppling from a throne, stumbling over a hidden pitfall, plunging through space. Well, perhaps "falling" in love is all of these—and more.

Somehow I pity those unimaginative folks who feel they will never fall in love again. In a dozen different ways—all minor, all fleeting, but gay and stimulating—I fall in love a little bit with so many people I meet. They have wit, or a thought that is challenging, or eyes that see, or a charming voice. And it doesn't subtract a bit from the big lasting loves of our lives to multiply our affection for those who can add a touch of humor or beauty to the daily design.

So, in the middle of gray, chilled February we exchange bright lacy hearts:

To you who wear laughter lightly and often.

To you who are young and pretty as springtime, and you who are old and noble as autumn.

To you who keep courage untarnished.

And especially to you who dare hope and believe and risk excitement and commitment in the annual round of routine.

By my Valentine?

A balanced diet. All through our lives we hear the pronouncement that everyone needs a balanced diet. And by this we mean meat, vegetables, fruit, milk, fats, sweets; strength, growth, endurance, energy for our physical selves.

But who speaks of the balanced diet for our minds and spirits? Do they need nourishment any less than our bodies? Do they not need replenishment, too? Do we lavish attention on our stomachs, muscles, skin, bones, and blood because these are our obvious selves, while we neglect the larger, more important selves and starve our intellects (curiosity, imagination, reason) and our spirits (dreams, ideals, love, faith)?

What contradiction is it that lets us stuff our bodies and starve our souls? We expand our waistlines and shrink our horizons.

Wondering about this, perhaps we could make a list of foods that are necessary for mental and spiritual health, growth, vigor. For a balanced diet, each day's menu should include:

Red meat of a new idea, a fresh thought—to be cut into sharply, tough or tender, and chewed thoroughly and swallowed slowly. Without this meat there can be no strength.

Vitamins from varied vegetables and fruits of experience —to be encountered in the back yard; on a different route to work some morning; by exposure to a book, a piece of music, a painting, a sport, which has been untried before. Without these vitamins there can be no growth.

Milk of human kindness and the cream of human charity —to be ladled out in generous portions both to those with whom we live and work, to those we love, and to ourselves as well, so that we shall not demand the impossible of ourselves or anyone else. Without these enrichers of life there can be little stamina for the long haul and little pleasure in the daily duties.

Sweets of patience and affection—to be a dessert crowning each day with special flavor. Without these the body as well as spirit wastes away.

And, with all, the salt of humor. Without laughter life has lost its savor. Try a dash with your main dish.

Wouldn't it be pathetic to waste away with pernicious anemia of the spirit? Perhaps it's time for a checkup, to see if our daily diet has been balanced.

That first murderer, among the dewy leaves and grass and ripening fruit, cried out his anguished guilt, "Am I my brother's keeper?"

And we echo the question today, needing no answer—we know the answer as we know the cycle of seasons—but crying for reassurance in our guilt.

Despite all the evasions we employ and the hypocrisies we practice and the indifferences we defend, we know the answer. Despite all the legalities which entangle us and the fears which ensnare us and the habits which imprison us, we know the answer. Am I my brother's keeper?

How strange it is that we mortal creatures should spend so many of the days of our lives seeking ways to divide ourselves from one another. How pathetic that we little human beings should use the strength of our fallible minds and feeble muscles devising ways by which we might be separated from one another.

The universe expands around us in awesome indifference to our loneliness. The ravages of disease and age lie in wait for each one of us. Winter's blast and summer's blister attack our frail bodies with vast neutrality. The questions at the edge of the abyss—of life and its evil, its good, its purpose—haunt the long nights for each of us.

How then can we be prodigal enough, stupid enough to use our precious little store of energy and time to attack not the common enemies and the common challenge—but each other!

Our stranger or our brother? Of necessity all those bound by mortal flesh and immortal spirit shall somehow come together and make life possible for one another.

We cannot come together in perfect equality of talents, hopes, resources. But we can and shall meet and live in equality of respect, humility, and pride.

The enduring literature of the world has one common characteristic: It reveals how man, in all his uniqueness, is still part of universal humanity. There is something more important than remembering that each is his brother's keeper. And that is to remember that he is our brother.

Among the happiest memories of my childhood are those long evenings in winter when my father and mother and I sat beside a blazing open fire and listened to my mother read aloud.

Sometimes she read a long and engrossing novel, and as we laid it aside at the end of certain chapters and made ready for bed, I could scarcely wait for the following night when we would come back to that book and re-enter its magic world. No country was too far away, no period of time too remote to be brought into our living room by the sorcery of words. I knew emperors and shepherds, murderers and explorers, witches and adventuresses, and they became as real to me as the schoolmates I knew each day. My mother's reading brought them to our fireside.

Frequently she read aloud a biography or a book of history, this usually of my father's choosing. We shared the struggles of many peoples down the centuries; struggles for power, land, religious beliefs, freedom. And always, behind the generals and the rulers, moved the horde of common men and women who carried the burdens and were the final victors or victims.

There was poetry, too, and sometimes my father would interrupt the reading and recite from memory the remainder of some familiar passage. I was invariably impressed when this occurred, for then I realized that an adult had found these lines so meaningful that he incorporated them into his daily life. Thus, by example, I came to know that the enduring poetry man has created is not some pretty adornment at the periphery of our existence; it is substance which nourishes us at the core of our living.

My father and mother were not scholars in the formal sense, but they both knew that a person who stays alive must keep on growing. They grew during long evenings of reading aloud. And so did I.

Sometimes now I feel a twinge of pity for boys and girls who have only wide-screen CinemaScope and plays and lectures and athletic contests and concerts and museums and recreation centers, not to mention color television, constantly at their finger tips. They can never know the enchantment, the liberation of imagination, which came from a firelit evening and a voice reading aloud the living words of the world's literature.

From the window where I write the view is bounded on its farthest horizons by the length of the Great Smokies. As I sit here today with pencil and paper on my lap, my eyes look up and out at the cloud-covered heights in the distance.

A few minutes ago their skyline stood out clearly against the opaque winter sky, but now it has disappeared behind a curtain that holds either rain or snow or a combination of the two, depending on altitude and shifts in temperature.

Gradually the curtain moves from the high Smokies across the intervening valleys and lesser ridges to the hill where I sit. A few minutes ago I looked out through pale February sunshine to the familiar Smokies, and now I am wrapped in a cloud that has no touch or taste or sound and yet locks the mountains yonder in invisibility.

This is something a lowlander does not understand about the mountains. This is something no casual visitor can experience and no lifelong mountaineer can fail to know in his blood and bones. "This" is the constant changeability of mountains.

Those who do not know the hill country in a variety of seasons, over a period of time, under shifting conditions tend to think that when they have seen a lofty range or towering pinnacle they have seen it once and for all time.

They have seen only once, never "for all time." Because mountains are like frozen seas of earth, ever changing, inviting, rejecting, enduring. The rains beat against them and the snows freeze and thaw upon them. Sun and fog and wind and frost touch them gently or ferociously. Their rock ledges crack and disintegrate with the stately passage of centuries, and their plants flower and fade in the brief passage of weeks. Slowly, or swiftly, they change.

Even the color of the mountains is never the same. The blue mists which seem to shroud them so often from a distance may be pale as wisps of gauze when seen in the light of early morning, or deep purple as bolts of velvet when seen late in the afternoon twilight.

Like the depths of the ocean yielding up a spectrum of greens and blues at certain seasons, so the heights of the mountains give similar richness and subtlety of color during various hours of the day and months of the year. For change is the essence of nature's process, and whether it be gradual as a snail's pace or sudden as the eruption of a volcano, mountains are part of that process, that inevitability.

They came to the New World looking for gold. And they found chocolate. It seems to be the fate of many explorers, and the irony of history, that those who search most voraciously shall not recognize wealth when they find it.

Four and a half centuries ago that Aztec Empire which is now Mexico was the most progressive and wealthy nation in the Western Hemisphere. When Cortez and the Spanish Conquistadores came to Mexico in 1519, they were looking for gold. They found instead chocólatl. This was a strong, bitter drink made of roasted and ground cacao beans flavored with spices.

The Aztec treasury was not filled with the precious metal that the Conquistadores had hoped would dazzle their eyes and weight them down on their return voyage to Spain. The royal treasuries of the mighty Emperor Montezuma were filled with cacao beans, some three thousand tons!

If those Spanish adventurers, intent on becoming instant millionaires, could have foretold the future they would have seen that in the long course of history these ordinary-looking beans would be the source of many fortunes. They did like the taste of that Aztec beverage, however, and they sent samples of the beans back to Europe.

The Spanish made the first great improvement in the use of chocolate: They added sugar. For a century they kept the secret of their goodies to themselves. Then Italy, Germany, and France learned the secret, and in 1657 a Frenchman opened a shop in London selling solid chocolate for preparing the beverage.

The next big step in the evolvement of this food came when the English added milk to chocolate, about 1700. (When we consider how long it takes to manage the simplest discoveries—two nations and almost two centuries to get sugar and milk into chocolate!—we might wonder how we ever got the wheel and the combustion engine together.)

Until the middle of the nineteenth century chocolate was for wealthy Europeans only. In several capital cities chocolate houses, which later became famous clubs, were the fashionable gathering places of the period.

And now, anyone with fifteen cents can buy a cup of hot chocolate and any child with a dime can munch a milk-chocolate bar. Montezuma's treasure has become our daily fare!

That night in late winter when the first peepers call in icy ponds and hidden swamplands, that night marks the first moment of spring.

Old-timers in the mountains say that the first frogs "will

look through glass windows three times before spring really breaks," but it is easy to accept three more veils of ice, knowing that those noisy little harbingers are laying their masses of eggs and the new life of spring is stirring under the frozen crust.

After those first frogs spring seems to rush forth on all fronts. Full streams tumble clear and cold out of the hills where winter snow and rain have made the spongy earth a reservoir of moisture soaked against days of heat and drought to come. Tall stems of trillium and jack-in-the-pulpit thrust up almost overnight. Suddenly, birds are busy everywhere—cardinal, catbird, crow, resident blue jay, and migrating grosbeak, and then one moonlit night the mockingbird sings.

Spring, like autumn, is a season for bypaths and side roads. The wide highways unrolling across our country are alluring enough, the thoroughfares and turnpikes save time, but occasionally it is good to turn aside from the new concrete ribbons, the easiest route, the quickest way, and follow old gravel roads and country lanes.

Perhaps that is what the simple life anywhere consists of: a momentary turning aside, a glimpse down a different path to see, hear, feel, ponder the uniqueness that is common to our lives.

On side roads wait the little farms, new lambs, new ground, pungent with the smell of fresh roots. You find pastures, too, with salt licks for cattle, abandoned orchards where gnarled old apple trees put forth hopeful bloom. Then there are the deep woods, inviting longer exploration, yielding themselves slowly to the stranger's probing. And all along the way—people—those who will share a moment or an hour in joking, remembering, denouncing, confiding.

Spring approaches—around us, within us. We may turn the new ground of untried appreciation, discover the salt of humor, the gnarled strength of old ideals, the variety of new ideas. There are old friendships whose roots may be strengthened and new friendships to be brought to blossom.

Spring is for sowing good seed, plowing fresh furrows.

Are there moments captured in your memory, like a moth caught in a cobweb or a flower frozen in its unfolding? They are not the large headline episodes of war declared or peace attained or personal grief and honor. They are simply those everyday minutes when some sight or sound or smell breaks through our consciousness with special force, carrying a heavy freight of meaning.

It is just such instants which we often remember most clearly from childhood. Our families ask us if we recall some important event that was supposed to be a landmark in our development. It is a hazy recollection. But we have vivid memory of the way the sun slanted across the grass where we played on a certain afternoon in spring; or how our father's hands looked as he stroked the grain in a piece of wood, or the sound of snow falling in the night on rhododendron leaves and bare oak branches outside our bedroom window.

It is not the gold pieces of special events that we hoard in our remembrance of things past, but the pennies of daily currency that have lodged with special brightness in some pocket of the mind.

Such a moment occurred for me the other day. I was passing through the bedroom of one of my boys. He was standing before the mirror tying his necktie. The tilt of his head, the skillfulness of the gesture with which he looped the knot in his tie arrested me in mid-passage. It was the stance and gesture of a man. Oh, a little man, a man in miniature, but nevertheless masculine, foretelling the adult waiting just around the corner of the calendar.

All at once I knew that I would have to look sharply, listen keenly, enjoy quickly and fully all the minutes of childhood left. Only yesterday, it seemed, this infant was groping with the challenge of a shoelace; this morning he was tying his tie with the forethrust chin, the tight neck, the unstudied care that has marked generations of males carrying out this daily ritual. He was not yet a man, not quite. But I could see the oak sprouting from the acorn. And I was glad.

I said to myself, watching, capturing the moment: All life is growth. But something also said: How does it happen so quickly? I knew my mind would not relinquish easily this instant of heightened consciousness, this stab of realization that our child was already part of another, larger world.

Each new precooked food which arrives on the market, each new utensil and gadget which is invented for the housewife arrives with the enthusiastic assurance of its creator that it will take the little woman out of the kitchen. It will free her from the stove, release her from the refrigerator, and liberate her from the dishpan.

Our attitude suggests that the kitchen today is only slightly more tolerable than the torture chambers of medieval ages, and that its victims live only by hope of quick and permanent escape.

Where we have not been able to eliminate the kitchen as an important part of family existence, we have tried to transform it into more of a Cinderella room. It has become, in some habitations, an extra lounge or den, complete with television and all necessary distractions. Elsewhere it has been expanded into a glorified play area, with recreational opportunities for all, from tots to teens.

Is it totally unenlightened of me to wish that someone might think of the kitchen as a place distinctive unto itself, where good food for the palate's delight and the body's rejuvenation is prepared with loving care?

I remember such a kitchen—and I smile at the words of that witty old rascal, George Bernard Shaw: "There is no love sincerer than the love of good food."

Isn't someone left to tell prospective young homemakers that imagination and intelligence are as much at home in the kitchen as in the laboratory or studio or office, and that affection can flower here and spill its fragrance over a whole house?

There was no talk of calories or cholesterol or schedules around my mother's kitchen. There was a spacious pantry smelling of soap, and sunshine from a casement window, and the subtle aroma of stored goodies.

There was a shining wood-burning range where soup that merited the name of soup (based on a rich marrow-bone beef stock) could simmer and blend the flavors of a half-dozen vegetables.

An ample refrigerator held flat pans of milk, and when my mother skimmed the cream, it was so thick it seemed to resemble dry ropes. That cream transformed fresh raspberries and wild strawberries, steamed oatmeal or tart apple crisp into a gourmet's dish.

There were pans in the cupboards that suggested my favorite dishes: a saucepan in which tiny green peas (never overgrown, never overcooked) were prepared in spring; a casserole which held the succulent oysters my mother scalloped so deftly in winter; the wide black baking pan used only for tender, spicy gingerbread; my favorite pie plate, which so often held a wondrous pyramid of meringue atop an incomparable lemon filling and flaky crust.

There were no short cuts in my mother's kitchen. But then there were no short cuts in her love for us either.

It "pure pleasures me", as my mountain friends sometimes say, to think on all the trees that flourish here where I live.

There are the broad-limbed beech trees with their silver-gray bark and oval leaves that spread a heavy canopy of green shade overhead in summer and a thick carpet of bronze underfoot in autumn.

Along the riverbanks sycamores multiply, the oldest of them standing like twisted skeletons, with their peeled trunks and limbs gleaming white as stripped bones in winter moonlight.

Oaks are the staples of our forest—heavy, sturdy, rough-barked, still clutching tightly their wizened leaves after all the other trees are bare. Their harvest of plump acorns, once called mast (along with the extinct native chestnuts), provides the wild game's winter provender. The oaks grow more slowly than many trees, but they grow stoutly, rugged as our own Appalachian hills, which form one of the great natural hardwood belts of the world.

Next to oaks in profusion and hardiness must come the maples, hickories, and poplars. They are the dye pots that splash our hills with color every fall: flashing reds and yel-

lows, mellow gold. And they are the graceful trees that lift a
fine symmetry of limbs and twigs and buds against the January sky. The poplars stand apart in their straightness, slim
and tall as young sentinels.

And what of the evergreens? Balsam, hemlock, white pine,
black pine, cedar—they are the year-round blessing and
beauty of our region. Their greenness on the heights of the
Smokies or along mundane hedgerows is a sort of immortality. The fragrance of their needles and bark carries the
freshness and pungence of life's essence. Often decimated
and wasted by careless, gluttonous cutters, they come back
again and again, the evergreens, spreading their branches
over the land's bareness, holding its fertility in a network of
roots.

There are the smaller trees—dogwood and sourwood,
sassafras and birch. As the dogwood bedecks spring with its
cascade of white bloom, so the sourwood is the first beckon-
ing of fall, with its clear red leaves which turn when all else
is still green.

No matter the season, the trees remain—gum and locust,
and the black walnuts with their rich grain and ripening
nuts, and the twisted little persimmons, and wild cherry,
redbud, ash. In their variety is the bounty and the beauty of
our hills.

The squarest fate that can befall a young person in his
teens is to be "taken in."

The watchword of the day is, "Keep your cool."

Remain aloof. Don't get involved. Love is an illusion, hate
a delusion; everything in between partakes of chicanery and

fakery. This is the code of the cool cats, the philosophy of the un-innocents.

Yet the great and original thinkers of mankind have always run the risk of being "taken in." Every artist worthy of the name must have as his goal to be taken in—by the experiences, the commitments of life. For those who can take the chance and pay the difference, a deep and abiding innocence may be their strongest forte.

Yet of all the endowments of childhood the one we rush to annihilate most quickly and surely is this one. Every year we watch the wry little faces of knowledgeable cynicism and shrewd wariness grow younger and younger. We must look in kindergarten now for the innocence once found in fresh and open high-school countenances.

Thoreau recorded this thought in his *Journal:* "A man had better starve at once than lose his innocence in the process of getting his bread."

How cheaply we trade our innocence today—not even for the nourishment of bread but for the gimcrackery of cake.

We have four Japanese magnolia trees on our place. There is one outside my kitchen window, near a stand where I feed the birds, and it is a deep purple shade when it blooms.

Another, near our driveway, is so pale a pink that, when it is in full blossom, it often appears to be almost white.

Two others—one beside the drive and the largest one of all at an edge of the front lawn—are a rich pink with shades of both the purple and the white along their petals.

When the largest of these trees is in full bloom, it reflects such a glow of color in the sunlight that the warm hues wash through the wide windows of our living room. When a spray is broken off for arrangement in a vase, it blows out to mature blossom quickly; overnight the petals grow bruised and brown. They flourish best on the tree.

Japanese magnolias always bloom early. Before forsythia has given more than fleeting hints of the gold to come, before hyacinths have fully thrust up their fat fragrant blossoms, before Emperor tulips have even begun to peep lipstick red, suddenly one morning we look out and there are whole trees of living springtime, exotic buds and full-blown petals of brilliant beauty.

Because they come out so early more often than not our magnolia buds are killed before they have finished blooming. This year they lasted only two days. The weather turned bitter during the night and in the morning the flowers looked as though they had been drenched with hot coffee. Brown and limp they hung on their brittle twigs. Since the flowers come before the leaves, there was no foliage to soften the harshness of their freeze. They had responded to spring before winter had relinquished its grip.

Doesn't it seem sometimes that human nature, too, destroys beauty through a sort of perversity? Is there a dark void somewhere within us all that resents the beauty that is not ours, the loveliness we cannot contain?

How often fragility seems to call forth the clumsy blow that can crush it in an instant. How often the unique and the charming find only the cruelty of the heavy hand that can deface and never know what has been wrought.

Not only Japanese magnolias are chilled by frost. So, too, are many young things stunted in the first fullness of hope and trial and confidence. So, too, can the human spirit, in a moment of quick fresh flowering at any age, be darkened and withered by indifference, jealousy, cynicism. Next year our magnolias will bloom again. People don't always have another chance.

Some people who want to become writers have had parents who helped them. But mine weren't like that.

Some successful writers have had parents who engaged in one long bitter conflict, striving to hurt and humiliate each other with barbed humor, double-edged sarcasm, searing scorn and deprecation. Such children's days were enlivened by torrents of language that is the devil's lightning, stripping the last fragile shreds of illusion and faith from human relationships.

Other famous writers have had parents who ignored each other as much as possible, maintaining only an icy superficial communication, while superintending the functions of a hollow shell of a home. Such children's lives could be surrounded by the submerged power of that glacial hostility, until suspicion and tension broke in one shuddering convulsion of wrecked dreams and poisoned hopes.

But I had parents who respected themselves and loved each other. They did not give me any opportunity to experience the nightmares of dread and panic which seize a child whose adult world is being torn asunder. They spent their energies—and they were considerable—and their imaginations, which were not feeble, on welding their lives into one strong eloquent wholeness. What opportunity did I have to hear the sullen threats and shouted insults which put such grit and sinew into our literature today?

When my father died, I was fourteen years old, and my mother went right on refusing to help me become a great writer. She reasoned with all my whims and treated my despairs with dignity, and never rejected me for an instant. Her banner was love—not selfish or escapist sentiment, but love—and her shield was common sense. She never smothered, but opened the windows wide for each test of wings I wished to undertake. How can I ever write a "daring," "honest," award-winning Broadway play about omnivorous mothers who claw their own flesh and cackle with glee, and utter pithy dialogue as they devour their own young?

My mother denied me an unhappy, selfish home and a grudging, bleak facsimile of love. She denied me quarrels and invective and discord and self-pity. She made me go out and find these for myself, if I had need of them—or wanted to be a fashionable writer.

Not that my mother—my parents—lived out somewhere on cloud nine. They knew the meanness and suffering of the world, and in both of them burned a deep hatred for injustice in any degree or form. They were very much aware of the world. But they made their home a refutation, not a replica, of the world's frequent tawdriness, conflicts, prejudices.

So I have had to get along the best way I could as a writer, since I had so little help from my childhood. My parents just didn't realize how hard it would be for me to try to live down such a past, especially in a period when moral bankruptcy is hailed as bold experiment, callous brutality is honored as strength, and swaggering expediency is called unvarnished truth.

What of the successful experiment of love my parents knew? What of their strength? Does none of their reality and my memory speak truth, simply because it is not destructive, distorted, hysterical?

Despite the fact that they did so little to help my writing, I haven't managed to stop respecting and honoring my parents. They infected me with love a long time ago, and I have never since been able to throw it off. Worse, I haven't even tried!

"It is required of a man that he must share the action and passion of his time at peril of being judged never to have lived."

How exhilarating to have one of the great Associate Justices of the United States Supreme Court use the word "passion" in a context larger than that of blowzy movie marquees or tawdry fiction. His challenge to share the commitment and action of our time suggests a modern mind, concerned with current problems.

Because Oliver Wendell Holmes, Jr., was concerned with the basic issues of human relationships, his thought will remain "current." He was born in 1841 and died in 1935. During that ninety-four-year span he was wounded in the Civil War, honored by President Franklin D. Roosevelt, and helped shape the decades in between. Many of the opinions he wrote will live in our literature as well as our legal heritage for generations to come.

At the age of eighty-three Holmes wrote to a young Chinese law student in Washington: "If I were dying my last words would be, have faith and pursue the unknown end." (How easy is the untested doubt many of us profess and how cheap the unexamined faith we profane.)

A friend of the Justice once said: "Holmes was skeptical of everything save life itself." In this his thought is not current; it is ahead of its time. For we have preceded ourselves and become skeptical, not of science, not of man, not of progress, but only of life itself. We must be reawakened to the passion of our time, or be judged still unborn.

Who can be happy enough or innocent enough at the Easter season? With nature's freshness and cleanness washing around us, how can we show adequate response, except through scrubbing our own minds clear of the little hates and the big prejudices that lurk in dark depths? With the mystery of a new beginning surging through all the earth around us, how can we be less than living hymns of praise for the possibility of fresh tomorrows?

Shall the bees that use the sweet spring flowers, the thawing streams that sparkle under the rhododendron limbs, the rising sap that feeds each tender bud and limb—shall these be more alive than we to the grand design and delicate tracery of Easter's renewal? Shall the brown thrasher and the mockingbird bear clearer witness than we to the glory of breathing and eating and mating and celebrating the season's return?

Isn't it interesting to consider that a virtue overintensified or misapplied can become a vice? And that the reverse side of a vice may sometimes be a virtue?

There is, for instance, curiosity. Curiosity may be the stock in trade of small-minded people who have so little life of their own that they must find a secondhand sort of existence in prying into the lives of others. On the other hand, curiosity may be the spur which prods man to search out new horizons, both within himself and in the universe around him. Curiosity may breed a Peeping Tom or an Einstein. It may prompt a tidbit of malicious gossip or it may promote a totally new insight into the psychology of man.

How often young mothers sigh and say that their children are "into everything." Their tender hands reach up and out —they feel, push, break, pull, grab, reject, caress. Their energetic legs carry them into investigations of hidden corners, closed drawers, forbidden territories of yard or street or woods.

Their bright eyes examine the world with fresh sight. A father's face, the shiny lids of kitchen pots and pans, a daisy's petals, the soft fur of a kitten or a puppy's clammy nose—each in its newness and variety claims the attention, the curiosity of the child in his first ventures beyond the realm of his own small continent.

Only the mother whose child is not "into everything" should be worried. Only the child with curiosity can come to know the world around him.

Only the adult with curiosity can grow in understanding of the world. Curiosity drove Copernicus to look up, and it drove Columbus to look out, and it drove Freud to look in. It compels each of us into meaningful investigation of our lives.

Perhaps it is as we distort this need, this gift, that we grow small and dissatisfied. What a waste it is that a person who might be marveling at man's walks in space and his need to know the stars should spend time peeking into his friend's shortcomings and cataloguing another's mishaps. How trivial we become when we pry into the little puzzles and fail ever to ask the big questions.

Is it virtue or vice, this inborn curiosity of ours? It may be either, or both—or neither. But when it is neither, when we are no longer curious, we are dead, whether or not the undertaker has been notified.

A young actor from New York came to visit us. The farthest south he had ever been was the Paramus Playhouse in New Jersey. And when we took him for a drive along some of the hill-bound dirt roads, his preoccupation was not with the scenery but with the people.

"They're so friendly!" he remarked again and again. "They smile at me even though I'm a stranger."

"Wave at some of them," we prompted.

He waved at the next man he saw, a tall, dignified old fellow who threw up his hand in a spontaneous response.

Then our visitor waved at a covey of small children who crouched beside the road as we passed. They all flung up their arms, and as soon as we were beyond them, they jumped out into the road again, laughing and saluting us.

I had scarcely imagined that a supposedly sophisticated fellow could spend a satisfying afternoon simply greeting people. And few of those to whom he waved failed to react with instinctive warmth.

I have sometimes wondered how the dwellers in apartments along New York's Park Avenue, or in the suburbs along Chicago's North Shore, or in the hills and canyons surrounding Los Angeles would respond to strangers who knocked on their doors looking for an insight, an "angle," from which they might write of the lives and customs of these quaint people. Yet these metropolitan pundits call mountain people reticent (ranging from shy to sullen) because they do not like to be addressed as guinea pigs and approached as if they were exhibits in some permanent side show.

It seems to puzzle reporters and sociologists that the inhabitants of our Southern mountains do not always yield up quickly and freely (with a few "typical" Elizabethan phrases tossed in for good measure and lively reading) their innermost values and ideas for public consumption—or even, on occasion, public laughter.

Most hill people are remarkably hospitable to strangers, once they understand why the stranger is in their midst. The majority of mountain men and women have an innate courtesy which might confound the rude flippance of many a more urbane social leader. I, for one, can hardly wonder at the chagrin and anger Appalachian dwellers have often felt in the past when they were depicted by their erstwhile guests as depraved buffoons or picturesque primitives.

Any researcher seeking an accurate picture of the mountain life of a century ago, for instance, is often hard pressed to discover the truth. Fiction and fact are the warp and the woof so tightly woven that one cannot be separated from the other.

It might or might not have been true, as one traveler through the hinterlands proclaimed in a national publication, that mountain people had more religion and fewer morals than any other people in the world, but naturally the subjects of the statement didn't enjoy having strangers make such unproved allegations.

Perhaps the report of an early missionary to darkest Appalachia balanced the view a bit more carefully when he reported on a certain looseness of family morals in some of the "secluded coves and highlands," and then went on to make this tart observation: "Laxity in such matters discounts a man's character no more than in some of the fashionable city circles."

Provincialism is not always confined to the provinces, and those who come to examine a region and put its people under a microscope must be no less hospitable to new ideas than they expect their hosts to be.

All of us know the date 1492, when Columbus and his intrepid voyagers discovered a new continent. But how many of us know a date only thirty-eight years earlier, when new worlds of the mind and communication were opened for all the generations of man yet to come?

In 1454, Johann Gutenberg, born in the city of Mainz on the River Rhine, printed the first book on linen paper from movable type. It is a date to rank at least with 1066 and Waterloo and those Councils of Nicaea and Trent and assorted other localities.

For the printing press and the manufacture of paper made it possible for every man to enter the kingdom of learning and become his own monarch. It broke the barricades behind which knowledge had been the possession (and sometimes the weapon) of a few—emperors and kings, princes of the church—a treasure to be hoarded and passed exclusively from one select mind to another. It made knowledge the common wealth of common men. The world would never be the same again.

Before the printing press, books were written by hand. The effort was long and laborious, and although the results were often extremely beautiful, the volumes were so expensive that their use and appreciation was limited to a few individuals.

People began to draw together to live in populous towns, however, and the need for a simpler and cheaper method of making books became increasingly evident.

As is the case with so many inventions, the triumphant breakthrough came not as the result of any one man's vision or single experiment, but as the achievement of a long, interlocking series of events. Printers in Holland and in Italy were working at the same time Gutenberg was, but the Latin Bible of this German innovator, who combined the inventions of many forerunners into the practical art of printing, is still considered the first printed book.

The manufacture of paper was equally important, for during the Middle Ages books had been made of parchment prepared from the skins of animals. When this costly product was replaced by linen paper made from the fiber of flax, the second essential ingredient for the production of cheap and abundant books had been achieved.

Books were no longer scholarly mysteries or highly decorated museum pieces. They had become tools and windows for all mankind. The movable type of Johann Gutenberg would shake the world in centuries to come. It would enable each of us to discover the continent of himself.

I just love being a woman.

I like it the year around, but especially in the spring it's fun to be a woman. I can buy a hat the color of dandelions and decorated with a froth of flowers; I can wear shoes with ridiculous heels; I can use my own hands to make deep-dish apple pie for my own menfolks; I can hang new curtains at my windows, throw the casements wide for the first warm breeze, wear rings on my fingers and bangles in my ears and long elegant gloves when I wish. I can pin violets on my shoulder or put them in the little cut-glass vase on my table. What man can have such fun?

I can work like an Amazon and pretend that it was play. I can soak up all the tears and troubles that come into this house and try to squeeze laughter out of them. What man can practice such sorcery?

I sometimes think that the most fun man has had through the centuries came from his witticisms about women. Britannia's Rudyard Kipling began his comments on the subject by saying that "The colonel's lady and Judy O'Grady are sisters under their skins." Five years later he had progressed to the opinion that a woman was a "rag and a bone and a hank of hair," and his summit observation was that "the female of the species is more deadly than the male." Surely he must have been stung by one at an early age!

Ambrose Bierce, never a man to mince words, threw out three "endearing" remarks: "He gets on best with women who best knows how to get on without them." And, "For study of the good and the bad in woman two women are a needless expense." His final warning: "Woman would be more charming if one could fall into her arms without falling into her hands."

It was a German who said, "Whoever trusts a woman plows the winds, sows the deserts of the sea, and writes his memoirs in the snow"; a Frenchman who said, "Woman inspires us to great things—and prevents us accomplishing them"; and an Englishman who wrote, "Women have always been picturesque protests against the mere existence of common sense."

Poor darlings! Isn't it obvious that one and all, they're jealous because they're not women? They want us to be the same as each other (colonel's lady and Judy O'Grady) because then we'd be so easy to understand. They want us to continue to be the same self day after day because then we'd be so easy to predict. And they want to understand us and predict us so that they can file us neatly away—perhaps under "W" (Woman or Wife), "S" (Sweetheart or Sister), "F" (Female or Friend). But we know the fate of that which is indexed and filed away: It's forgotten!

We don't let them get away with it! How dull such filing-cabinet personalities would be, as dreary as winter without spring.

I love to be a woman, because we can wear coats of many colors, on our backs and in our minds; because we know life most intimately; and, best of all, because of men. Yes, without men, being a woman wouldn't be any joy at all.

A plum tree of venerable years grows in our back yard. To my knowledge and to all appearances it has never been pruned, sprayed, or otherwise pampered by care and attention. Yet it provides a source of ethereal beauty at this season of the year—and it harbors one of the most delightful visitors that uses our premises.

The grace of the plum tree is Japanese in its form and effect. It achieves a bold simplicity of line in its black trunk and limbs and twigs that are twisted and knotty as they reach up and out. Blossoming from them are fragile white petals, so delicate it is a wonder they can survive the faintest breeze, much less the lash of quick winds and rains; yet they cling and flourish and finally fall away only to yield to the seedling fruit which follows.

As if to complete a color scheme that captures the motif of spring, the bright green leaf buds appear now too. Their bit of shading intensifies the white flowers and black twigs.

Seen in a mass, the plum tree is a foam of white with black and green high lights, but to break one twig and consider its burden of perfection is to realize the marvelous design of the whole.

I stuck a forked plum branch in a green glass jug and set

it in my kitchen window. When the morning sun outlines its angular sharpness and then spills over the soft freshness of flower and leaf, I feel that I have a painting-come-to-life before me. And the perfumes of Grasse are rank compared with this subtle breath of mountain wildness.

As for the visitor our plum tree attracts, it is a mockingbird that arrives at earliest light each morning and fills the air with an astonishing repertoire of melodies. He seeks out the highest branch of the tree and there, framed against the sky, he seems to fairly turn somersaults with the lyric flow of his song.

Plum tree and mockingbird, gifts of spring. I know that mockers are supposed to be ill-tempered, unlikable birds. I know that our plum tree is no longer a useful productive asset. But who heeds such irrelevancies when the first stray breeze carries the odor of the plum blossoms and the voice of the mockingbird?

Sometimes you can't help but wonder how these kids will turn out, what will become of them. Let me tell you about a couple of juvenile delinquents in our area. They were bright little fellows with sharp eyes and hungry minds, the kind you like to see have a chance and get ahead in the world, make a place for themselves.

The first boy was the fifth of nine children, and his father was unsuccessful at several occupations before he finally opened a little roadside stand on one of the main highways and managed to make a living this way.

At the age of twelve the boy went to work for a foster family in another state, but he ran away and returned home. When he was thirteen years old, he enrolled in school. By the end of the fourth day he had engaged in a major rumble with one of the gang leaders in the school, and he dropped out altogether. When his father tried to persuade him, by various means, to return to his studies, he ran away to an adjoining state where he worked at a number of jobs.

After this period of beating around on the road, as it were, he went back home, worked to help pay off his father's debts, and, finally, about the time he turned sixteen, stayed in school for six months. He learned to write his name, read a little, and figure a little in what he called Old Math.

He slipped out at night to dances in the neighborhood, hunted in any season with any bag limit he wanted, and went steady with several girls who were teenagers, too. His is a sad case of school dropout, untrained skills, low-income family.

The second boy was a first-generation American. His parents were from Ireland. The mother was widowed early in the lad's life, and this fact, coupled with his own temperament, may have contributed to an attitude of overcompensation, for his temper became a legend with friends and enemies alike. When he was in school he would fight as readily as he would study, especially if any of his peer group laughed at him.

By the time he was fourteen he had had his growth spurt and was already tall and gangling and when he got into trouble with military autocrats, he was thrown into prison. Before he was fifteen both of his brothers and his mother had died. He was a D.C.—dependent child—without anyone to depend on. So he went to a big city, where he took up horse racing, card playing, drinking, gambling, and, finally, schoolteaching and the study of the law.

Of course, one of these boys became a famous Congressman, Davy Crockett; and the other became President of the United States, Andrew Jackson.

You never know what will become of a boy. The most treacherous thing you can do is pigeonhole him or write him off too early.

Mothers are . . .

Well, precisely what are we?

Many things to many people. To small boys we are a voice that rudely interrupts ball games, television programs, and long thoughts at the breakfast table; we are hopeless addicts of soap and water, purveyors of galoshes and spinach.

To husbands we often appear as eternal sleepwalkers, domesticated Lady Macbeths lowering windows, pulling up blankets at all hours of the night; or, to shift images as swiftly as we shift characters, we're strange jungle creatures who can be transformed from mousy housekeepers to savage tigresses defending our young and our home against all enemies, real or imagined.

To teachers we are pitiable and troublesome females, with remarkable clarity of vision when viewing others' children, but afflicted with almost total astigmatism when looking at our own chicks.

To the gay, unattached wolves of the world we must seem a dreary lot, smelling by turns of pablum, fresh laundry, peanut butter, and the smoke of a hundred cookouts. Our witty repartee consists of Cub Scout jokes, and Paris designers never saw the teenaged daughter's rejected suit we're wearing.

To politicians we are a handy word to invoke in oratory; to stray dogs we are an easy "touch"; and to doctors a necessary evil.

We spank, scold, hope, pray, prod, defend, and sometimes we succeed in the delight and drudgery of rearing the best children in the best way we know.

And, yes, along the way we have also the partnership and influence of someone called a father.

We organize debut parties to put our daughters up for wedding—and then we cry when they are married.

We give our sons a dozen lessons in self-reliance—and then we choke back tears when they go out to put our preaching into practice.

When they're babies we think they'll never grow up, and suddenly one morning we wonder if they were ever children.

Something deep inside us often makes us saddest when we're gladdest, and if we could stop the clock several times each day, we would.

Bless us, protect us, forgive us—we mothers are almost as varied, contradictory, and wonderful as the human race itself.

For more than a week now the air has been filled with the fragrance of lilac blossoms. There were three lilac bushes of old and stately lineage already here when we bought our home. We have planted half a dozen more.

Two of these stand near the spot our boys and their friends have chosen for the home plate in their afternoon baseball games. It is both pleasant and amusing to think of that delicate odor surrounding those intense, shouting, dust-streaked, sweaty little ball players. Knowing the boys' openness to all of life, I cannot help but believe they will unconsciously absorb some of the quality, both of sight and smell, of the lilacs in bloom around them.

Perhaps in years to come the essence of lilac, blown on some random wind, will recall to their minds a memory of warm lazy afternoons and Saturdays, when making a home run seemed quite as important as making contact with the moon. For the fragrance of lilacs, at once earthy and ethereal, is above all nostalgic.

Around how many deserted old houses, from Maine to Mississippi, do the luxuriant heart-shaped leaves and lavender spires bloom each spring? How many abandoned homesites, from Pennsylvania to Oregon, are marked only by a lonely chimney or a vine-covered pile of stones and the presence of an ill-kempt old lilac bush?

When the lilacs bloom, we know that spring has come and summer is close behind. Their breath is part of the air as I walk up our driveway in the moonlight, or as I work in the yard in the morning sunlight, or as the boys play in the slanting afternoon shadows.

And I know why Walt Whitman began his great elegy for his President, Abraham Lincoln, with the line, "When lilacs last in the dooryard bloom'd . . ."

The day of the amateur is past. We shall all be a little poorer for the passing.

No longer can we take up a simple sport—golf, bowling, tiddlywinks—and pursue it with good-natured abandon and mediocre scores. From the moment that club, ball, or score card is placed in our faltering beginner's hands we must start striving toward professional form. If we apply ourselves with any diligence, this soon culminates in membership in a club or on a team.

This springs the trap, marks the point of no return. A guilty feeling for all flaws of technique intensifies; you sink, with your miserable score, not as an individual but as a partner, a team member. In desperation you either start practicing during every spare minute, or you give up the game.

A few years ago it was considered pleasant for every lady and many gentlemen to know how to play the piano or some other musical instrument. Now every boy who strikes a chord must consider himself an incipient Van Cliburn and enter strict competitions each year. Every little girl who has a sweet voice cannot simply revel in the joy of her gift, but must settle down to becoming a prima donna—or nothing.

The casual musician, along with the casual, nonprofitable, noncompetitive gardener or baseball player or poet can no longer be tolerated in our specialized world.

Furthermore, it is no longer permissible, when a few friends visit, merely to drop a needle on a record and enjoy the music. There must be highly technical discussions of hi-fi and stereo, amplifiers, speakers, and a vast variety of equipment. The amateur listener who plugs in a record player and succumbs to a Gregorian Chant or the latest ballad is outmoded. Before he can listen with authority he should become an electrician, mechanic, carpenter—and install his own hi-fi system. Then he can be a professional addict.

But much as I admire and enjoy the nuances rendered by my friends' record-playing systems, it is frustrating to think that I should be busy with screws and wires, hammers and ratchets, tape measures and precision instruments. For our family's inclinations just do not veer in this direction.

In fact, I fear we are inveterate amateurs in almost everything outside our chosen professions. (Let him whisper who would suggest we may also be amateurs there!) When we play a game we participate for enjoyment; to win is good, but not at all costs. When we partake of the arts, we seek enrichment of the spirit; to have excellent equipment is pleasant, but not if it overwhelms where it was meant to enhance. We would like to be occasional amateurs, with enthusiasm the watchword and scoreboards irrelevant. Our day is past, perhaps, but it was good while it lasted.

She was a tall woman with a big frame and a wide, weather-beaten face under dark hair streaked with gray and pulled back in a tight knot at the nape of her neck. Her arms were long and muscular; her hands were red, chapped, work-worn. She wore a neat print dress that was a little too long, and a sweater that was a trifle too large; and she carried a shopping bag when she got on the bus.

After she greeted the driver she looked down the aisle of strange faces. Her expression was hopeful as she waited to respond to the smallest sign of friendship from any of these people who were traveling through her native hills. Slowly she walked down the narrow passage.

The man on the front seat became absorbed in reading his newspaper.

The woman just behind him gazed intently out of the window.

The woman across the way rearranged her fur wrap on the empty seat beside her to demonstrate how little room there was there.

The boy on the next seat was asleep.

She came to me. "Would it put you out too much if I sat here beside you for a little ways?" She slipped into place apologetically, settling the shopping bag at her feet.

"I'm not going far a-tall, just into the next town yonder.

Time was when I'd a-walked it and thought nothing of it, but I reckon I'm not as stout as I used to be. Law no, child, nobody's got strength like the old-timers used to have. Why, even my younguns, when they were coming up, they worked. When they pulled up to the table they eat anything that was set before them—and liked it! Was thankful to get it!"

One rough hand rubbed across her face, as if brushing away cobwebs. "I tell you, the way half the children are today is an abomination. I had six myself. One of them, when she was born, was such a little weasley mite the doctor said she wouldn't be worth raising. She was just a little blue knot, a pinch of nothing. But we brought her through—and now all six of mine are married and gone.

"Seems like I just can't cook little enough now. Of course, my man and me we grow just about everything there is to grow. We don't buy nothing in the way of food but coffee and sugar and fruit-jar tops.

"Tobacco's where we make our dab of money. I can work in tobacco good as any man—and it's rough work too. I'm sixty-five year old and I never had no vacation yet. I reckon when you follow farm or house work this here 'time off' don't mean much.

"My flowers are a wealth of comfort to me. My man always says a woman that don't like flowers ain't worth a slick dime. My yard just looks like a flower pot from spring till first frost.

"Now you know, I'm glad I took this seat by you. Open-hearted folks are scarce as water in a desert place today."

She gathered up the handles of her shopping bag. "One of my grandchildren will be a-waiting right there in town for me." Her smile was proud and shy. "I hope the rest of your trip runs smooth."

The bus stopped as the driver called out the name of her town.

Past the boy who was asleep and the woman with the fur coat and the man who was reading his newspaper she went back down the aisle. And I thought about how much all these other travelers had missed.

An unknown blob of jellylike matter washes up on the shores of our consciousness. It dissolves and spreads, oozes out, covering all that it meets with a slime which clings and persists and cannot be scrubbed away quickly or with ease.

An old hag creeps out of the caves of our conscience. She is twisted with age and toothless with time; her eyes look but do not see, and her ears are deaf to all but the rasp and shriek of her own voice. The sound of her distorted laughter is worse than winter wind tearing at the hills and more bleak than the crumbling of earth before an avalanche of flood waters.

An invisible disease insinuates itself into the bulwark of our collective awareness. Its germ is minute and mobile, wriggling from victim to victim on its untraced passage of sickness, weakening the vigor of our natures, sucking at the strength of our innermost loyalties. It spreads with the speed of light, leaving injury in its wake, fastening affliction on some, misery on others, and loss everywhere.

This nameless blob, this ancient hag, this insidious disease? All have another name—gossip.

There was a time when gossip was considered only the pastime of the provinces, the relaxation or drama of bored rustics who had little else to occupy their talents. But today gossip is a way of life. It is the stock in trade of professionals who huckster it for money. It is a tool to undermine opponents and a weapon to destroy leaders. It is national in scope and import. It is fashionable.

Have you been touched by the insufferable, strangling, murky substance of gossip? Once poured upon its course, it can never be recaptured, can never be contained and confined again. Its clammy chill exudes a bitter odor, but it flows on, deadening and deforming all it touches, covering truth with a sickly mold.

Have you met the demented hag of gossip? Once set upon her course, she can never be recalled. Her ugliness blanches beauty wherever it is found, and her wretchedness destroys laughter and uniqueness, for her bony hands and clattering tongue are the instruments of death.

Have you encountered the repulsive malignancy of gossip? Once its infection sets in, it can hardly be rooted out. It spreads its feeders until they are open, running sores and it aggravates its fevers until they are deliriums of agonized fantasy. It is an underground poison, a sickness which rages and devours the health of a person, two people, humanity.

Brave men and gentle women strive to forswear the blob, the hag, the disease: gossip. As I have not been its victim (but have seen its devastation in the lives of others), so I would not be its perpetrator and spread it into other lives.

There lies gossip. May It Rest in Peace.

It was six o'clock in the afternoon. I went to the edge of the lawn to call a little boy in from play.

A fine spring rain was falling, and who would have thought there were so many children who didn't have enough sense to come in out of the rain? I paused to watch them; and it was one of those moments we would like to freeze in time, capture in essence, and preserve like a rare perfume or a fine painting on some indestructible canvas. Every color of sky and earth and bursting bud seemed washed and deepened to a new intensity. The moist air was sweet with a fresh purity. Perhaps, I decided, it wasn't sensible to come in out of the rain.

On the improvised baseball diamond, where a crucial inning was under way, the grass was a good deep green. Near first base our weeping willow showered chartreuse ribbons of leaves.

Behind home plate were two lilac bushes, a little the worse for stray baseballs that had zipped through their foliage in years past, but nevertheless in full and fragrant bloom. And nearby were the long lacy limbs of a sprawling old tamarack, blossoming with a misplaced sort of mauve-shaded elegance among these roisterous surroundings.

Oh, they were boisterous enough—the shouts of advice, the cries of urgency, the screams of defeat and victory as clear as bells in the evening air and just as sweet, at least to one listener.

Over the thick spring grass the boys ran and slid, hair growing damper, plastered to their eager, bobbing heads; shirts sticking to their sturdy shoulders; feet as ceaseless in motion as if they were attached to tireless springs, which could never lose their bounce.

Adding to the general activity, but too excited to be banished from the scene, were the little black dog (of varied origin) that had come with a player to our west, and the doleful-eyed beagle, that had come with a player to our east. They helped celebrate—and slow—each home run.

The game was over in a matter of minutes. One player picked up assorted gloves and bats and balls and came across the lawn toward me. He grinned sheepishly in the misty rain.

I heard a robin and smelled the lilacs and felt the fresh dampness on my face and skin. And I laid up for myself a little treasure in heaven, a moment's memory no moth nor rust could corrupt and no thief could steal.

Every woman needs two fathers, two of those dear, delightful, complex, cantankerous creatures. They come in assorted shapes and sizes—36 stocky, 44 long—and a wide variety of beliefs, opinions, and abilities. None of these assures their success as fathers, however.

Some of them like to hunt and fish and watch the wrestling matches and sing old ballads. Others like to play the violin and hear Eric Sevareid's news reports and go for long walks in the woods. Some like baseball and others are all for golf and some like both—or neither. None of these has anything to do with their success or failure as fathers.

Some of them are Presidents of the United States (one was called, in the highest tribute his fellow citizens could bestow, the Father of His Country); some of them are street cleaners. None of this means that they will succeed or fail as fathers.

A father—the real, honest-to-goodness, 100-per-cent, full-time male half of a parent team—the kind that we pay tribute to on Father's Day, is a marvelous combination of tender heart and tough mind. He knows that tenderness (warmth, sympathy, forgiveness, understanding) of heart without a tough mind may wind up as ineffectual sentimentality. He knows that toughness (strength, courage, inquisitiveness, conviction) of mind without a tender heart may wind up as arrogant brutality. But met together in even proportions they make a man.

And isn't that what a good father is, first and last—a man? A man confident enough of his own strength to stoop and help those who are weaker, sure enough in his own faith to speak with those of lesser faith, rich enough in the treasure of his own mind to envy no one else's money or prestige, and self-disciplined enough to administer discipline to others.

Such a man can take his child's hand and lead him through the darkest and brightest moments of growing up, because he can fulfill a father's task: to set an example, to preach through deeds a daily wisdom, counseling through the conduct of his own life.

It is hard to be such a father, such a man. The only thing harder, in the long run, is not being such a one.

Every woman needs two fathers: one when she is born, to be her own; and one when she is married, to be the father of her children. Whatever else she has—or lacks—in this world, she will be rich, if she can look with pride to the two fathers in her life.

I know.

So monumental is the conceit by which we human beings live that we may be genuinely astonished when we make some discovery of the small and secret lives going their own way all around us every day. How much more astonished we might be if we could realize how insignificant we may appear in the patterns and routines of these other lives.

A few nights ago, walking along the street in front of our house, I came upon the body of an owl that had just been killed, perhaps by the car which had passed me only a few minutes before.

Of all the birds I know, owls have always seemed to me the most secretive and mysterious. Perhaps this feeling has been fostered by their nocturnal habits and their ability to sit absolutely motionless when they are discovered abroad in daylight. Or perhaps it has come from the peculiar lonely quality of their cries or hoots.

At any rate, as I looked at the crumpled wings and limp neck of this dead owl, I wondered what mission of foraging for food or nest or pleasure had brought it to swoop down into our domain of blinding headlights and fierce mechanisms. In what tree, on the steep slope behind me or on the wooded bluffs beyond, did other feathery creatures now go about their business of existence, all unknown to me, and I to them?

Yesterday I dislodged a rock at the edge of our back lawn. Underneath where it had sat, the ground was raw and damp, and wriggling through a tiny web of paths or channels was a long shiny earthworm. As it disappeared into some underground abode, I thought of the vast excavations of earthworms, loosening the soil, keeping it porous, aiding thus the life of every other creature dependent on the earth. Indifferent to me, and I to it, the earthworm and I had crossed paths in our mutual processes of existence.

This morning I startled a lively rabbit in our shrubbery. He jumped straight up and so did I; we were equally surprised. As he disappeared into adjoining acres, I wondered if he were scouting out future springtime gardens where he might find tender ready-made breakfasts. Where was his secret nest or hole, and how many homes of other creatures were all around me at that moment?

How do our personally consequential affairs appear, I wonder, seen from the perspective of owl, earthworm, rabbit? We are not sole proprietors of this earth, and perhaps we do not possess it as completely as we sometimes believe we do.

At the apple orchard we once owned there lived a child who seemed to be part of all the outdoor world around her. In summer she was brown as the hard-baked earth; her curly hair was a tangled auburn mass above her round, ten-year-old face. The skin of her square little hands and bare feet was tough as saddle leather. She knew where the cardinals and brown thrashers nested, where lady's-slippers grew and chipmunks hid; and treasures of tender cress or juicy berries or spicy herbs were her special knowledge.

One morning in spring she led me to a big old apple tree in one corner of the orchard. There, where the ground was rich and shaded, she knelt down carefully and folded back the tall grass with gentle hands, revealing clusters of ripe red strawberries.

After letting me pick a handful and enjoy their flavor for myself, she produced a small panful already picked and presented them to me, shyly and proudly. "They're plumb dripping with shu-gar," she cooed, and the way she elongated the word and savored it brought the taste of sweetness to my tongue again.

The following day we entertained at lunch a distinguished couple from other regions. For dessert I gave them some of my little friend's berries.

"*Fraises des bois!*" the husband exclaimed. "Very *recherché*. Delicious!"

So these world-traveled gourmets and a mountain child who had traveled only, as Thoreau had, extensively in her own back yard, shared a connoisseur's pleasure of one of nature's gifts. So often the best is free and near—if only we will part the grass and look.

Whatever happened to romance?

Under the weight of the world's problems has it withered and died, or is it simply unfashionable and therefore in hiding somewhere in the alcoves of our daily lives?

I look for its shimmer in the clear eyes and wind-swept hair of Sweet Sixteen, but it is difficult to detect under a curtain of mascara and a hairdo stiff with lacquer.

I search for its glow in the talk between young people, but it is hard to find above the din of the latest combo or between the lines exchanged about the latest T-birds, and SAT scores, and golf records.

Romance, of course, is rooted in dreams and nourished on hope. It believes that impossible and wonderful things not only happen, but that they happen all the time, and to the most ordinary people. It may be based partly on deception —of self or others—but it is the lightest, warmest sort of deception in a world where many things are not what they seem.

Perhaps it is this whisper of being deceived that makes romance so suspect today. Above all else, we don't want to be fooled. We hesitate to dare if there is much chance of losing, especially our heads or hearts. And so the little girls and boys "go steady" (and put themselves in the most difficult situation possible), when they should be dancing forth on unsteady dreams to find the vast variety of the world.

At an age when one might hope they were dreaming with stars in their eyes as well as in the drawing-board plans of a space mission, they are making down payments on automatic dishwashers and laying up Social Security benefits.

Ah me! No wonder the little wives sometimes cast a wistful look beyond the door as they push the baby stroller along the aisles of the supermarket. No wonder the fathers occasionally stand gazing down the fairway as though contemplating a horizon beyond the golf ball.

Romance may be the caviar and crepes suzette of living, but to be well nourished a person must have appetizers and desserts as well as meat and potatoes.

Or perhaps romance simply wears a different disguise today. Instead of the cap of the Foreign Legion, it dons the insulated suit of an astronaut. Instead of the black lace of Mata Hari, it fares forth in the trench coat of a Peace Corps volunteer. I hope so.

A world in which only the probable were possible would be a burned-out cinder indeed.

That clean sweep time of year comes again, that season when "things must go." Closets shall be thinned out; cupboards shall be inventoried; and shelves of accumulated sundries shall be emptied to make room for new accumulations of not-quite-necessary, not-quite-useless sundries.

And it is that time of year and that season when I begin to wish that everyone at my house was illiterate.

What do you do with in-between magazines at your house? I mean those magazines that poured in during the year just past, the ones in which you read the first story or the lead article, but never quite finished the rest. The ones in which there was something special you knew you'd get around to reading just a little later.

But before you got around, another week's, another month's, another quarter's publications arrived; and you had just time enough to glance through them and see that there was something special you'd get around to—and the circle began all over again.

The procedure at our house for dealing with this problem takes the same form each season. In fact, it's as ritualistic as a Polynesian coming-of-age rite or as precise as the ballet movements for "Swan Lake."

A burst of energy and a quick reminder of Thoreau's dictum "Simplify! Simplify!" brings the initial flurry of activity. Quality magazines of all vintages, shapes, and contents are plucked out of their crannied nooks and piled up for sorting.

At this point my allegro movement suddenly slows to andante. The first magazine is picked up. . . . A quick flip of its pages reveals hidden nuggets I can't throw away. I turn to one of the absolutely essential articles and lay it, open, in a separate pile.

I pick up the second magazine. A peek into its contents reminds me that these were pieces I could not afford to miss. I turn to one of the articles, stories, poems, or cartoons I cannot part with—and I lay it on that separate pile.

Presently, of course, there is no "separate" pile, only a transferred pile. Undergirded by thick slabs of Sunday newspapers, it's the same big stack—in a different place on the floor—tottering like the tower of Pisa as I add to the semi-permanent file all those publications I intended to discard.

But I have made some progress. I now have them opened to the pages I'm going to read—tomorrow.

It requires at least a century to create a really lovable martyr. And then it should be a stranger who discovers and announces that the person was in truth a martyr in good standing.

In other words, martyrdom, like good wine or cheese, requires an aging process. We encounter too many people who don't realize this basic fact, who want to become Instant Martyrs. And they will not recognize that they cannot announce the achievement themselves; recognition must come from outside, like being tapped for the Nobel Prize or the Social Register.

There are few people more studiously to be avoided than do-it-yourself martyrs. They are a fretful, frowning, fearsome lot. Their banner is a wet blanket and their coat of arms is a prostrate goat beneath the inscription "No one really appreciates me."

When it comes to creating a first-rate, everyday, durable martyr, women seem to have the edge over men. Perhaps martyrdom, self-confessed, is one of those roles society has thrust upon the female. But personally I prefer the little lady with a meat cleaver or a rapier, who can defend herself in the wars of the world.

Be that as it may, I shudder to think of the fragile females with pursed lips and accusing eyes who are carrying on their housework, their church work, their social work, unappreciated by those for whom they sacrifice their precious time and talents.

"When I think of all I've given up for you children . . ."

"I've devoted the best years of my life . . ."

"I work my fingers to the bone for this organization and what thanks do I ever . . ."

They are a dreary lot, these hoarders of their own martyrdom, and if they expected to be repaid, they haven't actually given anything, have they? They've only made a grudging, self-imposed loan.

Masculine martyrs seem to be less plentiful, but when they do appear, they win the gold ribbon for unattractiveness. The husbands whose wives don't understand them; the fathers who are tied down by their wives and children; those perennial failures who just are not lucky, like some folks—it's a wretched coterie.

Someone should remind these characters of the English proverb: "It is not the suffering but the cause which makes a martyr." And selfishness has never been considered a very noble cause.

On second thought, it requires *two* centuries to create a lovable martyr.

The smell of freshly cut grass comes through the window. It is a pungent odor of green juices drying in the hot sunshine. It is the essence of summer.

Besides water, air, and sunshine, grass must be the most bounteous gift of nature. Its presence, or absence, has shaped the lives of generations of men, and much of the early destiny of this country was determined by the vast prairies of grass our forefathers found here. Much of that green wealth we wantonly destroyed.

"Grass," a United States Senator once said, "is the forgiveness of nature—her constant benediction. Forests decay, harvests perish, flowers vanish, but grass is immortal."

As a child, did you ever lie on a thick bed of grass and luxuriate in its tenderness, its fresh sweetness? Did you ever walk with bare feet in summer grass, soaking up its coolness through the pores of your skin? Have you ever known the gentle relaxation that comes from contemplating an expanse of grass? (And have you ever considered how that restfulness would vanish if grass were red instead of green?)

Few things seem more common than a blade of grass.

How seldom we look at one separate, lovely stem. Walt
Whitman, America's poet of common men and things,
looked. And he sang: "I believe a leaf of grass is no less than
the journey-work of the stars . . . Or I guess it is the hand-
kerchief of the Lord . . ."

Was there ever a time when so many people were telling
so many other people how to live, and getting away with it?
Not only getting away with it, getting paid for it, too.

There was a day when a neighbor who advised her friends
about how they could improve their lives was looked upon
as a busybody. There was a day when children could take
some chances on their own and learn thereby—without
knowing all the answers beforehand.

Now we're all so busy telling each other how it could be
done better—or cheaper or quicker or easier—that we seem
never to get around to really dipping the paddles of our
own canoe into the water and shoving out into the mainstream of life.

Movie stars who have had more husbands than their pub-
licity agent can count are paid to write lengthy articles telling less morally agile females how to win and hold a man's
devotion.

Business tycoons whose financial manipulations resemble
the writhing of Laocoön lecture on the secrets of success.
Government officials who have ferreted through the run-
ways of a dozen minor frauds and swindles stand before
college audiences and tell young people how to serve democracy and preserve it in our time.

Parents who have all the upright honor of a rag doll on a

string advise their children to stand up to the bullies of the world, and armor them with glowing platitudes to strengthen them when the going gets rough and the answers must come from inside.

Perhaps that is the key. We have all forgotten that the only answers which endure are those we dig out, blast out, sweat out for ourselves. Neighbors can't dish them out like a cup of borrowed sugar. Celebrities can't hand them out like stenciled autographs. One generation can't pass them on to the next like family silver. No instant answers to the ancient questions have yet been devised.

Yet it is surprising to find so much unsolicited advice from so many unqualified people showered upon us daily. For my own experience I have found that a few minutes' counsel with grass and trees, a few hours' communication with woods and wind can serve me better.

I have been watching a summer storm gather.

It began slowly at first, moving out of the west-northwest, visible in the beginning only as a dark mass on the far horizon of an otherwise brilliant day. Its forerunners were ripples of wind, shivering the leaves on the tallest trees, then becoming stronger until small saplings and shrubs shook, too, and finally whole limbs of leaves were twisted until their paler undersides glinted like silverfish in the diminishing sunlight.

The clouds began to move faster. They rolled in now in long sweeping billows, some dark as soot, others light with a hectic sort of illumination that only made the growing darkness more weird, mysterious.

Above all, the gathering storm infused a sense of mystery into the commonplace afternoon. When will it break? Where will its fury center? Will it be helpful friend or ancient foe? Life-giver or life-taker?

This one was a deceiver. With all its dramatic prelude, its jagged streaks of light and deep-throated mutterings, it managed only a quick hard burst of rain, the sort that does not soak in to nourish roots and land. Then it moved on.

But in its gathering and in its approach was reminder of all the poetry and power that is possible in a summer storm.

A new house is going up in our neighborhood. It is not visible from where we live, but it is within hammer-hearing distance. Every morning the tattoo of the carpenters' hammers fills the air. Occasionally it is broken by the sustained grating of a saw through a two-by-four or a piece of siding.

With songbirds less plentiful than usual around our place, this sound of construction has filled a void. It is a homely, humble sort of symphony, reaffirming the fact that some of man's building is still done by hand and that all he builds must be done in co-operation with others.

There is a deep optimism underlying these ringings of hammer and saw, too. It is the optimism of every home-builder in whatever part of the world he may be putting up his tent or thatch, adobe or brick or redwood. It proclaims that wars have come and gone; peace has been won and lost; fortunes have flourished and perished; but the family outlasted all of these. The home is still the stage where the greatest dramas take place: birth and death (the physical event may occur in hospitals, but the ultimate confrontation of the reality still comes in the privacy of home), love and hate in their subtlest and strongest forms.

Elsewhere these mornings there are men creating and accumulating explosives powerful enough to blow up the world and every little dwelling on its face. The thought is so staggering we cannot even accept it, and yet it is not powerful enough to silence the tap-tap-tap of those hammers joining together rafters and flooring for a new home.

Around the world men hate each other, especially those they consider different from themselves, with a fierceness that burns deeper than the sun. Yet these smoldering tinders cannot dull the bite of those saws shaping the walls of a new home.

No matter what stories blaze into headlines, no matter which glamorous international personalities seize the spotlight for an interval, this is the continuing story binding families one to another in the human drama—the building of a home, the search for identity and fulfillment there.

I like to hear the hammers in the distance.

They say a cat has nine lives.

I wish I were as lucky as a cat.

One of those lives I would spend out of doors. Right after breakfast I would walk into the yard and if I saw a rosebush that wanted trimming, I would trim it; then I would go on and trim the next one, and when the pruning was finished, if I saw a weed that needed pulling, I would attend to that, and since there would be another weed nearby that had to come out, too, I would pull it. . . .

One of my lives I would spend on the sea, in the air, on

the highway, traveling to a nearby county or a distant country, anywhere on earth so that I might discover other people, other scenes. . . .

Another of my lives I would spend indoors. I would do all the little tasks I postpone now. Violets and begonias and philodendron would be repotted; bookshelves would be rearranged in better order; letters would be answered promptly. I would polish crystal and shine silver and move furniture. . . .

The fourth of my lives would be spent listening to music. I would enjoy old popular songs that make me nostalgic and new songs with a jungle beat; symphonies that have uplifted me and marches that have roused me and waltzes that have enticed me and ballads that have moved me; I would experience the feast of the best music of all times. . . .

And I could spend one of those lives on the reading I'm going to finish someday. When I consider the messages waiting for me in the incomparable books of all countries and centuries, the laughter and sadness, knowledge and insight, I become impatient for a lifetime in which to read. . . .

Then I could spend a life in classrooms studying anything from archaeology to zoology. I know now just how exciting any subject may become. . . .

Another of my lives I could devote to playing games, all the games (with and without balls) which I have liked and at which I've never had time or talent to become proficient. How exciting it would be to pick up racquet, club, paddle, stick, mallet, or other appropriate equipment and feel that you might win your next encounter. . . .

And perhaps my most important life I could spend in contemplation of man and his Creator, in communion with the questions that stir us all, sooner or later: Why are we here? What is life's value and death's meaning?

Nine lives? I could use a dozen.

"To every thing there is a season, and a time to every purpose under the heaven," the ancient wisdom advises.

"A time to be born, and a time to die; a time to plant, and a time to pluck up that which is planted . . .

"A time to get, and a time to lose; a time to keep, and a time to cast away . . ."

It is not recorded that there is a time to travel to foreign lands as a family, and a time to refrain from traveling to foreign lands with a family. But this is just as true as any of the passages about gathering stones and casting away stones, embracing and refraining from embracing.

The hour struck for us when a letter from our prep school son casually (too casually) mentioned student tours that were being organized for the coming summer.

A letter went by return mail from the Great Smoky Mountains to the environs of Boston: "Hold everything! Sign nothing. Maybe we can go as a family to Europe this summer."

The die was cast. Soon we were awash in a sea of maps, folders, books, proposed itineraries, and revised proposed itineraries.

"Summer in Europe is crowded, expensive, and definitely not chic. Travel during the off-season." Thus the sage old hands in all this printed matter repeated over and over, *ad nauseum*. They overlooked one small fact: School administrators are notoriously inflexible when it comes to revising their vacation schedules to fit in with seasonal travel fashions. For us, it was summer or nothing. And we strongly felt it should be *this* summer.

There was already restlessness in the ranks, as that broadly hinting letter had revealed. Given another year's accumulation of independence, curiosity, and awareness of the peer group (jargon for other boys—and girls), added to an already sufficient supply of each quality, it seemed likely that our sons might not only reject any thought of going with us to Europe; we might not make it together as far as the supermarket.

During the past ten years our family had had its share of happy travel. By car we had meandered twice across this continent, following the dictum to "See America First." We had seen it first, last, and in between from Hungry Jack's camp on the Gunflint Trail in northern Minnesota to the jungle maze of freeways in Los Angeles; from the sumac-shrouded stone walls of Vermont glistening under early morning dew to the vast silence of the Grand Canyon washed in pale white moonlight. In Canada we had gone from the winding roads of Gaspé Peninsula and the lonely green farms of Cape Breton to the towering majesty of Rocky Mountains at Lake Louise and Banff and Jasper.

Remembering, too, the advice of the ancient Greeks to "Know Thyself," we had explored in our hills of home more peaks and hollows, side roads and highways, villages and crossroads and creek beds than we could count, even with the help of the New Math.

Now it seemed time to bestir ourselves, to beg, borrow, pool our resources, and, throwing fiscal caution to the wind (which we knew would not accept the gift, but return it with interest), go as a family "across the waters," in the words of our mountain neighbors.

Europe, any part of it, seen through the eyes of three generations, would be an exciting adventure. We included two Teens, one Senior Citizen (to translate "Grandmother" into a euphemism of the day) and two In-Betweens (statistically "middle-aged," so long as we manage to enjoy fantastic health and extraordinary luck during the coming years).

Since the nomenclature for the four years at our son's Massachusetts school was: Juniors (for beginners), Lower and Upper Middlers, and Seniors, we adopted these to use on occasion as our travel titles for each other.

On our past journeys we had discovered that five pairs of eyes see many times more than two or three or four pairs see. Five pairs of ears hear in stereo—from all angles, in several ranges. Five pairs of hands and systems of nerves and pores feel with an awareness which more than quintuples what one can absorb on his single personal radar.

Most important on this European adventure, however, would be the three-dimensional experience of encountering a richer past, a more sharply defined present and future through the triple vision we would bring to people, places, historic events. In short, we planned to see several corners of Europe in triplicate. But our views would not be carbon copies of one another.

Of course, we soon discovered that it was not always age that defined our different roles as observers either. Naturally we knew from which source we might expect a question about the best antique shops, or the nearest beach, or the morning edition of the American newspaper. But many times it was the eldest among us who had the most eager anticipation for the future, and the youngest ones who had the most forceful insights into the past. Richness grew from the fact that it was both yesterday and tomorrow we took with us in our lively contrast of ages, and the creative tension between the two made today certainly more lively and, hopefully, more meaningful.

Our cast of characters for the summer itinerary might have read something like this then: Lower Middler Wilma and Upper Middler James, Two Squares; Keepers of the Exchequer, Assorted Vouchers, Eurail Passes, and Letters of Introduction. Juniors Dyke and Jim, Two Semi-Swingers; Holders of the Maps and Money Exchange Computers, Re-

Revisers of the Schedule, Interpreters in All Matters French. Bonnie, one Senior; Keeper of the Kleenex, Holder of the Foot Lotion, Ambassador of Good Will Without Portfolio (with warm heart and ability to make friends any time, anywhere where two or three are gathered together).

Previously, one of us had been to the majority of west European countries three times, two of us had been once, and two of us had not been at all. Our reactions therefore would also reflect varying familiarities and freshness of acquaintance.

One of the questions we asked each other before we began our trip was this: What do you think is the most important thing we can take with us on this journey?

We had five different answers.

"Enough money."

"Anticipation."

"Some helpful guidebooks."

"Light luggage, and a foreign dictionary."

"A sense of humor."

When our trip was finished, we would ask the same question again.

But would foresight really have changed much if we could see with such perfect 20-20 hindsight? I doubt it.

One piece of freight we did not take with us on this journey was the compulsion that we must See Everything Worth Seeing.

This getting-your-money's-worth syndrome (perhaps it could also be called the impress-the-folks-back-home syndrome) afflicts many travelers, and especially those who go to foreign countries. Its victims crowd every museum, night club, cathedral, stately home, and historic battlefield from the Mediterranean to the North Sea, from Edinburgh to Venice.

The symptoms are easily recognizable: First and most apparent is the glazed and ever-wandering eye. No matter where the travelers may be, or how much of importance lies in view close by, their eyes cannot focus on the immediate scene but wander to other horizons, distant groups, a different scene, apprehensive that whatever is *there* must as a matter of course be superior to whatever is *here*. The glazed look derives from the strain of trying to see everywhere at once and therefore seeing nowhere.

Other symptoms include a furrowed brow, constant shifting of attention, nervous patting of the foot ("We've got a lot of ground to cover"), and alternate dedication to and rejection of the guidebooks.

The wisest decision anyone can make before he ever sets foot beyond his own doorstep is to squarely face the fact that neither he nor his wife nor his children nor his aunts (nor his mother-in-law) can See It All.

Trying to do so is somewhat like going to your first smörgasbord determined to sample everything that is offered. The result is either frustration or gluttony. Neither is very desirable.

This, then, is not a travel log in the usual meaning of the term. It is not chronological. It is neither a do-it-yourself guide, advising others where to go and what to avoid after they get there, nor a we-did-it-ourselves journal, recording every place we visited and every breathless moment of a long summer.

It is perhaps, rather, a sketchbook of an experience shared by three generations. Here is what they had in common—and what separated them. Here, too, are a few of the old familiar landmarks, the ones that seem to await each visitor, century after century, forever fresh, forever beautiful, no matter how often they are waited upon by the stranger. And here are some lesser-known places, where a moment or a day suddenly became unforgettable.

Or could we say it is a patchwork of personal impressions, facts and figures, conversations, reflections, observations, perhaps akin to the bright patchwork quilts our mountain grandmothers used to make. Each piece in those quilts was distinctive with its own color and design and shape. Yet set together with loving care and daring, they blended into a unique and unified pattern.

Maybe our record is best likened to a mosaic. It is not meant to be a systematic panorama of daily events, and it does not aspire to definitive portraiture of any country visited, any people encountered, any event celebrated. Here are only numerous small hard blocks of personal experience and fragments we might call "shocks of recognition." As they are related to each other and to our total life and as they fasten in our memory, there emerges a sort of inlaid design.

Sketchbook, patchwork, mosaic—whatever the form, the hope is to intrigue others even as we were intrigued by the joys and surprises of travel; to share some of the riches we assayed; to stir conscience, wonder, laughter, horror, self-consciousness—all in their turn as they were stirred in us. And the hope is also to encourage others to discover the variety and revelations of traveling as a family, a three-generation family, if possible.

One reality must be faced at the outset, one fact frankly acknowledged: Travel is hard work.

Those naïve homebodies, secure in their own three-mile orbit, who envision a journey nowadays as being one huge festival, a sort of cross between the bacchanalian revelries of the Emperor Nero and the bucolic reveries of the Countess von Trapp, have a shock in store for them.

Travel is for the stout of heart and sturdy of limb, and unless you are an international duke and duchess or a jet-set movie mogul, you had better go into training for your jaunt. It is not likely that you will be met at every dock and airport and railway station by rows of eager baggage porters, and unless your luck with taxis is phenomenal, you may find yourself depending on the ankle express in many a city and town.

Incidentally—or not incidentally at all but very pertinently—the one of our five who was really in shape for all the walking, standing, stretching, sitting, climbing, riding, which was demanded during the summer was our Senior. Which only proves that nothing can equal a lifetime of conditioning: walking in the mountains; gardening among chrysanthemums and tomatoes, roses and rhubarb; attacking household chores with relentless daily energy. The two Juniors among us had merely undergone rigid school athletic programs of soccer, wrestling, swimming, and something called Search and Rescue. They could not be expected to have the stamina of a real old-timer.

At any rate, it did not take us long to reiterate what we had long known: Travel is work. It is demanding. It is exhausting. But so is trout fishing. So is golf. So is chess. And so is everything else worth the doing. The more you put into it, call it play or what you will, the greater the pleasure it will return to you.

Successful travel requires the instincts of a Bedouin chief, the strategy of a Napoleon (before Waterloo), the adaptability of a chameleon, and the energy of a volcano in full eruption. It involves being as gentle as a dove to the sensibilities of other people and cultivating the hide of an alligator with regard to their insensitivities toward you. If you also happen to have the physique of a football blocker, the stamina of the long-distance runner, and the tenacity of a pit bulldog, it won't hurt a bit.

With these rugged requirements, and if it is work, why does anyone travel? Perhaps we travel because we are creatures of curiosity. We have a compelling hunger to look, hear, feel for ourselves the wonders of the world—nearby or far afield. We are snoopers into history, scrutinizers of geography, experimenters in the adventure of life, and we are inquisitive about all its aspects.

We climb the mountain, cross the ocean, prowl the city, explore the wasteland, because we wish to see the stranger's face for ourselves, taste his food on our own tongue, feel a different weather through our own skin. We want to discover the bleak or the baroque, the grand or the trivial, the past or the present. But to do it for ourselves, to satisfy a deep and greedy urge to *know:* For this we travel. And the work resolves into pleasure and the hardships are transformed into enchantment.

Ripe color and teeming motion, a counterpoint of sounds and a rich stew of smells—all these are the essence of Europe's markets, from the smallest village square to the huge Les Halles of Paris.

A traveler who unwittingly bypasses or deliberately shuns these markets misses much of the savor of the Continent. For here, bursting with juice, plump and tender, are the prototypes for those hundreds of still-life paintings of fruits and fowls and vegetables which solemn tourists flock to see in the Louvre and the Prado and the Uffizi. Here, too, are the unadorned faces, the raucous voices, the hungers of a cross section of each city, brought together for a lusty interval in their common daily chores.

One of the most readily apparent differences between Americans and Europeans is in contrasting attitudes toward food. To many European people the gathering of food— whether from field or marketplace—is still a daily ritual to be undertaken with dedication and delight. To most Americans, the gathering of food is streamlined drudgery to be checked off as soon as possible as seldom as possible.

And after this choosing of ingredients, the difference persists: in attitudes toward preparation and serving, and even in eating the finished products. We often rely on pre-cooked items and meals in a matter of minutes; they are still accustomed to the habit of peeling, paring, slicing, and simmering on a schedule of hours or even days. In achieving efficiency we have frequently sacrificed flavor.

Because many Europeans still value flavor more highly than convenience, and because not every family owns a refrigerator, shopping in the market is a daily necessity. Each morning the housewife carries her string shopping bag to the little shops or the open stalls and fills it carefully from the foods arrayed there for her scrupulous inspection.

Fruits and vegetables rise in colorful pyramids of red and orange, white and yellow and brown; wheels and slabs of white and yellow cheeses fill another display; there are stacks (like cordwood) or baskets (like fagots) of long unwrapped loaves of fresh bread; every cut of meat, including tails and feet, is on display at the butcher's stalls; and always there is the rabbit—hanging in long, skinned nakedness except for the ruff of fur still at his feet and head and cottontail.

Pricing, bargaining, pinching, testing, purchasing, the

housewife makes a social occasion of her marketing as she greets the familiar vendors and her neighbors. So food brings her double daily nourishment.

Feeding the hunger of a great capital city is another matter, however.

It was just growing daylight as we walked along the deserted streets of Paris to that vast central market called Les Halles. Our hotel was near the Louvre, and the symbolic fact that Les Halles and the Louvre are only a few minutes' walk from each other had led to our early-morning excursion.

To see Les Halles at the height of its frenzy, it would be necessary to arrive even earlier than we did. But we were in ample time, it seemed to us, for we were unprepared for either the size or spirit of this "stomach of Paris."

To begin with, there are a dozen enormous pavilions, gray and black structures built with iron girders and skylight roofs through which the pale light of dawn pours. Each is as large as a railroad station, and more filled with activity. From the central areas of these halls the surge of trade spills forth into a vast network of streets, where trucks, pushcarts, retail merchants' stands carry on the overflow work of providing food for an impatient metropolis.

Les Halles has been here since the beginning of the twelfth century. Ten of the present pavilions were built during the time of Napoleon III, and the two newest ones were added in 1936. Thought of the past gives way to the pressures of the present at Les Halles, however. It is not for the dainty or the delicate. This is a place of brawny men, vegetables by the barrel, fruits by the bushel, eggs by the crate, and the blood and carcasses of animals and fowls of every edible description.

Dodging wheelbarrows and carts and other vehicles, side-stepping puddles of blood, listening to the shouts and curses and laughter and haggling of husky men and hearty women (whether or not we understood their French), we prowled through one looming pavilion and crowded street after another. A barrel full of sheep heads momentarily threw us off balance. A case of fine lettuce which had spilled in one alley made walking slippery for a short interval.

At one point we were blocked until a load of veal calves, freshly dressed, was transferred from the market onto a truck. Along the way we passed several of the all-night restaurants that are famous with Parisian polite society and tourists for the delicious onion soup that is a traditional ending for a night on the town.

And even as we walked among the fish, meat, cheeses, fruits, vegetables that would go to hundreds of thousands of homes and restaurants, the cleaners—with old-fashioned twig brooms—were moving in. The debris of another morning's wholesale flow of food would gradually disappear. We thought of the plans underway to move the market to a new site.

We returned to our hotel by a slightly longer way, along the Seine. The river flowed gray and quiet as the morning. Overhead, leafy branches of trees spread an atmosphere of green country freshness. People were stirring—opening doors and windows, beginning their round of chores and errands— moving a bit slowly as they tested the day.

We spoke of the shopkeepers and vendors who were even now unloading and arranging the foods bought at Les Halles, and of the women who would be coming presently with their string shopping bags to choose a succulent cut of meat, a few scallions and some firm potatoes, a kilo or so of mushrooms perhaps, tender greens for a salad, a carton of sweet juicy cherries—and a loaf of bread, most surely. A cycle, a ritual was ready to begin again.

I shall be content if I never see Versailles again. Having made two pilgrimages now to this palace some eleven miles outside of Paris, this vast network of chambers and ante-chambers, ballrooms and halls and receiving rooms impresses me as just one big status symbol under twenty-seven acres of mansard roof.

Louis XIV, the so-called Sun King, who built this royal urban complex allegedly because he was mad about the country, has been delineated by French historian Pierre Goubert as a man of energy and ability, but lacking any real insight. That is precisely what I miss in Versailles: It boasts the energy of a creator who had set out to be recognized as the head of Christendom, and it displays the ability that an unestimated investment of royal wealth could call forth—but it lacks insight.

For all its silk wall coverings, its priceless paintings and tapestries and porcelains, its celebrated Hall of Mirrors, and its two satellites, the Grand and the Petite Trianon, there is a deadness at the core of Versailles, a futility which perhaps reflects the recent statement of an English scholar that "there was a strange pointlessness to this reign, so full of outward activity, which is the measure of the hollowness of the aims Louis set himself."

Versailles, too, with its thousands of residents, its strict pecking order, and its complicated etiquette, which masked a brutal lack of gentleness more often than it revealed gentility, was awash with "outward activity" around a hollow center.

As we hiked across those hard cobbled courtyards and surveyed the forest of windows, doors, statues, even the fabulous formal gardens and fountains grew oppressive. Here was the reflection of an artificial, contrived society— when 1,000 great lords and 4,000 servants lived in the palace itself, with hundreds of frequent visitors and the bulk of the court (20,000 people) housed in the nearby village of Versailles.

There was little contact with those whose vitality was essential to keeping the money pouring in for the Sun King's extravagant palace and his endless wars—and these were the bulk of his 20,000,000 subjects.

Silks and tapestries and elaborate furniture decorate room after room with gorgeous colors and designs, but eventually we longed for the spirit of the human beings to unify and illuminate these objects. And that is where Versailles, for me, is hollow at the core: a royal wasteland.

Two facts do almost endear Louis XIV to me, however, even if I do not wish to visit his palace again—he had bad teeth (poor soul!) and he liked tulips and jonquils. I wish there were a few thousand more jonquils and a few thousand less bricks at Versailles.

Discussing this visit after we returned home, there was a difference of opinion. One of our Juniors said, "I liked Versailles. I would like to have lived there when it was in full swing."

We assumed, of course, that he was thinking of living there as one of the 1,000 great lords, not as one of the 4,000 servants.

On a bright morning in early July, James signed numerous official, fine-print documents and several crisp traveler's checks. In exchange he received a set of car keys and the briefest briefing on record as to a Mercedes' steering equipment, braking apparatus, and gear arrangement. The hood was flung up and down. The trunk was an open-and-shut sleight of hand. Tires were perfunctorily kicked and dashboard lights were snapped on and off. Then the rental agency's Man in Paris gave a smart little salute—and departed.

As he disappeared, he left us food for thought, however. With a smile that balanced feverish gaiety and sympathetic anxiety, he said, "On the highway today—ah, you will not be lonely!"

We glanced toward the streaming thoroughfare which ran in the distance beyond the quiet pool of the square where our hotel basked in the sunlight. The roar of traffic assured the accuracy of his prediction.

"But we got up early this morning," we protested.

"So did everyone else in Paris!" he cried triumphantly. "It is the long holiday weekend. All go to the seashore." And he disappeared under the arcades of the Rue de Rivoli.

Bristling with road maps, exuding good will for our fellow man, we lurched forth onto the river of traffic. We promptly abandoned both the maps and the good will. Nothing in our national scheme prepares an American to cope with European driving in the summertime. It partakes of all our national sports: the speed of baseball, the brute force of football, the finesse of golf, and tennis with the net down.

There are few speed limits. Certain cities or specific stretches of certain highways will post limitations, but on the new autobahns, autostradas, and most of the lesser roads individual prudence is the regulator on the speedometer. Unfortunately, prudence is not standard equipment on every model of the human species.

Reading traffic signs that convey their messages by picture rather than word; interpreting the minds of strangers who zip in and out of lanes beside, behind, and in front without the slightest warning; propelled to greater and greater speeds by the lemminglike push of cars crowding each other down to the sea, we careened along Parisian streets, missed our correct turns, passed several picturesque landmarks, and headed generally in the direction we wished to take.

Just before hysteria gripped our ménage, we emerged from the roaring riptides of city traffic into the calmer streams of the country roads. Long avenues of trees beside these highways cast their tranquilizing shade across our route. The carefully tended fields and neat farmhouses were peaceful. Eventually we came into the valley of the Loire River, which has been nurtured for centuries as one of the royal garden spots of France, and we were reconciled once more to the pleasures of life—and driving.

This was the pattern, more or less, which our experiences behind the wheel seemed to follow: from chaos to calm and back again, from suicidal desperation to dilettante loitering.

Europe's drivers, like its wines, have been the subject of many an authoritative tirade and many a lengthy discussion. Who are we to remain aloof from this mainstream and not share our opinions and knowledge on the subject?

The basic assumption behind European driving seems to be that people are more expendable than cars. Numerically there are more, many more, people than automobiles. Spain, for example, has 12 cars for every 1,000 people. (The U.S.A. averages 339. Italy has 49 cars per 1,000 persons, England 110, and France 123.)

Financially, cars are a bigger investment than people. It takes, proportionate to income, an extremely high outlay to get a car, and a very small layette to beget a baby. And in most places, even as in America, a car is one indisputable status symbol.

So, in any encounter between man and automobile, the watchword is: "Let the human beware."

In Naples one afternoon we heard a bump at an intersection along the street where we were walking. We turned to look behind us and saw a car with four men in it which had just struck a young sailor who was attempting to cross the street. The front right fender of the small auto had caught him on the thigh and bruised his leg.

The mystifying part of the incident was the attitude of those involved. The men in the car were upset and angry. They hurled furious verbal blows at the sailor, glared, and shook their fists at him.

He, a perfectly innocent victim who had been within all the traffic regulations and his own rights, cowered apologetically. The shouting quartet in the car leaned out to examine the fender and make certain their machine was not injured. For all they knew, or apparently cared, the unfortunate boy's leg could have been shattered. But the sailor seemed to share their evaluation. With murmured regrets and shame he crept away from the scene. In his unsought contest with the hallowed car, he had definitely come off second best.

Germans told us of the deaths on their great autobahn system, a network comparable to our turnpikes, but usually having only two lanes in each direction. In 1965 there were 15,710 people killed on this one West German complex of some 3,000 miles; 432,770 were injured.

Although there was no apparent cause and effect between the two events, the week before we departed from Europe there were news items in the papers telling of English, German, and French attempts to establish speed limits on main thoroughfares. The German dispatch asserted that four out of five people polled wanted a speed limit imposed. England simply stated that "accidents causing death or serious injury have been cut by 13 per cent on main roads since speed limits of 50 or 70 mph have been imposed." The French report concluded: "A government study group said preliminary studies showed speed limits contributed to road safety.

It recommended a nationwide study to see whether France should adopt speed limits on all its roads." Apparently speed is not one of the afflictions besetting these commissions.

With the general do-or-die atmosphere that exists on many highways on the Continent, as well as in our own country, we were impressed to read what one American colonel said about his experience with the English: "A British advantage over the United States is the inherent courtesy and consideration of the British driver. Nowhere else have I seen people who seemed to be thinking of the other driver, his rights and privileges on the road, as is the custom in this country."

It is precisely that courtesy and large consideration which is a basic ingredient of civilization. Without it a good many of us seem to be returning to the jungle—at 125 mph.

We live in a violent age and in a violent country. Four of our Presidents have been assassinated while they were in office. Murders, assaults, and deaths on the highway are increasing. One of our national pastimes is watching two men punish each other in a ring until one suffers enough brain damage to fall down and be counted out.

If we sometimes seem to be making no progress at all in the long, slow process of civilizing ourselves, it is encouraging to contemplate the history as well as the architecture of some of the buildings in Europe.

Talk about gang wars! Visit the castles where those Lancaster and York partisans met each other. They may have boasted red and white roses as their emblems, but they dispensed with enemies, friends, relatives, and threatening infants by a variety of methods and with a thoroughness of purpose that ranged from simple hangings to messy stranglings.

Talk about muggings and stabbings and brain-washings! Along the beautiful, gentle valley of the Loire River are scattered chateaus soaked in the blood of past conspiracies and reprisals. It is difficult, for instance, in the quiet rooms, turrets and great halls, on sun-washed battlements of Amboise, overlooking the peaceful river, and in the green gardens and woods of the surrounding countryside, to visualize those days in March, 1560, when Francis II and his wife Mary Stuart and his mother Catherine de' Medici were spectators here to a massive blood-letting. Conspiracy by religious and political enemies was suspected, in some cases partially proved.

On the first afternoon thirty-one victims were put to death. As Ralph Roeder, biographer of Catherine de' Medici, describes the event, the meanly born culprits were tied in sacks and drowned in the Loire, like unwanted dogs. Some of higher station were hanged or beheaded, and a few were suspended from the ramparts. The next day a larger number were slaughtered, among them a leader whose body was "spread bat-wise on a bridge." On the thirtieth of March came the crowning spectacle. "It was a command performance at which not only the Court but the inhabitants of the outlying country within a radius of miles were compelled to appear. Tiers of seats were erected about the courtyard of the chateau." It took a long time to behead fifty-six people, a long nerve-wracking time. One or two of the spectators became hysterical.

After this, as Roeder points out, "the atmosphere of Amboise became unbreathable, and for the sake of the health of the King it was decided to move to Chenonceaux."

Today's American violence—shocking and deplorable as it is, and still to be diminished—yet seems tame and accidental by comparison with some of the violence embedded in the bones and bricks of Europe's past. Those ancestors were strong builders of forts—and brutal destroyers of life— capricious lovers and vengeful haters.

And none of them achieved those goals (obliteration of opposition, destruction of different religious faiths, annihilation of ideas) for which they were so ready to resort to the garrote and the noose and the sword.

Chartres is more than a cathedral. It is an architectural astonishment in a rural landscape. It is a massive monument set in a simple village. It is a triumphant testament of total belief which has survived into a present of fragmented faith and shattering doubt.

Chartres, as much as any other single experience of architecture and religious history, left its impression on our three generations—even though the majority had not been entirely enthusiastic at first mention of a visit there.

"Think of how we could use that extra time in Paris! Do we have to go to another gloomy old tomb?"

"We saw a pretty fair sampling of Gothic on our other visit—do you think this one is strictly necessary?"

But our Upper Middler, assuming a dictatorial stance not customary to him, insisted. "Yes," and "Yes," he answered to both of these, and all other doubts.

After our first glimpse of the splendid spires of Chartres none of us asked another question.

So must it always have been for visitors throughout these centuries: doubt diminished by affirmation of that stone grandeur, pride dissolved before the aspiration of those two upthrust towers. We may have rejected along the way the belief that made Chartres possible, but we still share the hunger that it reflects.

For sixty miles southwest of Paris the highway runs through the granary of the Beauce region of France. On the route are small towns with names that stir memories of history, and there are industries that testify to the twentieth-century realities, but the predominant landscape is neither of towns nor factories but of wide rolling wheat fields. Occasionally a windmill tilts picturesquely against the horizon.

The road is lined with trees along most of its passage. The drive is pleasant. There is a rustic, tended fairness everywhere. It makes a minimum of demands on our thoughts or senses.

Then, suddenly, reaching the crest of a small rise, "Look! There it is!"

And there, rising out of the golden wheat fields in the foreground and the gray stone cluster of the village in the background, there in the distance like a dream is the crowning glory of Gothic religious achievement.

As if on signal we stopped our car and climbed out and stood in one of the fields, looking at the dreamlike scene there beyond us. It was a mirage soaring into the sky, and yet not a mirage; it was a statement of all the hopes that were not hopes but solid faith that once made life on earth soar to new heights.

The most satisfying and surprising feature of our own experience arose from the fact that we all responded to Chartres; none remained indifferent to it; and our response was not as architects or historians or experts in any field but as seekers. We came as most people do to their search for truth or beauty: innocent of overmuch erudition or the niceties of dogma.

Chartres was not built by seekers, however. It was made by people who were supported and buttressed by belief. The difference between our doubt and their certainty, between their idealism of another world and our cynicism of this world is made visible in Chartres. It is a gulf we may not span, but we can look at this superb structure and appreciate what was theirs and is not ours.

"But as I remember the Middle Ages . . ." I began to no one in particular that day.

"Do you remember them?" One of our sharpies pounced on my slip.

"As I remember *studying* about the Middle Ages," I persisted, more or less—mostly less—patiently, "they were a dismal time of downtrodden serfs, superstition, dirt and disease, and no plumbing, crusades against the infidels in the East and burnings-at-the-stake of heretics at home."

Our Juniors, rather more recently immersed in history than were their parents, comforted me that this was accurate —as far as it went. As is often the way with facts, my smattering of knowledge concealed about as much as it revealed.

Here and throughout our journey we were to discover that the Middle Ages might have been steeped in gore, but they also left a legacy of glory. No period that could mark the rise of our great Western universities—Bologna, Padua, Paris, Salamanca, Heidelberg, Oxford, Cambridge—or that could give birth to Dante and Roger Bacon and Thomas Aquinas, or that could build Chartres cathedral could be altogether backward. And if the rough brawling daily life of the time included plagues and torture and slop pots emptied into the streets, it also included vision of another life and a great community of men who would work together to make that vision real on earth.

For one of the remarkable facts about Chartres and all the Gothic cathedrals is that they were the accomplishment of an entire community in a way no building today can be. Perhaps because the people believed in a common faith with a passion and unanimity that seem inhibiting to us, they could more readily release their talents and riches into a mutual enterprise of stupendous proportions.

Fire after fire ravaged the churches which stood on the site of the present cathedral. The first one, at the foot of the Roman wall, burned in 743. Danish pirates leveled the second one in 858. Its successor was destroyed by fire on a September night in 1020.

The bishop of Chartres laid even more ambitious plans for the new structure, however, and it was under his influence that the present church began to take form. Again, in 1134, fire took its toll. The front of the building and the bell tower were injured. As a result, the two towers were begun which are today so unique to Chartres: the ornate north spire with its numerous trimmings and adornments, completed about 1150; and the more solid, simple, and splendid south spire, finished about 1160, which has been called "the most perfect piece of architecture in the world."

In June, 1194, the fifth devastating fire burned all of the renowned church except those two towers, the crypt, and the new front. Once more the clergy and the people sifted hope from the ashes and vowed to raise an edifice to the Virgin of Chartres. There followed one of the most massive outpourings of wealth in Christendom's history. Kings and peasants, princes of the church, powerful nobles and their vassals—all shared in the offerings. The great cathedral, begun in 1194, was completed, as it now stands, in 1260. It proved beyond doubt the success of the Gothic experiment, for it has never been altered or needed to be strengthened. How marvelously it fulfills the Gothic purpose of making closed areas seem spacious, of making the small seem infinite, and of lifting the eye (and spirit) upward is immediately evident to anyone who stands inside its nave.

The miracle of Chartres arises not so much from the liberality of kings and queens, the gold and jewels and treasures they had plundered from one another and foreign lands and now laid on the altar, but from the enormous and continuing gift of enthusiasm and toil contributed by all the population.

Gothic architecture came about largely as a result of building with stone. The quarries of Berchères are some five miles from Chartres; they yield a very hard limestone. The massive blocks we see in the cathedral today were transported and put into place by human effort alone. Looking at the edifice from the wide steps of the south entrance or from the open square before the west front, we could almost see the scene of the building here as a contemporary had described it:

"Who has ever seen!—Who has ever heard tell, in times past, that powerful princes of the world, that men brought up in honour and in wealth, that nobles, men and women, have bent their proud and haughty necks to the harness of carts, and that, like beasts of burden, they have dragged to the abode of Christ these waggons, loaded with wines, grains, oil, stone, wood, and all that is necessary for the wants of life, or for the construction of the church? But while they draw these burdens, there is one thing admirable to observe; it is that often when a thousand persons and more are attached to the chariots—so great is the difficulty —yet they march in such silence that not a murmur is heard, and truly if one did not see the thing with one's eyes, one might believe that among such a multitude there was hardly a person present . . .

"When they have reached the church they arranged the waggons about it like a spiritual camp, and during the whole night they celebrate the watch by hymns and canticles. On each waggon they light tapers and lamps. . . ."

On the cobbled streets, between the stone buildings today, it is not difficult to imagine those creaking hulks of burdened wagons encamped before the church, with pale flames of rude lamps flickering in the darkness. As small and constant as the light from their tapers, as sturdy as the slow, sure wheels of their wagons was the faith of these builders.

It has been said that "the splendor of Gothic buildings, their variety and versatility, came as much from the liberation of skill as from the structural revolution." Craftsmen of every sort found their talents dedicated to a grand design beyond the immediate mundane world. They were translating the transient into the eternal, celebrating the compassion of the Virgin Mother, who could heal their body's frailties. They were small men (who had little voice in the daily life they were forced to follow), but they knew they were engaged in large purposes. The result was—and is—an achievement of inestimable value.

After the stones were hauled, masons set them in place under the direction of architects and builders. Sculptors, wood carvers, weavers, metalworkers, painters, and artists—all set up workshops in the vicinity and with their numerous helpers worked for years and decades on the cathedral.

Then there were those who served the artisans who were serving the Lord, feeding and clothing and sheltering them. Obviously, it required a town's resources, drawing on a wide swath of the surrounding countryside, to undertake a cathedral.

It is interesting to consider, too, for those of us who live in the liberated present world, the freedom of expression permitted those who built Chartres. No detailed plans set forth the precise nature of each small aspect of the cathedral. As a result, the creative imagination and personal mood of each worker could be expressed as he saw fit.

With our American background of standardization—one of the biting paradoxes of our vaunted individualism—we are surprised to discover that many of the artistic features of Chartres have no sequence. Each creation is to be read in its own context and meaning. Yet we are even more astonished to realize how unified is the whole. As one observer has summarized, "All this combined effort produced a final result that was at the same time magnificently harmonious and infinitely varied."

Can Chartres perhaps tell us something that we tend to forget: that it is not things (their common production or consumption) which unify people but ideas (a common faith and dedication)?

And still we have not spoken of the windows. "Chartres is all windows," Henry Adams, New England historian of half a century ago, said; and he contended that they were not only a triumph of the glassmakers of the Middle Ages but were a miracle of the Virgin herself.

They seemed indeed a miracle to us. We entered the quiet, cool dusk of the church at noon. Even with other people there, although not many at that hour—a group of French schoolchildren, scattered individuals, and families— the interior, built to hold 10,000 people (15,000 when crowded), seemed relatively deserted. How small the two six-footers in our family appeared when I glimpsed them, as we went our separate ways to discover the cathedral, in the forest of tall pillars under that vaulted ceiling!

As we came into the nave, our feet stumbled on the un- even pavement of the floor. It was first constructed thus so that it could be washed down after the encampments of pilgrims who came to worship Our Lady and seek her heal- ing, and were allowed to sleep inside. But we stumbled be- cause we were not watching the floor. We were looking up. Up, up, up at the brilliant windows—and at the light falling through them, around us, transforming that dusk to an iri- descent glow.

Two of us sat down, as if to absorb the first wonder and become attuned to it. Two of us began slowly walking (in opposite directions), as if to measure the scope of these riches, their radius, their outermost reach, and better allo- cate appreciation. One of us focused his camera on the rose window of the west front (that huge superb rose nearly 44 feet wide in its exterior surface), as if to capture immedi- ately the color that might fade at any moment.

But it did not fade. It has not faded during seven centu- ries.

Oh, yes, Henry Adams, you were right: "One becomes, sometimes, a little incoherent in talking about it; one is ashamed to be as extravagant as one wants to be. . . . One loses temper in reasoning about what can only be felt. . . . Still, it may be that not one tourist in a hundred—perhaps not one in a thousand of the English-speaking race—does feel it, or can feel it even when explained to him, for we have lost many senses."

Yes, we have lost many senses. Can we really plumb the depths of that famous Chartres blue, as clear as the depths of the sea, which are of course not clear at all, or penetrate its luminous height, as high as the blue arch of sky at an autumn noon? Or absorb those other amazing colors?

The great Viollet-le-Duc asserted that "the first condition for an artist in glass is to know how to manage blue." The reason? "It is that luminous colour which gives value to all others. . . . If there is only one red, two yellows, two or three purples, and two or three greens at the moment, there are infinite shades of blue."

And although they were made by amateurs, it has been claimed that these are "the most splendid colour decoration the world ever saw. . . . The effort to make such windows was never repeated."

In 1939, when war clouds were gathering over Europe, the glass from these windows was removed and protected. As long ago as 1200, their value was so well known that the windows were carefully preserved from earlier demolition or defacement.

Perhaps only a canny New Englander would have tried to assess any of the cost of Chartres. When Henry Adams privately printed 150 copies of his book about Chartres and Mont-Saint-Michel in 1904, he wrote: "According to statistics, in the single century between 1170 and 1270, the French built eighty cathedrals and nearly five hundred churches of the cathedral class, which would have cost, according to an estimate made in 1840, more than five thousand millions to replace. Five thousand million francs is a thousand million dollars, and this covered only the great churches of a single century. . . .

"Expenditure like this rests invariably on an economic idea. Just as the French of the nineteenth century invested their surplus capital in a railway system in the belief that they would make money by it in this life, in the thirteenth they trusted their money to the Queen of Heaven because of their belief in her power to repay it with interest in the life to come."

We could not—nor did we try to—appreciate at a first visit the many facets of Chartres. We became aware of its presence, grew acquainted with its character—and came under its spell. For the totality of Chartres somehow communicates itself even to the modern visitor, perhaps especially to the modern visitor.

From that first amazed glimpse of its two spires, rising above the gabled roofs of the village and the wheat fields of the surrounding countryside, to the final burst of brilliance from any one of its jewel-toned windows, the cathedral was a revelation and a joy.

Are we so much better satisfied today, building our patterned swimming pools and interchangeable houses and suburban churches cut from a design devised at some distant central headquarters, than were the medieval men who had a common faith so strong and full of wonder that they could shape a cathedral in their own individuality and have the result be a rare universality?

"There's no progress ever made but something is lost," one of our family said.

"But still Chartres is here," another reminded us.

"Chartres came from an age of belief. . . ."

"There are many beliefs. Keats stated one when he said, 'Beauty is truth, truth beauty—that is all ye know on earth, and all ye need to know.' "

We considered that for a while, as we walked down one of the narrow streets. Along this way coarse and dedicated swarms of men had once pulled and heaved dead weights of stone to build their living church.

"Chartres has two spires and several doors and many colored windows. Perhaps it has more than one truth, too."

"That's why it has survived so long."

In the Midi, or southwestern part of France, we discovered the hill towns that were so much a part of feudal history, and the dark green vineyards hanging heavy with fat clusters of grapes; the orchards of peaches, pears, and cherries; and the fields of grain that are so much a part of the present.

Then one morning on a bridge crossing the Aude River we looked up, and there, hanging against the blue sky like a dream of distant kingdoms in a Brueghel painting of boisterous peasants, like the fantasyland of a Walt Disney movie, like all the imaginary kingdoms of childhood and knights in armor, rose the city of Carcassonne.

Five pairs of eyes beheld it simultaneously for the first time, and it was the single most breathtaking moment of our summer.

As we drove from the "modern" lower city beside the river—it was founded in 1247 and has about 40,000 inhabitants today—we were stunned by the size of La Cité, as the historical Carcassonne is called. We had included it on our itinerary because we knew it was the most authentic depiction extant of ancient and medieval fortifications. But we had not envisioned it as a living museum of such large proportions that it would incorporate us into the flow of its life and transport us back into another age.

The old Cité of Carcassonne is the most complete fortified town in the world. It covers an entire hilltop overlooking the Aude River as well as the pink tile roofs and green patch-work of small fertile farms in the surrounding countryside. It is encircled by not one but two immense walls, which are strengthened at intervals by some fifty massive towers. Within this fortress is a castle, a cathedral, a town of about 800 people and their small shops and cafés, and two hotels, which preserve the atmosphere and scenery of the Middle Ages but also provide the comforts, service, and good food of the twentieth century.

Carcassonne, even more than other unique and historic sites of Europe, demands to be known by walking its narrow winding streets, climbing its precipitous spiral stairways, following the paths atop its giant ramparts, exploring its round towers with their sharply pointed roofs and the stolid square towers. And then, within the moat (long since dry) and the Outer Wall and the tiltyard and the Inner Wall, wait the final defenses of La Cité: the castle and the cathedral. The castle was an independent fortress in which the people of Carcassonne and the surrounding countryside could take refuge if all other protection failed.

The Basilica St. Nazaire is famous for its stained-glass windows. Its Romanesque and Gothic features date back to the eleventh century. Perhaps its most significant feature, however, is an empty tomb marked by the lion and the cross of Simon de Montfort. Here, for a few years following his death in 1218, was buried the man who probably brought more death and suffering to the region of Languedoc—with Carcassonne at its heart—than any other single conqueror in its history. Simon de Montfort led the crusade of northern nobles and defenders of the faith against a group of heretics known as Albigensians. The intensity and bloodiness of his onslaught may be divined from the reply he is reputed to have given when asked which of his opponents should be put to the sword and stake and which should be spared.

"Kill them all," he said. "God will know His own."

The entrance to Carcassonne, like that ascribed to heaven, is straight and narrow. A one-way bridge across the moat leads under the Narbonnaise archway, jammed between two great stone towers, and into the well-worn streets of La Cité.

From that moment forward we felt that we had passed into another world, a time before cannon had rendered walls obsolete, before motors and wings had diminished hilltops into easy reach, before ideas had become part of the free commerce of man's life. Above all, it was a world and time of war.

From its very beginning Carcassonne was a site of bastions and defenses. Early Gallic tribes built primitive forts here. During Roman rule the hill overlooking the Aude River was on the frontier between what are now Spain and France; it was on the main trade route between Bordeaux and Rome.

When the Roman encampments were conquered by the Visigoths in 462, Carcassonne began to assume even larger importance. The first wall was built around the city. About a third—all of it in the present inner wall—remains today, with some of the distinctive towers constructed by those German warriors.

The energetic Visigoths were, in 725, besieged by the Saracens, who had swept across Spain and taken all before them. Their turn at ruling Carcassonne lasted a little more than three decades before they melted back into the Arab world and the city became part of the Frankish Empire under Pepin the Short and his famous son, Charlemagne.

During this time the first dynasty of the hereditary counts was established, and now La Cité reached one pinnacle of its development. During these two centuries of the feudal ages the castle and the cathedral were built, and the age of chivalry—with its valiant knights, fair ladies, and wandering minstrels—flourished.

The saddest period of Carcassonne's past came during the Albigensian Crusade, when that Simon de Montfort we have already mentioned led one of the religious wars which, as one observer has said, "took on a character at once religious and political, the latter in the end prevailing over the former." Under relentless attack and cruel siege the fortified towns of the Midi fell; those who had parted faith with the Church were killed; pacification was a long and brutal process.

In 1229 Carcassonne came under the rule of the kings of France. New fortifications were added, especially the enormous Outer Wall, which was kept along its entire course within bowshot of the Inner Wall. Other strongholds and towers were added and, with the establishment of the Inquisition here for some two centuries, a prison.

But France's conflicts moved to other regions. The boundary between Spain and France was set farther southwest, along the Pyrenees. Weapons and methods of warfare changed. Gradually, almost as Carcassonne had reached its zenith of power, it fell into decline. Its walls and structures were used as a quarry by people of the countryside who carried off quantities of its stone.

Then, in 1835, the writer Prosper Mérimée rediscovered Carcassonne and published a book which brought it to the attention of his fellow countrymen. Fifteen years later, however, the entire military works of the old town were condemned to demolition. A local archaeologist and that renowned and controversial architect, Viollet-le-Duc, who lived from 1814 to 1879, protested this destruction and spent the rest of their lives preserving and restoring La Cité.

There are those purists who argue that the Carcassonne we see today is more Viollet-le-Duc than it is Visigoth or Louis IX or Philip the Bold. Perhaps. But there are historical sites the world over where all that we find is the authentic fragment, the indisputable particle from which our imagination must construct the whole. Permit us a La Cité, where we may actually experience history, where the past of crossbows and lances, battering rams and catapults, parapets, drawbridges, and narrow tower rooms becomes a part of us. For thus we can enter the mind of an earlier age.

At sunset and at sunrise and at noonday we watched the play of light and shadow on the gray pebbles and red brick of the old Visigothic towers and walls, the yellowish and the square gray stones used by later Viscounts and kings, the conical dark (at times irridescent) roofs of circular towers and the looming ramparts of the square towers, the buttresses of the quiet cathedral, the impregnable façade of the gloomy castle, and the small squares with their public wells. And gradually we comprehended that, although these were built, in large measure, during an era of faith and devoutness, these bristling turrets and forbidding walls reflect— above all else—fear.

La Cité seemed to us, finally, a testimonial to fear of one's fellow man and of change. For the tragic flaw of those Middle Ages was the subjugation of curiosity, the suspicion of all inquiry. It was a time when man had all the answers—and none of the questions.

"And now," one of our family said, "we have all of the questions—and few of the answers."

As we drove back down the little street and through the Narbonnese gate, we passed the crude statue of Dame Carcas. On one of those stone walls high above the city we had heard her story only the day before.

When Charlemagne laid siege to Carcassonne during its Arab occupation, Dame Carcas was the Saracen ruler's wife. Her husband was killed in the fighting and she became the leader of the city's defenders during a long, bitter siege. At last, with the people on the verge of starvation and surrender, Dame Carcas threw her wit into the breach. She ordered the town's inhabitants to sweep the last grains of corn from bin and corner, and these she fed to her last sow. Then the stuffed pig was thrown over the walls. When it burst open and the besiegers saw that the inhabitants still had sufficient corn to be feeding it to their pigs, they concluded that their siege was having little success.

As they parleyed among themselves, Dame Carcas watched and ordered the trumpets to be blown. The blasts rang out and the people shouted to their attackers, "Carcas sonne, Carcas sonne!" which means, in English, "The trumpet sounds."

And when Charlemagne finally rode with his hosts into the city, he was so impresesd by the wit of Dame Carcas that he permitted her to remain as La Cité's ruler, and married her to one of his noble followers who became a founder of one of the most famous dynasties of powerful counts in Languedoc.

"Is it true?" is not the question one asks upon hearing a legend. A legend exists—because if it is not true, it should be.

Carcassonne, on its lofty hill, should be true. For us, during one brief interval of exploration and imagination and historical search, it was.

La Cité was imprinted on our senses: sight of ancient sun-warmed, rain-washed stone; damp smell of chilly cells and dark chambers; sound of footsteps echoing along labyrinthian pasages; hardness of stone and brick and iron softened by the touch of a summer breeze blowing up from the vineyards and orchards and grain fields; taste of ripe fruits, aged cheeses, full-bodied soups, an assortment of sauces from meat course to dessert.

As we turned our car southwest toward the Pyrenees, we looked back for one last full glimpse of Carcassonne.

Then, "The trumpet sounds," James said. And we took out our road maps. We had glimpsed yesterday. Now we would look to this day.

Whenever I see hydrangeas, I shall be reminded of two of the great resort cities of Europe: Biarritz and San Sebastián. In my imagination I smell the sea again and feel the warmth of the sun on the beach and the sand curved beside the sparkling water like a Turkish scimitar.

Biarritz was probably the most fashionable resort in France at one time. It was in part the creation of Empress Eugenie, wife of Napoleon III. Naturally there were many who followed such a royal example, hoping to find the air a bit more rarefied, the scenery a shade more vivid if it had been enjoyed by an Emperor and Empress.

Today the great baroque villas and hotels boast a fading opulence, a mere reflection of that earlier era of crowned heads and less mobile summers, when an entire season was spent in one locale. The hotels along the water front are as obsolete in the motel age as the dinosaur or the mastodon.

We found our way to one of these landmarks on the promenade above the sea. Banked along it, clustered on the steep terraces, were giant hydrangea bushes. Their round blooms were as plump and plentiful as the pretty women who once thronged these walks and beaches.

Inside, the ornate drawing room of the hotel remained largely deserted through most of our stay. The writing room, with its beautiful little Louis Quatorze desks and tables, was as desolate as an artifact displayed in some museum. The numerous doormen and porters and maids and attendants at the front desk wore an air of genteel resignation, as if they knew that only the hydrangeas would flourish without change in a future which had already overtaken all else in this hothouse little world.

San Sebastián, some thirty miles southwest, on the Spanish stretch of the Basque coast, was lavish with hydrangeas and tamarisks, too. In addition, it had an atmosphere of verve. The present seemed to be free of the velvet clutches of the past.

It is the most popular seaside resort in Spain. Certainly it is situated on one of the handsomest sites imaginable, along a bay surrounded by three hills, each of which provides a panorama of the multi-green and azure ocean and the sprawling colorful city and, from two of the peaks, a view of the majestic Pyrenees in the distance. Along the drives winding up these slopes were frequent thick plantings of ever-present hydrangeas, and the sweeping views from the summits dazzled even two jaded Juniors. (As someone remarked along the way, our Juniors were old and sophisticated; our Senior was young and enthusiastic; and our two Middlers were alternately eager and weary. Spirit was all, age nothing.) Brilliant sunlight, tiled roofs, blue sky and ocean, clean cool breezes from the bay, beds of scarlet cannas in flower along the boulevard and in the park.

The two beaches of San Sebastián were beautiful, and their facilities for swimmers and sun worshipers were excellent. This won the prompt approval of the two youngest.

Biarritz and San Sebastián sit like two queens on the Bay of Biscay: one a dowager, still affluent but with waning influence, the other at the crest of beauty and sociability; each bedecked with banks, borders, enormous beds of flourishing hydrangeas.

We came into Spain through the mists of the Pyrenees and ate our first meal on a terrace in San Sebastian. We left

Spain via the commercial capital of Barcelona and the scenic Costa Brava on the Mediterranean.

Between arrival and departure we wandered, somewhat like Don Quixote—with our own contingent of Sancho Panzas—over that vast plain known as La Mancha and beyond: across high mountains and wind-swept plateaus where both sun and shadow are harsh and bold, through arid desert places and luxuriant tropical gardens, from ancient capitals and bleak villages where yesterday still reigns to hustling cities where today invests the air with noise and industrial fumes.

Seville, with its horse-drawn carriages and canvas-shaded lively bazaars, its Gothic cathedral and Moorish Giralda tower, we found conspicuously unlike Madrid, so manifestly a "capital" with its huge government buildings, wide avenues, modern offices and shops, and jostling automobiles. Alicante, with its palm-shaded promenade and public bandstand, modern hotels and cafés is far different from Avila of Roman times, girdled by massive medieval walls 40 feet high, 10 feet thick, with 88 immense round towers of pinkish cream-colored stone, where storks now nest and bitter winds howl in winter. In Alicante we saw a vendor peddling ices from his portable cooling machine along the boulevard; in Avila we watched a milkman plod door to door along a narrow street, measuring out milk by the cupful or jugful from straw-covered vessels hanging on either side of his patient donkey's back.

We adapted to the dining hours of two until four in the afternoon for lunch and ten till midnight for dinner. We were aware of the ever-present military, the Guardia Civil, which was more apparent here than in any other country we visited.

And in the Basque region, as we entered Spain, we came upon a solitary sheepherder disappearing over the brow of a hill beside the highway with his dog and flock in front of him. He was a slightly built man, wearing the typical black

Basque beret, and his face was alert—bright brown eyes above a stubble of beard. We slowed our car and he responded with such a cheerful grin and hopeful little salute that we stopped to stretch and stand with him a moment. The only solid information we managed to exchange was, on our part, the fact that we were American and not English and, on his part, the name of the valley in the distance. But he took such a warm farewell of us when we drove on, leaving him there with his sheep scattered down the steep green slope in front of him, that we felt the encounter had been a good omen for the rest of our visit.

Reaction of our three generations to Spain reflected some of the extremes of the country itself. (One interpretation of its name says that Spain means "Hidden Land," and we agreed that, more than most countries, this one demands a personal discovery and calls forth a personal response.)

Our two Juniors pronounced Spain harsh and difficult and, despite numerous de luxe hotels and occasional excesses of luxury, living for the most part too much in another time. Perhaps our preoccupation with the riches of the Prado, Madrid's museum of art, which may be the most impressive in the world, and the gold and silver and jeweled treasures of Toledo's Cathedral, and our concentration on yesterday's strongholds rather than today's commercial centers helped shape this particular reaction.

Precisely because it was harsh, however, with a distinctive and definite character all its own, and because, especially in the country, it did still follow many antique ways, our Senior decided that Spain was her biggest surprise and most unique experience.

The two of us who were Middlers found Spain a tortured paradox of independence and dictatorship, hopefulness and despair, gentility and coarseness. It is not easy to understand this country of the poet Garcia Lorca and the dictator Franco, of St. Theresa and Pablo Picasso, of Marcus Aurelius and the bullfighter Ordoñez.

Of all Western European countries, the one that Americans probably have most difficulty understanding is Spain. There are doubtless many causes for this, most of which remain unknown to me. Among the reasons I would suggest, however, drawn from limited experience and extensive thought, are these: the proud, somewhat formal and reserved individualism of the people, contrasted with their equally warm courtesy and quick passion; the essentially rural nature of the country, despite its distinctive cities; the sense of tragedy, rather than the spirit of "success," which broods in the shadows of the busiest street and deepens the lines of the most urbane countenance.

None of these paradoxes—or even anachronisms, if you wish—lend their possessors to ready familiarity or easy friendship with strangers. Americans, especially, may be puzzled and even alienated by such characteristics.

Yet these very qualities which put off others of our countrymen are, I suspect, the bonds which should make American Southerners best able to appreciate, enjoy, and comprehend Spain.

Spaniards may often be as difficult for other Europeans to understand as Southerners are frequently difficult for other Americans to understand. And there may be a common reason for this.

Spain is the one country of Western Europe whose people for several successive centuries came under the powerful influence of an African people living within its borders. The South is the one region of the United States whose white population for several successive generations were influenced from infancy to dotage by an African people living beside and with them. The influence in each instance was profound, and could be expected to produce a nation disparate from neighbors who had not known such an influence.

It has been said that the Spaniard combines "Roman hardness with Eastern sentiment." Certainly the delicate fluted arches and the limpid fountains, which the Moors bequeathed to Granada, add grace and beauty to a land dominated in large part by dark Romanesque cathedrals and ponderous fortresses. Likewise, in the Southern United States perhaps a certain European hardness has been tempered by an African sentiment, an unself-consciousness, an ease of pace and gift of enjoyment which deeply affected all the life of the region. In each instance, Spain and the Southern region of the United States, an original white majority had its physical existence shaped and its view of life affected by a dark minority more subtle and patient than itself.

Geographically, of course, Spain was long cut off from the rest of Europe by the Pyrenees Mountains. (One of Napoleon's best-known comments was his assertion that "Europe ends at the Pyrenees.") The Renaissance and the Reformation and the Industrial Revolution—each of which had a decisive impact on the other Western countries—bypassed Spain altogether or touched it only slightly.

Without belaboring the parallel too much we might say that the Southern states, too, lagged behind their neighbors to the north in experiencing industrial revolution. And the extractive nature of both the agriculture and the use of natural resources was a plague common to Spain and to our Southern region. Until recent decades wanton deforestation and unwise planting of corn and tobacco led to major problems of erosion and soil exhaustion in the South, especially in the Appalachian mountain areas, while the one-crop economy of cotton in the Deep South impoverished both land and people, with the exception of a small minority. Coal and other minerals were largely controlled and developed by corporations or people outside the region.

Spain, also, over the centuries, was systematically relieved of its mineral deposits by foreign development companies in league with a few sympathetic Spanish businessmen. The agricultural resources were likewise depleted. In this instance, however, the native was more responsible than the outsider for the creeping plague of erosion. Careless cutting of trees and laying bare the soil to the elements sacrificed the future to the greed of immediate gain. The scars remain.

Both the Spaniards and the Southerners have known poverty, then, a poverty partly of their own making and partly that of strangers who battened on their raw riches, and all the more exasperating because of the affluence of their neighbors. And each responded to the plight all too frequently by intensifying a trait of character (independence resentful of any criticism and shunning any co-operative effort), rather than by changing daily habits or farming practices.

From the past flow reasons for some of the present differences from the majority "norm." To look again at the three we have named:

First, the prickly pride and aloofness which co-exists with the outgoing warmth of the people. Our initial major experience of Spain made us feel in many ways that we were back home in the Southern mountains, where our Appalachian natives can be both the most reticent and the most unreserved of acquaintances.

We had found ourselves stranded in a village in the province of Burgos, between car rentals, and we had resorted to the train to reach Madrid. The railway station where we had landed appeared to be deserted. The dusty square and sun-baked buildings in front of the station drowsed in the afternoon sun. A lonesome wind blew in from the high tableland surrounding the little town. It was evident that no passenger train for the great and distant city of Madrid was due to depart from here in the next sixteen minutes as our schedule indicated.

But we had climbed off our previous train, which had paused here for only the space of a breath, without any railroad employee or fellow passenger setting us straight about our erroneous information. This hands-off policy, we came to realize a little later, was born in part of an excessive courtesy, which recognizes that most people resent being corrected in any error. It is a courtesy which grants each person the right to his mistakes as well as his triumphs—unless, of course, he has directly requested help. We had often encountered this maddening and endearing trait at home. ("I never was one to tell the other feller his business," an old mountaineer once explained after he had watched us make a dreadful misjudgment in our gardening.)

The comparison went even further, as we asked for help in finding out just how bad our predicament was. A Civil Guard—in full military regalia distinguished by the round flat headgear with its sudden wingspread—promenaded slowly along the platform. We stopped him and promptly learned that the language gap between us was indeed a gulf. Four other husky members of the Guardia Civil suddenly appeared as if from nowhere, and now we were evenly matched, five to five, in numbers if not in size, each using sign language to supplement our loud repetitions in native tongue. At last *they* understood that we were expecting to go to Madrid momentarily; and *we* understood that the next such train departed this place at 23:30 hours, or 11:30 that night. At 2:00 in the afternoon we were either very early or very late.

Further gyrations and efforts to find common words led us to comprehend that this 23:30 train, when it did arrive, would have no sleeping accommodations and would stop at many places along the way, was, in short, a very local local.

Our military escort was joined by an attendant of the railway, a small man wearing ragged trousers, a beret, and a wide smile. He indicated a gloomy little café across the square where, he made us understand, we could wait in convivial comfort for the next nine and one-half hours. Looking at our pyramid of luggage, which had appeared quite modest in other surroundings but took on the aspect of a Shah's entourage here, we suspected that five new customers—none of whom could be considered petite—and their attendant suitcases and tote bags, would tax the facilities of that cranny-in-the-wall café to the bursting point.

There was much animated discussion as to our plight. Then James spied, at one side of the square, a solitary row of four cars. They seemed quite empty as the five of us, abandoning baggage, station, and all but hope, rushed to ask if any of these were for hire. Several men, hands stuffed in their jacket pockets, materialized on the scene.

The nearest car at hand was a Seat, one of Spain's own manufacture, and we finally gathered from its dark, heavy-set young driver that it *was* for hire; he *could* drive us to Madrid; and he *would* do so for 2,600 pesetas. It was a reasonable price. (Friends in Madrid later pointed out just how reasonable it was, and that this man had not tried to take advantage of us, although we seemed ripe enough for the plucking at that point.)

Our lengthy negotiations attracted quite an impressive audience, especially considering the deserted aspect of the surroundings before the action had begun. The total attentiveness of the listeners, the grave concern with which they regarded our dilemma, the approval with which they accepted the driver's statement of his fee to us, and their eager anticipation of our response to his offer—all these revealed a natural provincial curiosity, but they also suggested a genuine interest in human undertakings and reactions.

We pointed to the 2,600-peseta figure (the equivalent of about $43) which the driver had written on the edge of a newspaper we were carrying; we repeated the word "Madrid" and waved our arms in a southerly direction; and then we all nodded. A little sound, almost a sigh of relief, went up from the Civil Guards, the assorted taxi men, and the accumulated onlookers. They smiled at us, nodded to our driver, broke into rapid conversation with one another.

A sense of comradeship swept over us, too. In part it was a vast relief at this simple solution to our transportation-shelter problem, but in larger part it was appreciation for the unabashed concern of these strangers.

All that concern soon found a new focus. Our two Juniors—anticipating Madrid more eagerly than an impromptu visit in an isolated rural village, no matter how picturesque or friendly—set to work on the double transporting our bags from the station platform out to the little car. Our Senior citizen climbed into the back seat and forthwith removed herself from the great debate, which now raged between those who thought the limited space of the Seat's trunk could best be utilized by standing all the bags up, and those who contended they should be laid flat and piled one upon the other.

At last the perpendicular school of thought prevailed, and several intense and brawny men shoved our suitcases into the order they thought would be best. But this left two bags still outside.

Then the opposition had its test run, and left one bag without a place. At last, to a chorus of shouted instructions, grunts and gesticulations, a compromise horizontal and vertical placement of bags was undertaken, and all were fitted in. Of course, James and our two sons were chagrined to discover that our Senior had assessed the space situation of the trunk at a glance and had already dragged the two zipper handbags into the back seat with her. Which only meant that she had overestimated the space in the car itself. Our faithful audience now watched as we folded our long legs and arranged ourselves in the narrow seats. As we drew our shoulders together, hunched up our legs, and struggled to slam the door (much as a floodgate might seek to contain bulging waters), the driver started his motor with a roar and there was a small cheer from our friends.

We smiled and waved and tossed a few "Gracias" and

"Adioses" into the general atmosphere. They waved back—the Civil Guards in their heavy uniforms, the other men with their thin clothes and their grins that revealed in two or three instances broken or missing teeth.

As we careened out of town and broke into the open country and narrow two-lane highway, leading toward the city of Burgos and eventually to Madrid, we recalled the many times we had seen boys and men in the mountains at home clustered around a broken automobile (their favorite sort of problem), and how they responded just as spontaneously as these had to any stranger in need of help. The rural Spanish people had almost stranded us by their deliberate reticence and congenital unwillingness to interfere in another's private affairs; then they had rescued us with ready and generous response when their help was sought. It was the most minor of incidents, but it served to make us aware of qualities with which we had coped lifelong in our Southern mountain friends, and which were also possessed by these strangers.

As visitors in America frequently remark on a hospitality which seems readier among Southerners in the United States than among Northerners, so we soon discovered that many travelers in Europe comment on the comparative friendliness of Spanish people. One Englishman observed neatly a number of years ago: "The French man or woman I meet, however polite, seems to be viewing me as a possible enemy. The Spanish man or woman, on the other hand, even if less formally polite, seems to be viewing me as a possible friend."

To touch briefly on the other two distinctions I have mentioned, which Spanish Europeans and Southern Americans have in common, yet which serve to set them somewhat apart from their fellow dwellers on the Continent or in the region:

There is the rural nature of the country, or region, which

still prevails in an industrialized world. This ruralism has its attendant virtues of jealous individualism and family pride, and its attendant problems of a passive "community spirit" and massive emigration. (To illustrate simply the latter problem: During the first half of this century two million of Spain's people went to live in other countries; during the single decade from 1940 to 1950 the Appalachian South lost one million of its people to other areas of this country. And they went in each instance despite a strong loyalty to family ties and familiar terrain, because their land could not support them and their towns could not employ them.)

Such a rural orientation may persist in attitudes, mores, customs, and habits of thought even amidst increasing industrialization. The tension created between old patterns and new pressures may make a people seem original and fascinating to visitors from more homogenized societies. The necessity is to balance the excesses of their virtues and the enervation of their flaws.

There is, too, the sense of tragedy which often seems more dominant than that spirit of "success" which characterizes most of the Western world today. This tragic sense is reflected in Spanish painting and in Southern literature, and it has been largely sustained by the strong religious convictions and the formal church affiliations of the people.

That the majority of Spaniards and Southerners are on sharply divided sides of the Christian faith perhaps matters less in our age of massive skepticism and nonbelief than the fact that each remains convinced, often to the point of intolerance, regarding his own faith's infallibility. And each of their religious convictions lifts man into a relationship with God which at least permits tragedy. These religious beliefs do not seem in either instance to guarantee a keen sense of social justice or personal freedom, but they do provide for man a vision of himself, a vision in which he has the capacity for tragedy as well as that absurdity of which the secular world is presently so enamoured.

The fundamental religiosity of these two people de-emphasizes getting ahead in worldly affairs. Man's business becomes less impressive when placed in the perspective of God's service, and success in today's transactions seems unimportant when related to eternal commitments.

In addition to the strong religious orientation influencing the tragic sense, there is also the historical fact that both Spain and the Southern United States have known the excesses of Civil War fought in their own gutted fields and narrow alleys and village squares, brother butchering brother, kinsman betraying kinsman. More than a third of a million people were killed in the American Civil War, and most of them died on Southern soil. A million lives were lost in the Spanish Civil War, all of them on this native ground. Experience of such bloodletting fosters a sense of tragedy, and in a proud, romantic, rural people, who are given less to abstractions than to the concrete, less to ideas than to the senses, its memory remains green and bitter for a very long time.

To set forth these few comparisons suggesting why Southerners, especially Appalachian Mountain Southerners, with a bit of effort and imagination may be better able than the majority of Americans to understand Spain and its people, is to invite immediate rebuttal and numerous citations of contrasts and differences between the two peoples. My purpose, however, has not been a definition but simply an indication of similarities which may exist between widely separated groups.

Our own little family felt that, had we spoken their language with any facility, we might have eaten in the high mountain pastures with the Basque sheepherder we paused to greet one morning, or that we might have visited in the white sun-baked little house among the olive trees with the Andalusian woman from whom we asked directions one afternoon; with each of these and many others we could have established a warm and easy friendliness. For we have stopped too often to talk with shy yet responsive strangers in our own Southern mountains, and had them finally welcome us into their homes and their loyalty, not to recognize their counterparts anywhere we meet them.

Perhaps Hemingway voiced something of our feeling in his novel, *For Whom the Bell Tolls*, when he had Robert Jordan, the American who loved Spain and the Spaniards enough to die for them, say: "There is no finer and no worse people in the world. No kinder people and no crueler. And who understands them? Not me, because if I did I would forgive it all."

The morning was good. It was Sunday morning and Sunday is a good day in Madrid.

The sun shone but not too hot, even though it was July and the July sun in Spain can be harsh. There were people along the Calle de Serrano and the Avenida de José Antonio and many streets, and in parks, and in the lobbies of the big hotels; but they were not the people who had been at cafés along the streets or in clubs at the hotels late the night before. At least not many of them were the same. For the Saturday night people for the most part did not appear until after midday Sunday, which was all right because that is when the Madrilenos, too, become sociable once more.

In the afternoon there is the bullfight.

After the good morning of church bells and walking slowly only where we wished to walk, we ate. We ate well, with much food and much time to enjoy it.

Then we went to the Plaza de Toros. The bullfight began at five o'clock; not five minutes till or ten minutes after, but at five in the afternoon. The people were there—the late Saturday night ones and the bright Sunday morning ones, rural and city Spaniards, and curious tourists—streaming across the pavement and then the hard-packed dirt on the shadowy walkways under the immense tiers of seats overhead, emerging into the dazzling sunlight and vast circumference of packed seats.

It was good to sit in the shade and look at the colorful clothes in the sun and feel the anticipation rippling through the crowd. The anticipation was not simple, as if awaiting some single event or experience. It was complex: excited, as for a sports contest; sophisticated, as for a ballet or ritual dance; and somber, as for an encounter with death. It pulsated, warm with enthusiasm for spectacle and courage; and receded, aloof with chilly loneliness. A stranger to the bullfight could sense but not share this intoxication. It was too ancient (born of the Moors and Romans who influenced Spain in these animal contests), too deep (rooted in character inured to, enamored of suffering?), too alien.

At five o'clock in the afternoon there was the blare of the *paso doble*. To the sound of the music the matadors entered —three stiffly formal young men dressed in skin-tight pants, pink stockings, brilliant beaded jackets weighing many pounds, and black bicorn hats. They were followed by their *cuadrillas*, or assistants, dressed only a little less splendidly. Their procession around the arena was well hailed. They remained grave and formal.

("At last," one of our family whispered, "I've seen someone on whom stretch pants look good!")

They left the arena, three matadors and their helpers on horseback and on foot. The great round sweep of sand was empty. The music had stopped. For the space of a half-beat there was silence.

Then, into the sun erupted a black fury. The bull came swiftly, skidded to a halt, raised his head, pivoted to find an antagonist, and lowered his ponderous head again. He was a splendid specimen of the animal kingdom: more than one thousand pounds of ancient breeding, care, and murderous intent. In twenty minutes he would be dead.

The sport-drama-death ritual had begun.

No, Mr. Hemingway, and all other less articulate, equally romantic aficionados of the bull ring, it was not "good." The myth dies in the moment of truth. . . .

The brave bull trots around the arena, horns and head held high above his sleek black neck.

The *toreros* come from behind the protection of the wooden fence and offer their capes for his lunges and hooks. Then the slim matador walks forth to match wits with his deadly adversary. Muscle and brute force confront skill and courage. The austere matador will, before the rites are concluded, face the full fury of a savage beast and in one superb moment of truth plunge the sword to its hilt and into the bull's heart, releasing man's artifice and courage back into life and the bull's bravery into death. The mystique of the *corrida* is ready to reassert itself.

But . . .

The bulls are not always brave. They are—by specification—big (more than a half-ton in weight), mature (between four and eight years old), with horns that hook in varying degrees of surprise and danger. But they are not always brave and eager to die.

The matadors are not always skillful. Sometimes their grace fumbles and their courage falters.

Then the elaborate mythology of the bullfight tumbles from its realms of rhetoric and romance into the sand.

Of course, the tauromaniac's first warning to a novice is invariably, "See only the top matadors. Don't watch the beginners, the unknowns."

But how many Manoletes and Ordoñezes and El Cordobéses are there? It is simply impossible to follow such advice.

Also, there seems something awry in any philosophy or discipline or art or sport—however its enthusiasts may choose to label it—which cannot expose its amateurs as well as its stars to public vision, which reveals itself as primitive when once (and frequently) stripped of a fragile veneer of ceremony and symbol. If we cannot know the novitiates and apprentices and find some admiration for their achievements, how shall we cultivate respect for the final triumph of the masters?

And, since there are dozens of aspirants for every Dominguin who has arrived, what of those spectators who do throng all the bull rings of Spain and Mexico to watch less-than-the-best in matadors? Are they, the numerous, the "insensitive" ones, drawn there by sacrifice or spectacle? Do they satisfy hunger for style or thirst for blood?

The aficionado's second advice is usually that no one should go to the bullfight before he has learned the subtleties surrounding the afternoon's procedures. Anyone who does not know what *faena* means, and that *veronicas* are the passes the matador makes with his cape, and something about the niceties of footwork will not even know when to shout "Ole!" But how shall he learn except by seeing and knowing for himself?

So strangers flock to the Plazas de Toros from Pamplona to Seville, from Barcelona to Madrid. Some are fascinated by what they find. "I thought they [bullfights] would be simple and barbarous and cruel," Hemingway once wrote, "but the bullfight was far from simple, and I liked it. . . ."

Others are shaken by the experience. Not all of these are little old ladies in tennis shoes, contrary to that assumption as displayed by the weary shrugs of the followers of *la fiesta brava*.

There are those who respond not only to the thrilling danger of the cruel horns as they graze the swiveling hips of the unflinching matador, but respond, too, to the unequal contest with numerous men systematically punishing and wearing down the brute toward ultimate defeat.

We sat in the *sombra* (shade) on a fine Sunday afternoon and watched six bulls die. Three of us had seen Manolete, he of the tragic mien and icy daring, in 1946 in Mexico City, but even his celebrated skill had not managed to blot out the final picture of the *corrida* in our minds. But there was no Manolete in the Plaza in Madrid. There were only three less-experienced young men whose splendor at the beginning of the afternoon crumbled steadily to chagrin and shame. One of those encounters we saw will suffice, one which the great prose-poets of the *corridas de toros* always fail to include.

The bull was released into the arena. His shoulders were powerful; his stance was proud; his horns hooked danger-ously. In the middle of the amphitheater he paused and pawed the ground. His short angry digs sent hard pellets of dirt flying.

The *toreros* attracted his attention, played him with their capes, retreated at a run as he charged them too closely. The matador, watching behind the wooden fence, had opportu-nity to note how this bull responded, if he were quick or slow, whether he hooked to right or left, and if he betrayed any peculiarities which might become important in a mur-derous lunge.

The matador took the field, tried a few veronicas. The bull responded, charging and missing. There were small cries of "Ole." Then the matador retired.

The picadores arrived. Two heavy-set men, each carrying a long lance, they wore wide hats and colorful jackets and sat astride gaunt bony nags. The horses' right eyes were bandaged and their right sides were covered with a thick padding.

The shock of the bull's assault on that padding made each horse shudder in turn, but caught between fence and horns as in a vise, the poor glue-factory candidates could only stand and endure while their riders jabbed the sharp steel knives of the lances deep into the bull's shoulders. At the first picador's encounter they stood locked for a gory interval: terrified, blindfolded horse; bull shoving his horns into the padding, seeking the horse's belly (and sometimes, although not this particular time, finding it and ripping it open in a messy spectacle of guts); and picador, burying the lance's hurt into those powerful muscles. (The muscles are cut so that the bull's head will be lowered to the right position for the eventual death thrust of the sword.) Then the tableaux broke. Another charge, another exchange between bull and horse and man. The picadores rode gravely out of the arena, the steel ends of their lances rich with blood.

There was yet another act before the final drama of matador and bull. Three men called *banderilleros*, each carrying two spikes decorated with bright streamers, took turns facing the enraged and wounded animal. Each, in the moment of the bull's charge toward him, leaped aside even as he plunged the barbed darts firmly into those huge, bleeding shoulders. It was a daring precise dance of defiance. When it was finished, five beribboned spikes hung hooked into the terrified bull's withers. One dart had gone astray, dislodged by the frantic tossing of his head.

At last, the matador, carrying his sword and muleta (red cloth attached to a short rod), and bull faced each other.

Slowly, hissing *"Toro! Toro!"* and grunting short gasps, the matador minced toward the snorting, angry beast. As it charged, he drew it, with the muleta, to pass beside him. Its heaving sides barely grazed the man's tight pants. A murmur of approval went up from the spectators.

It was their last sign of approval, however. On the next confrontation the bull did not charge. He walked away. And the young matador signaled for the picadores to work with the bull once more, weaken those mighty shoulders still more. Neither the bull nor the man appeared to have the careless courage that arouses spontaneous adulation.

When the picadores had finished gouging again, the matador resumed his play, winding the bull around him as his feet stayed frozen and the red cloth seemed to become his mind and will.

He did not do badly. But the bull was disinterested and seemed to seek an escape rather than a fight. The matador spit *"Toro! Toro!"* at it, and waved the muleta ever more desperately.

An ironic rhythmic hand-clapping arose from the audience.

At last the matador brought the bull into place for the kill: directly in front of him, its head lowered, front feet together. With one long movement the matador sighted and thrust forward between the horns toward the crucial point between the shoulders where the sword would sink to the hilt and the bull would collapse, dying, dead.

But the man missed. The sword did not find its target, but struck bone and dangled on the wounded animal as he retreated across the arena. The sword was pulled out. Blood followed it. The bull's flesh on this forepart of his back was torn and clotted, lacerated and raw.

The stance once more. The instant thrust. And a second miss. The sword clattered to the ground.

The crowd reverberated with disapproval. The misery of the young matador distorted his face. The bull stood still, panting, blood streaming from nostrils and mouth. Its butchering proceeded. At last the sword found its target. The legs buckled. Slowly the bull sank, head forward, and then toppled to one side.

No ears or tail as reward for that matador, only hisses and murmurs of disappointment.

A gaily decorated mule team crossed the arena at a gallop and dragged away the carcass of the bull-that-was-not-so-brave. The sand was raked and the blood erased.

The amphitheater was quiet.

Suddenly, a great black bull, powerful with life, erupted into the arena. . . .

Six times in an afternoon the furious arrival, the departing carcass, and the ceremony in between.

It was not a good afternoon, Mr. Hemingway. But that was the way it was, recorded in the realism of five vigilant senses. It was an experience of unnecessary suffering, ill-matched odds, risk without reason.

And yet, what of the tortuous prize fights, the ordeal by automobile, the casual allusions to atomic warfare, the death and brutalization in the human rituals that surround us all the time?

I arrive at my own private moment of truth. The blood of the bull ring offends. Then how shall we forsake and forestall the infinitely larger offenses of civilization's ceremonies of death?

Doctors tell us that patients who, through fear of becoming helpless, take to their beds and refuse to exercise limbs or muscles do, in fact, soon grow helpless.

Psychologists assure us that the child who is protected from making any mistakes on his own while he is growing up will, in fact, make the biggest mistake of all and never grow up.

In similar fashion travelers who doubt their own resourcefulness and refuse to exercise it, who want to be protected from the unknown even though they are going out to seek it, do, in fact, miss the very experience for which they grope. A traveler who lets someone else do all his thinking, planning, buying, arranging for him is yielding to a sort of dictatorship; and although it may be a benevolent dictatorship, and carry with it the acknowledged rewards of efficiency, it is nonetheless stifling to both imagination and self-confidence.

Certainly no one but the sturdiest student who could always rely on his hostel or sleeping bag would propose that a middle-aged couple or a family group or a party of friends should set out for Europe in the summertime without at least some expert advice and planning ahead. Since tickets for the Salzburg Festival, for example, are sold out a year in advance, it would be illiterate to advise anyone to wait for a spur-of-the-moment inspiration before he decided to make the birthplace of Mozart part of his musical memory. But what we might suggest is that some time along the predestined way be left free for frequent personal exploration, that some daring always be reserved for individual side expeditions. Exercising curiosity is the best way to keep it healthy. Feeding knowledge will make it grow.

There was, for instance, no prearranged plan that we should go to the city of Segovia when we were in Spain. But we had a car; we had a day; the weather was co-operative—and the name Segovia stirred memories formed somewhere long ago.

Besides, there is special reason for an American to be interested in a pilgrimage to Segovia. It was here, in 1474, that Isabella (she of the pawned jewels and the three small ships —*Nina*, *Pinta*, and *Santa Maria*) was proclaimed queen. It was in Segovia, in 1505, that Ferdinand bore witness to the last will and testament of Columbus, six months before America's discoverer died, still ignorant of the dimensions of his achievement.

The sixty-three miles from Madrid to Segovia cross the Sierra de Guadarrama—or go through it. The tunnel is new; a superhighway flows through its darkness swiftly. The route over the mountain range is old and winding; it offers views of the vast plain of New Castile below. We took the high road.

Beyond the mountains is Old Castile and Segovia. Out of a barren landscape it rises dramatically, situated on a rocky eminence more than 3,200 feet in altitude. Buttressed to the furthermost point of this great upthrust is the turreted Alcazar, overlooking a sheer drop to the two rivers which converge near its base. From a distance the castle seems to pierce the blue sky itself. As the traveler draws nearer, the ancient walls enclosing this proud city come into view—and the tall cathedral, built of warm rose- and golden-colored stone. Streets wide and narrow lead to busy squares, other churches, photogenic houses with weathered façades.

But the distinctive feature of Segovia, which overshadows all other attractions, is its colossal aqueduct. The largest Roman structure standing in Spain today, it inspires awe in any beholder, from Teens to Senior Citizens; almost 100 feet tall, it stretches across the busiest square in Segovia, nearly 900 yards in length. Its two tiers of 165 arches, built of massive blocks of granite from the nearby Guardarramas, dominate the town and dwarf the buildings and people who swarm at its feet.

And if anyone should doubt the genius of those ancient Roman builders, let him consider two facts: This mighty structure has stood these eighteen centuries without any mortar, and today it still serves to bring water to the people of Segovia.

In the shadow of the aqueduct is the Meson de Candido, a rustic restaurant with narrow winding stairways, numerous small dining rooms, informal service, and succulent roast lamb and pig, the specialties of this region of Spain. Here we enjoyed a flavorsome, lively dinner.

We came to Segovia without direction. We explored it without guides. We felt that it became ours by right of discovery and appreciation.

Following a different route back to Madrid, we climbed through splendid pine forests (in the countryside where Hemingway laid much of the action of his novel of the Spanish Civil War, *For Whom the Bell Tolls*) and found ourselves in one of the most scenic corners of this varied and dramatic land.

Along several slopes, as we wound up the mountains, the Scotch broom was in full bloom. The contrasts of the scene created what we might have called a portrait of Spain itself: the luxuriant yellow undergrowth of the shrubs flowering richly up the rugged inclines, overshadowed by the dark green tops of the towering pines; the opulence and lightness of the golden bushes mingled with the proud, storm-beaten old evergreens.

Nowhere had we come closer to the essence of ancient Spain than during this memorable day of a "side trip."

The town of Avignon manages, at least in the summertime, to be both a museum of the past and a stage for the present, and our interlude there served both antiquity and youth.

Avignon is in the heart of Provence, that celebrated region of southern France where grapes and olives yield rich juices and abundant oils; flowers splash brilliant colors in fields as well as gardens; and grains and cypresses and such sweet herbs as thyme, rosemary, and lavender flourish.

This countryside does not seem new or alien, even to the stranger, however. We have known it through the eyes of Van Gogh, the frenzied visitor from those chilled Low Countries to the north, who tried to capture on canvas all this southern vividness and the blazing heat of the sun itself. We have seen it through the impressions of Cezanne, a native who absorbed Provence through his pores as well as his eyes, and gave us the translation in subtle lucid shades and strokes. In the landscape of Provence, life and art frequently appear indivisible.

In similar fashion, in Avignon history and the present often seem indivisible. This is because of a truncated bridge thrusting its mutilated reach out into the Rhone River before the masonry abruptly ends, and because of encircling ramparts and the massive papal palace which dominate the town. The bridge remains alive today in a familiar children's song, "*Sur le pont d' Avignon*," but its actual importance came when it originally served as the spur transforming this little crossroads into a major city. Merchants and traders of the Middle Ages found few bridges to ease the hardships along their routes, and when, in the twelfth century, one was erected at this crossing of the mighty Rhone River, their traffic changed the village into a prosperous town such as it had never been before.

During the fourteenth century the seat of the popes was in Avignon rather than in Rome (for a bitter period of schism it was in both places), and this in turn transformed the town beside the Rhone into a powerful metropolis such as it has never been since.

With the power of the Church centered in Avignon, its population swelled and its treasuries overflowed. Royalty and rogues (sometimes in the same person) came and went; pilgrims brought their prayers and offerings; persecuted Jews and criminals sought asylum; worldly traders and ascetic saints came, and all formed an endless procession. Riotous festivals and religious celebrations created a steady succession of diversions. Money was so plentiful that within a space of only twenty years the monumental Palace of the Popes was begun and completed and decorated with rare tapestries, frescoes, statues, and rich furniture.

Today the interior of the Palace is bare. It was stripped soon after the papal power was permanently moved back to Rome in 1403; for a while it even served as a barracks. But the physical impact of the Palace itself is made even more overwhelming by this barrenness. The popes who constructed this ponderous building must have been convinced that the awe men felt toward God should be reflected in the dwellings of His commissioned servants here on earth. The vast audience chamber, banqueting hall, conclave, grand staircase, numerous chapels, hallways, courts, and other public and private rooms *do* inspire awe rather than any sense of identification.

We passed through these labyrinths with little hesitation and then came out into the Great Court, where we had entered, and through the gates back into the broad passage leading to the heart of town. Above us loomed the square towers of the Palace, some of them 150 feet tall. We needed perspective.

Our walk through the town followed numerous narrow streets where well-stocked specialty stores invited much window-shopping, and flowers in pots and tiny gardens called forth frequent comment. When we came to the area outside the city walls, we followed the Rhone for a distance. On our left its waters flowed full and swift, gray-white flecked with occasional patches of green. Later on our journey we would stand where the Rhone is born, more than 6,000 feet high in the St. Gothard massif of the Swiss Alps. Now we could witness at close range the power of its glacier-born waters. Their force had influenced numerous invasions of France; even the mighty Hannibal had had some of his army destroyed and his fantastic elephants alarmed before he was driven farther north in an effort to ford the Rhone.

To our right rose the stone walls which once protected Avignon, sheer cliffs of battlements. Where we rambled there had once been a deep moat, which would have rendered this barricade even more impregnable, and higher.

As we walked, the chill, cutting wind which, since early

morning, had been blowing down the valley from the northwest increased its tempo. We turned up our summer-coat
collars and wondered if this were the mistral of which we
had read and heard legends.

The mistral is a dry, cold, often violent wind which sometimes scourges this Edenlike Provence. Its name comes from
the Provencal word for master, so that it is the "master
wind." A folk rhyme says that it is the mistral which keeps
Avignon's people healthy. Wind has always seemed to me,
however, a willful, mischievous force, which assaults our
tranquility and shatters peace; and I could appreciate the
assumption, which may or may not be accurate, that in the
courts of Marseilles, the great seaport just south of Avignon,
the mistral may be taken into account when crimes of passion are being judged.

A little farther along we came to a rough-hewn flight of
stairs, which climbed the steep hillside, and the wall which
abutted it here. The wind tore at our hair and coattails and
urged us upward. When we reached the top, we could look
back down on the gray Rhone surging past the stump of the
old bridge in the distance.

Before us lay the charming Rocher des Doms, a park built
on the crest of this bluff. It is a quiet green oasis of pine
trees twisted by the mistral, of grass and flowers, and an
artificial grotto and pond where swans glide peacefully un-
perturbed by winds or people. While Middlers and Senior
found a bench where we could pause and catch our breath
and enjoy the white swans and emerald grass and multi-
colored flowers, the two Juniors went their own way.

"Think of those poor rich popes," James said presently, as
we sat under the clear blue sky arching away into the distance over pleasant rolling countryside. "There they were
entombed in that cavernous palace, wrapped in lifeless
tapestries, weighted down by keys and accounts and the
fears of attack these walls were built to repel. And there

were the poor rich peasants and minstrels out working under the sun, frolicking under the stars, tending vineyards and gardens, smelling the fresh earth and ripe grapes. . . ."

Our Juniors returned, informing us that the Cathedral was just beyond this park, on the slope of the bluff, and a short distance farther, the Palace of the Popes. We had come full circle in our pilgrimage. The boys had decided they wanted to attend the drama festival that night and they went to buy tickets.

This marked the moment of the Avignon schism, or division, in our family. We felt its full impact when, after a delicious dinner eaten out of doors under an arbor protected from the wind by surrounding walls, we all walked back toward the Palace. And three of us were abandoned as our two youngest joined the people streaming into the Great Court, where we had seen bare stage and empty seats earlier in the day. The boys understood French well enough to follow the drama being presented. We did not. They were part of this varied, lively, questioning, youthful crowd. We were not.

The Avignon Festival of Dramatic Art was founded some twenty-odd years ago by the brilliant actor-director, Jean Vilar, and its aim was serious theater at low prices for large and especially for youthful audiences. From the first season of seven performances before some 3,000 people, the productions had grown to thirty performances with more than 50,000 in the audience. And, as one New York critic has said, there had been "an inundation by youth, animated and serious, on a pilgrimage such as the Avignon popes never dreamed of."

Avignon, it seems, will through the generations live up to its reputation as a site of festivals. Our participants returned later that night chilled by the mistral which had gone through the heavy sweaters they wore, but stimulated by the play, *God, Emperor and Peasant*, and the vocal, responsive audience of which they had been a part.

The ponderous surroundings of that immense Gothic Palace, with its reminders of the medieval power which had been wielded here for almost a century, had affected the atmosphere of the drama, too, and heightened its impact. Both antiquity and youth had been served at Avignon. And perhaps, despite the eternal schism between the two, they had drawn a fraction closer together.

At Nice, on the beaches of the Riviera, bodies lying in the sun. Bodies long and short, lean and thick, glossy and rough, muscular and flabby. But all exposed to the broil of the sun like carcasses turning on a spit. Flesh cooking on the most famous strand in the world. Pink, medium rare, well done to a dark brown. Bodies lose all their allure here. Mystery is dispelled in nakedness, the thrill of subtle confrontation is devoured by the mass exhibitionism. All that remains is cannibalism—person to consume person, without hunger, without nourishment.

Cannes—Antibes—Nice—Monte Carlo. Man made flesh, his body only meat. In this world of the beautiful people, where to consume all is to be all, the only gesture left at last is to turn in upon the self and destroy that flesh which, when it is made all, becomes nothing.

Our first two stops in Italy were at the Villa d' Este on Lake Como in Lombardy—the varied, energetic, northern region of mountains and industry and the Po River—and at Siena, in the golden, fertile, central region of hills and art and the river Arno, Tuscany. The contrasts between our stay at Villa d' Este and at Siena were deep and instructive. They conditioned us for the rest of our visit in Italy.

"Listen to this." One of our Juniors held up a travel folder as we entered Italy. " 'The Lake of Como, the harbour of many famous personalities, marked by well-known events, enthusiasting and inspirating poets and artists of all over the world.' Are you ready to be enthusiasted and inspirated?"

"I'm no artist," his brother replied. "I'd just like to swim."

But when we caught our first glimpse of blue Como disappearing into distant folds of the hills, surrounded by rugged green mountains, dotted with red-tiled roofs of villages and villas, we were all ready to be poets and artists. Unfortunately, too many amateurs in the past had tried to capture Lake Como—deepest, clearest, most romantic of the three great Italian lakes—in thin water colors and garish oils which recorded only nature's surface sheen and little of its character or atmosphere. In calendar art this was a picturesque playground; in reality it was a multitudinous, breathing landscape.

We came to the little village of Cernobbio and the entrance to the Villa d' Este. Down the driveway, which wound like a tunnel under tall old chestnut trees, between thick green shrubbery which screened it from the outer world, we approached the Villa.

It is a stately building, decorated with bas reliefs and stucco works in Renaissance style, sitting on a level ribbon of land caught between lake and hillside, and after we had been welcomed and conducted to our accommodations, we flung open the long windows of our three adjoining rooms.

They looked across a limpid expanse of water to the massive hills and to the shore stretching on either hand in a broken, breathtaking line around the lower reaches of the long meandering lake. It was a view of such perfection that it seemed a parody of all its feeble reproductions.

The rooms themselves were no less lavish than the scenery, spacious, luxurious in all the creature comforts. Here we had our first taste of the Italian ability to enhance the flesh and surfeit eyes, limbs, taste—all the hungers of the senses—with a baroque abundance. Richness of draperies and carpets wrapped us in a cocoon; softness of mounds of pillows and silk spreads and eiderdown comfortables enveloped us in an enervating cradle; enormous gilt-framed mirrors and highly polished, finely wrought furniture reflected our presence and invited enjoyment.

When we walked outside, we found formal gardens of tall neat cypress avenues, begonias and other brightly flowering plants, carefully trimmed box, velvet-smooth grass, and statuary. We preferred the informal plantings—the winding gravel walks, wisteria-drenched pergola, scattered pines and elms, poplars and palms, and above all the giant old beech tree which dominated the promenade and park along the edge of the lake.

To our Senior and two Middlers the Villa and its gardens were the epitome of all that we had visualized from reading long-ago novels of English and Americans abroad in an exotic Italy, or from the genteel reproductions of villas and landscaping which some of the returned travelers had scattered across our country in a naïve longing for culture by transferral, art by adaptation rather than revelation.

To our Juniors this spot was a taste of *la dolce vita* (without big-city excesses and aberrations) of which they had heard such exciting reports. Certainly they assured us that although some of the salons and parlors were stuffy and oppressive, they found it sweet to discover the floating swimming pool, the tennis courts and golf course, and especially the terrace and "Empire Room," which blossomed at night with music and dancing and the possibility of meeting someone special.

As we lay in our rooms that first night, listening to the occasional gentle slap of the waves lapping the dock just beyond our windows, watching the play of shadows reflected on the high ceilings, it seemed to us quite a feat that this estate had survived through four centuries. Only sixty-five years after Columbus sailed from this land of Italy to discover America, the Cardinal of Como purchased the site and shortly afterward began building the villa.

We were reminded several times during our stay of the royal guests and owners who had preceded us, and we were assured that, although the years brought changes of ownership, there was no diminishing of reputation for scenic beauty and luxurious comfort. Princes of the Church, generals of the battlefield, and an Empress of Russia had spent intervals here. It was Caroline of Brunswick, Princess of Wales and wife of England's George IV, who brought *la dolce vita* to the Villa, and scandal to the royal name.

The birth of Villa d' Este as a hotel came about as a result of the legal entanglements following Caroline's death. For almost twenty years the lawsuit to determine her heirs dragged on.

"Almost as long as some of our feuds at home over a line fence or the disputed corner of a mountaintop," James remarked when we heard the tale.

Although it was never definitely cleared up, the problem of ownership was resolved by the dictates of common sense and the pressures of the modern age. A company of political and financial leaders was formed to operate the Villa d' Este as a public hostelry. Thus we—one dowager of a sixteen-acre empire, two pretenders to a four-acre hilltop kingdom, and two princes of an undetermined realm—came to be at the Villa.

The day after our arrival we drove around part of the

lake, shivering at the narrow roads, trying to keep our cli-chés on a leash while a succession of superb views unfolded around each curve. (One of the discoveries we made early on our trip was that affliction by cliché is almost solely a malady of middle and later years. Our Teens reflected a necessity to see, sense, appreciate, or reject for themselves. The trite, even in photography, drew their scorn.

"You know the perfect picture we're looking for?" our photographer Teen asked one day. "A little old lady with a black shawl over her head carrying a long loaf of bread in one hand and a bundle of faggots in the other, leading a donkey loaded with straw or pottery in front of a thatched cottage bedecked with flowers. Corny, but absolutely corny."

"Faked on," his brother agreed.

They were frequently eloquent, however, in their single simple admonition: "Look!")

As we continued our drive during the afternoon, rain came. It gave us a different, less artful view of lake and countryside. Mists descended like gauze curtains over the mountains and patches of heavy cloud settled on the peaks. Wind stirred choppy waves on the lake whose color, no longer reflecting blue sky and green hills, was a leaden gray. Traffic thinned and it was possible to drive slowly and look more closely at some of the homes.

"A number of the villas belong to Milanese industrialists. Others are owned by wealthy foreigners from all parts of the world. As for the villages in these hills, many are shrink-ing," the transplanted young Englishman with us said, as we passed a cluster of small houses. "A man I know who works at a garage in Como lives in a town near here which used to be a bustling city of sixty people." He grinned. "Now it has a population of six. There wasn't enough work for the others to support themselves. The mountain land is unproductive."

"That's the story in part of our Appalachian region at home," James said.

"So Milan booms and draws these workers," our friend continued. "There is silk manufacturing in Como and heavier industry in a few of the towns. But probably half the residents and homes on these hills are summer season only. They and the tourists support a large segment of the rest of the population. Farming and fishing can't do it."

That evening rain dripped from the pointed cypresses in the gardens and the spreading limbs of the beech tree and soaked the terrace. The Villa's night life moved from "under the stars" into the Empire Room. So did our elder Teen, who saw again the winsome brunette he had met the night before.

He was the only one of us who found much of interest at the Villa after the initial impact of the setting had worn off. Because, for the most part, the other guests in this limbo were altogether too closely related—by attitude and dress and pastime and ennui, if not by blood or nationality. They represented the money which can obliterate differences, build a Renaissance-style villa in Ravello or Palm Beach or Acapulco, and reduce each unique scene or people to a boring sameness. Their spiritual ancestors had built and maintained the Villa over the centuries, and now they were its natural heirs, by right of purchased permission if not legal documentation.

We went from the Villa d' Este and Lake Como southward to Siena on three hills. Through narrow passageways we wound up to the old heart of the city and, when we located our hotel, it opened directly off a cobbled street and faced a piazza which was a veritable history of architecture in itself, since the three palaces surrounding it were fourteenth-century medieval, fifteenth-century Renaissance, and sixteenth-century Baroque. People filled the street between the hotel and the piazza, walking, talking, and we were astonished by both their numbers and their animation.

Once more we were greeted and guided upward to our

rooms. But this time the halls were dim, the damask upholstery on chairs and listing sofas was threadbare and tattered. When we reached our quarters, they were the bleakest we had faced in Europe. The beds sagged like sway-backed horses. There were no closets, only coat racks in a corner boasting a few tangled wire hangers. A couple of thin rugs awaited our first step to wrinkle into a wad like tissue paper. The years had left their marks on the walls. A single medieval bathroom, with fixtures stained to match the city's name—burnt siena—opened off the dim hall which connected our rooms. Our spirits sank.

We edged across one of the rooms to open the shutters, hung slightly askew on the wide windows. At a little distance, on an opposite hill, rose the great dome of the Cathedral and the slim pointed finger of its campanile, or bell tower. In between stretched a sea of red tile. Roofs of varying heights, angles, and slopes fell away below our windows, sheltered the shops and homes in the shallow cup of that section of the city, then ascended the opposite hill.

In the slanting afternoon rays of sun the shades of tile ranged from an almost rosy-red to a sallow sort of orange, but the predominant tone was that of the rich baked color, siena. The sky was high and blue and the light was as golden as the legends of Tuscany had promised—and that sweeping expanse of tile seemed to be the heart of the clay earth itself scooped up and molded into useful shapes, burned by sun and centuries until its very sight and smell and grain was that of time and solar heat transforming clay to a substance of nature's essence and beauty. Our spirits rose.

Outside the entrance to our hotel streamed part of the life of Siena, and we soon went to be part of it. We discovered then that lodgings can be all-important on a journey, but not in the way we usually believe them to be. The comforts they provide may cost more than money. They can be bought, and frequently are, at expense of intimate knowledge of the people among whom we are visiting and the places we have come so far to see.

"After all," one of our Middlers said, as we left our rooms and headed for the streets, "remember old George Bernard Shaw: 'I dislike feeling at home when I am abroad.' "

Our two Juniors were still enamored of the physical delights of the Villa and were not to be quickly reconciled to what they considered quite a fall from grace.

"Well," the Senior responded, with a little smile, "I wouldn't dislike feeling just a smidgin more at home than I am going to on that bed tonight. But I can tell you now, Siena has my heart."

"And the Villa d' Este," the youngest Teen replied, in a stab at wit, "has our pocketbook."

It was a coincidence that our Senior had spoken as she did, for moments later we learned that the city's motto is "Siena opens its heart to you." There was little to wonder at in the sense of kinship between the two, however, for the words that seemed to us to summarize Siena's spirit most accurately were energy and independence. And they could have been the biography of our Senior, too.

We were no sooner in the street than we became part of the flow of its people. The majority were men, conservatively and well dressed, mature, vigorous men, walking side by side or in little groups that had their traffic problems, and invariably talking. As we passed them, we noticed the mutual attentiveness and forcefulness which alternated in their exchanges. No wonder that a national poll had revealed Italy's most popular pleasure to be "conversation with friends." These people knew how to converse— with passionate gentility, with tempered conviction.

Orson Welles is supposed to have said that Italy is a country of fifty million actors, the worst of whom are on the stage. And I do not think he meant that as a disparagement. An actor is an empathizer. He can put himself in another person's place. He is more aware than the average person and more attuned to the nuances surrounding "reality." He simultaneously affects and reflects the life around him, and because of this he may be more intense and more paradoxical than most of his fellow creatures. The same seemed to us true of many Italians.

The two women in our family agreed that nowhere had we seen as fine-looking men as in Siena. They seemed to possess some of the qualities of the two chief mineral resources of their region: iron and mercury.

And as we had experienced at the Villa d' Este the Italian flare for satiating the body, now we encountered the Italian gift for stirring the mind and the imagination. The Villa was built by and exists for the beautiful consumers. It is a rich haven. It is a temple of relaxation stretching into indolence, a carefree interlude inviting permanent indulgence. Siena was built by and survives for the vital creators. It is a poor city. But its buildings are testimonials to the dynamism of a people who could not be daunted in their past by the destructions of plague or defeated by successions of bloody conquest, and its art is of permanent inspiration.

We could not help but wonder at the skill and variety of a people who have managed so successfully the two quite opposite roles of consumer and creator. It was a duality we discovered again and again throughout Italy, to our delight, to our enlightenment.

Siena is a city of medieval towers and monasteries and encircling ramparts; Gothic palaces, baptistry, merchants' loggia and, above all, narrow Gothic streets. These streets are more than passages connecting various parts of the city. They are also club, forum, park, theater—all rolled into one. We were especially happy that we were three generations of walkers. This made us practically Sienese, except for our hostility to the occasional motor bike that roared past us, scattering people to each side like flocks of geese, causing us once or twice to dive into the nearest doorway, since there was no sidewalk for retreat.

So we came afoot to the two greatest sights of Siena: its Piazza del Campo, or public square, and its Duomo, or cathedral. Each was evidence, in its own way, of a people's remarkable vitality.

The Campo is the most unusual place of its kind we have ever seen. We approached it down a flight of steps from one street level to another. There it lay before us, sloping toward the focal point of the handsome town hall and its 286-foot tower of warm red brick. Eleven streets lead into the Campo, which has been described as a huge cockleshell or fan. It is surrounded on all sides by buildings. But it is this unique slope and fan shape which makes the Campo interesting, along with its color and atmosphere born of centuries of sun and use.

Naturally this was the site of sumptuous celebrations in the past. Two persist today, as distinctive as the people who observe them. Each July 2 and August 16 these colorfully costumed festivals reach their climax with a dangerous and exciting horse race called the *"Corsa al Palio,"* run in the Campo. Then the banners of the various *contrade*, or parishes, of Siena boast once again of that tenacious strength and independence which made Siena historically the despair of its despotic neighbors, even as its bankers were shaping the financial affairs of Christendom and its painters were influencing the art of the Western world.

The glow of early evening light in the Campo was blotted out by sudden clouds. An approaching storm roiled the sky. We found a little *trattoria*, or café, where we ate a lengthy, leisurely supper, and between showers we returned to that hotel which did not seem so disappointing now that it had proved so handy for our explorations.

That night it rained. We lay on our thin hard beds and listened to the splash of the rain on the ancient tiles of the roofs and the worn cobbles of the streets below. There was no other sound now except the rain as it fell and then ran in whispering streams. A breeze through the window brought the smell of wetness on dry tiles, rain and dust mingling in the scent we sometimes knew at home when, after a drought, showers drenched dusty pavement and fields and withered weeds. The steady sounds and cool, pungent breezes soothed the sharpness of our rooms and wrapped us in a luxury of rest as surely as silk or eiderdown could have done.

The next morning we found the Cathedral. Our Senior and our younger Junior had aroused at first daybreak and gone again to prowl in the great Campo while it was still deserted, walking the narrow streets before they had begun to teem with activity. So they were ahead of us when we all came to the hill crowned by the imposing Duomo.

The Cathedral and its campanile stand apart in the city because they are not of the color or construction that characterizes most of the rest of Siena. They are white and black and dark green, fashioned in bizarre patterns. They are both Gothic and Romanesque and highly decorated.

As we stood before the Cathedral, the first rays of a rising sun glanced the top of the campanile, that tall tower designed like a convict's suit of alternating stripes of white and dark green marble. The sun touched the ornamented spires and then the dome of the Cathedral itself. Swiftly it flooded the rich façade of arches, many-colored marbles, statues, the gilded sunburst clock, and delicate exterior paintings, until the whole Duomo was brilliantly visible—and we saw what the people of Siena had awakened to each day for five centuries since its completion and the two centuries during construction.

Inside, the black-and-white heraldic colors of the city achieved another unusual effect in the pillars which alternated across the vast interior. In their Cathedral, as in their horse racing, their strolling the streets, their history, the people of Siena maintained a difference.

They were also remarkable, at least in our judgment, in their courtesy. No village or city we visited, and neither of the ones from which we came in our own country, afforded people as consistently polite as the Sienese.

The first of numerous examples occurred soon after our arrival. During our first venture into the streets, our Senior paused suddenly to look at some of the local black-and-white and siena-brown ceramics in a small shop window. This caused a woman walking close by to jostle her unavoidably. The well-dressed woman, whose posture was beautiful, stopped immediately and turned and spoke her apologies swiftly. Our Senior smiled and nodded. Then the stranger laid a tentative hand on her arm and with genuine concern made what was obviously an inquiry about any hurt or disarray. Again our Senior smiled and this time shook her head. The lady quickly removed her hand, and smiled, looked at the rest of us, and spoke liltingly words we could not understand but whose meaning of apology and good will was perfectly clear. We all nodded. We all smiled. Our Senior shrugged to show her perfect composure. We all shook hands, and the dark-haired, bright-eyed lady went on her way. It was a trifling episode, yet it stuck in our memory long after larger occurrences and Meaningful Events had faded.

"Give us a few more days of communicating by gesture and I guess we'll be fairly acceptable Italians," our Senior said.

Again, in the café where we had eaten the night before—a family enterprise carried on by the mother-cashier, two daughter-waitresses, one son-handyman, and father-chef— we had found that same spirit of thoughtfulness and readiness to communicate with strangers.

After his daughters had relayed our five orders to him, the

father had come out from his kitchen and sat down at our table and discussed precisely what each of us wished, so that he would make no error of preparation and we would make no error of judgment. The whole transaction became as personal and important as buying a watch in Lucerne or a pipe in London.

When, during that preparation, we saw each of the daughters leave the restaurant on two different occasions and return momentarily with some item necessary to filling our order (each time flashing us a smile as they hurried by), one of us finally remarked, "Well, I'm glad I ordered the *bistecca alla Fiorentina*, if that's the grilled T-bone, instead of roast chicken. Much as I like Siena and these nice people, I'd hate to spend the rest of the night here waiting for them to pick a chicken and roast it."

Just then the youngest sister dashed in from the street carrying the cup of hot tea I had ordered. Where it had originated, or why it had not been available in their own kitchen, we never knew. And I did not dare order a second cup, necessitating another sally outside.

Eventually we ate a delicious meal, under the slightly disconcerting gaze of five pairs of watchful eyes. After each course the chef-father appeared from the kitchen. "Was O.K.?" And we assured him it was O.K. Then there were beams and nods all around, and new flurries of activity. No meal at the Villa d' Este was more memorable than that supper in Siena.

The ghosts of two women dominate the Villa d' Este and Siena. One was a princess and the other a saint. Their personalities and accomplishments summarize much of the spirit of the two places.

Caroline of Brunswick was a lumpish German who was married for political purposes by the dissolute Prince of Wales, eventually George IV of England. To escape a miserable married life and to find some sort of hectic happiness in living beyond her means and beneath her dignity, Princess Caroline went to Italy. There she purchased the Villa d' Este in 1815. It was she who gave it its present name.

She lived there for four years. Her gaudy clothes and adornments brought her no admiration; her coarse manners and extravagances won her no respect; but her lively continuous parties and pleasures accumulated numerous guests. Reports of a lengthy love affair with an Italian courtier who became her chamberlain brought divorce proceedings, but no divorce. When George III died, the Princess returned to England, prepared to become Queen upon her husband's ascension to the throne. But when she tried to enter Westminster Abbey for the coronation, she was turned away. Two weeks later she died.

It is still as "a former residence of Caroline Amalia of Brunswick, Princess of Wales and wife of George IV of England" that the Villa d' Este is distinguished today.

Catherine of Siena was an intense, disfigured girl whose father was a dyer. She had twenty-three brothers and sisters, and she was born (in 1347) and died in one small room that remained her modest home through life. When she was a child she became so enraptured with religion that her parents were worried and gave her the hardest household work to do in order to distract her thoughts and attention from heaven above to this world below. They learned, as powerful popes learned a little later, that Catherine was not to be distracted.

In her early teens she entered the Dominican Order. She had visions. (Her vision of a marriage with Christ became the subject of countless paintings through the ages.) Eventually she went out into the earthly community to nurse the sick and help the poor. She became aware of the evil men do to each other, and of the corruption within her own Church. She denounced the mighty with all her might. She told the Pope, Gregory XI, who was in Avignon at that time, that when she went to visit at his papal court in France, "her nostrils were assailed by the odors of hell."

Her voice must have carried conviction, for it was her persuasion that moved Gregory XI from Avignon and returned the Church's seat to Rome, where it is today.

Catherine was neither pretty nor comfortable. Her face had been scarred by smallpox; she was gentle with the ill and harsh with the dissolute; and she must have been both wonderful and wearisome as a woman. In 1939, six centuries after her short, profound years on earth, she was declared the patron saint of all Italy. But it is still as "Catherine of Siena" that she is revered today.

Between the personalities of Princess Caroline and Saint Catherine stretch the contradiction, the enigma, the enchantment of Italy. In our first two encounters we met that tension—or that universality—which reaches its epitome finally in the Colosseum and St. Peter's in Rome. Perhaps that is why every visitor seems to wish to return to Rome someday, because both his flesh and his spirit are exalted here.

The one creature that neither the Villa d' Este nor Siena was built for is mechanized man, the statistic, the number on a punch card. Each has recognized the variety and bounty of human personality, the anomaly that is man: stomach and spirit, consumer and creator, flawed and flawless—but alive!

By detail and by contrast, perhaps, we come to the whole: the solid mountain and fluid water at Lake Como, the subtle shifting of molten light and threatening shadow on the stones of the Campo in Siena, the frantic gaiety of the Princess Caroline, and the visionary ardor of Saint Catherine. The question, so often asked by friends, of where we stayed along the way was trivial. The question of moment was how we stayed.

Whether or not it is true that all life began in the ocean and that the sea's salt is still part of that vast and intricate bloodstream throbbing through our veins, it is true that water is both necessity and poetry of our life.

The ancient Romans and the Moors, who were part of medieval Europe, understood this. The Romans left enduring monuments of water's utilitarian nobility; the Moors left graceful mementos of water's transient poetry.

From the sunny fields of Provence in southern France to the harsh highlands of Britain's northern reaches, massive stones laid under Roman direction and design march across Europe's landscape in relics of aqueducts, mute witnesses not only to the superb engineering and construction talents of their builders but also to the regard they cherished for pure and plentiful supplies of water.

In Rome itself, writers and travelers and composers have celebrated the Eternal City's abundant fountains. Picturesque and practical, they embody that dual nature of vitality wedded to antiquity which strikes many visitors as Rome's peculiar charm.

An ancient title for the city was "Queen Of Waters." Today's plentiful supply from springs and streams in nearby mountains might make it the envy of many a modern American metropolis plagued by pollution, drought, and the twentieth century's wholesale debasement of our natural resources.

No one claims to know exactly how many fountains there are in Rome, but most estimates arrive in the vicinity of 3,000. They range from hydrant-like street-corner fountains, where the thirsty may gulp a drink in simple satisfaction, to the Baroque splendor of the Fontana di Trevi, where statuary, rocks, and cascades of water combine in one huge spectacle while enchanted tourists toss coins of hope into the pool, anticipating a return to Rome some day.

The Trevi is massive and ornate, but its display of water is natural and free-flowing. Old Triton and the sea horse and assorted statues bring fable and art to the tumble of rocks which appear almost more synthetic than real, but the result is a deft combination of wildness and artifice. Fed into the topmost basin, water cascades down the sides and spills over the edges of the boulders to the waiting pool below. Its fall and splash fills the hot golden afternoon or the warm irridescent evening with a sound of revival and renewal.

We came upon Trevi late one night after our teenagers, in an orgy of do-it-yourself exploration, had led us through some of the labyrinth of the city's streets and over at least a half dozen of its fabled hills. But suddenly we emerged into the square where coveys of young people had congregated like bright-plumed, chattering birds come to rest momentarily beside these falling waters. A fluttered scarf, a sudden shout—would they take flight and disappear? The moon rode high in the sky; the air was sweet and cool; and the fountain splashed in the background, binding man with nature, the strong imperious city and its mighty structures with the fluid constancy of life and the changing, changeless caress of water.

Everywhere in Rome—the fountains. Those of Bernini, who created the colonnade enclosing St. Peter's Square with its own two geysers tossing dazzling jet streams high toward the heavens, and his fountains in the Piazza Navona and the Piazza Baberini. Those of unknown origin—grotesque faces with water pouring from the mouth, fish spouting streams into cupped basins, and the ever-present prosaic drinking fountains for housewives and shopkeepers, flower vendors and children, any weary, lucky passer-by.

The noise and rush of Rome threaten on occasion to

explode out of control. But as long as the sight and sound and spray of living water can be experienced on every hand, perhaps the spirit—and thirst—of stranger and native alike will remain eternally refreshed.

While the Romans were interested in magnificence and durability and utility, the Moors who came to Spain in 711 and remained powerful until 1492 found their life-style in delicacy, in elaboration, and, above all, in exquisiteness.

They came—those fierce, sensitive, able conquerors—from northern Africa, parched land of blazing heat and glare; and they were enchanted by the water and fertility of Spain. They introduced irrigation; they created gardens whose beauty delights us today; they brought pleasures of the senses into daily life.

A visit to the Alhambra, fantastic relic of Moorish splendor, provides a charming surprise for most Westerners. At least, it was a surprise for our family.

The ancient city of Granada is blessed with more than a beautiful name. Its backdrop is the snow-capped Sierra Nevada range of mountains, and its setting, more than 2,000 feet above sea level, is an arid, dramatic landscape which provides sharp contrast to the well-watered productive belt of land where Granada flourishes. Fields of grain, green or gold according to the season, immense blue-gray groves of gnarled olive trees, acres of sugar beets grow around Granada. Its climate is more agreeable than that of Madrid or Seville. Here was the last stronghold of the Moors in Spain and here is the crowning achievement of their culture. An American author, Washington Irving, helped rescue it from oblivion. The surprise of the Alhambra is due partly to its size, partly to its variety, and especially to its combinations of pools, streams, fountains, and gardens.

As we looked up from Granada toward the Alhambra, 500 feet above the city, and then as we drove up the steep winding route to the hilltop which was enclosed in a reddish wall rising and dipping with the contours of the land and punctuated by tall towers, we were astonished by the spaciousness of the site.

The Alhambra is not just a single structure. It includes two palaces, a citadel (the Alcazaba), and covers some thirty-five acres. Alhambra means "the red," and its walls and towers glow with earthy ruddy shades in the strong light of a summer run.

There are two main attractions: the older palace built by the Islamic rulers and the gardens of their Generalife, or small summer house of "love, dancing and pleasure."

It is not architecture but ornamentation that makes the Alhambra unique. Its walls and ceilings, arches and porticos, halls and salons are decorated with honeycombs of intricate geometric designs wrought in wood and plaster. They appear as fragile as frosting, yet they survive the centuries. There are ceilings that hang with stalactite decoration and others that seem canopied with lace, arches that frame the colorful scene of Granada in the valley or the nearby groves of elm trees. Mosaic floors and arcades lead to ever-more-elaborate traceries and embellishments. And this excess of decoration would be cloying; it would grow tiresome and decadent but for the courtyards and the gardens with which it is interspersed.

In the Court of the Myrtles and the Court of the Lions the sultans brought the relaxation and grace of water into the heart of their dwelling. The first is a long open courtyard centered by an oblong pool. Here the water is green and still, surrounded by hedges of myrtle and reflecting at each end a graceful arcade and gallery supported by slender columns. The quiet water and its limpid reflections are restful.

Farther within is the Court of the Lions. Washington Irving said nothing gave a more complete idea of the Alhambra's "original beauty and magnificence" than this most famous part of the edifice. Here the water is not still and contained but spewing, falling, tinkling. The figures of the twelve marble lions—squat, square, unferocious looking beasts—support an alabaster fountain. From their mouths spout twelve streams of water, and from the basins above water drips to the pool below. Surrounding this oasis are marble columns supporting the gallery and stucco work of unusually profuse design. It is, however, the simplicity of the lions and the water which have brought proportion and its reputation to this court.

In the gardens of the Generalife, the Moors achieved their most subtle harmony of man with nature. Everywhere we walked through the grounds of the Alhambra we were captivated by the sound of water. It flows in conduits alongside many of the streets and paths, and its pleasant whisper is more welcome than anyone could realize who has not experienced the heat and thirst of that arid country which stretches just beyond Granada.

When we came to the Generalife, shortly before sunset, we discovered the innermost enchantment of the Alhambra. Here was the sultan's summer residence, a little palace with views down into the old Moorish city and toward the distant mountains, but its charm lay in its gardens. And water— bubbling, spraying, flowing, splashing—is the essence of their beauty. Water feeds the luxuriant orange trees and tall old cypresses, the oleanders, myrtles, and cedars. It gives life to the brilliant flowers and to the carefully tended hedges.

Fountains play across long, flower-decked pools and throw sparkling streams high into the sunlight. They ripple with constant music and fall in quicksilver showers from one pool to the next.

The terraces of the Generalife are neither large nor extensive. Yet they yield hidden loveliness and restorative moments of green quietness to those who will give them time and attention.

The last glow of a setting sun was deepening the red of the Alhambra's walls and towers in the distance as we gathered up our final impressions. There were no other visitors left in the gardens and only the scent and sound of water permeated the gentle evening air. As we walked back down the steep slope beneath tall green trees, the liquid voice of the water accompanied us, flowing in a little channel beside the walkway.

We thought of the Romans, with their masculine civilization—majestic, aggressive, dominant—and of the Moorish civilization, more feminine in its grace, ornamentation, fluid adaptability. Yet both Roman and Moor knew something that we are only in the slow and painful process of learning. It whispers across the centuries from the Roman aqueducts and the pools of the Alhambra: Water is the irreplaceable gift. It is life. Use, cherish, celebrate, preserve, enjoy.

We were heavy with the material intoxication of the world. Rome, the sheer physical power of the city, had engulfed us. There were the massive ruins of Empire—Colosseum, Forum, catacombs, the ancient roads—and the luxuries of the present embodied in sidewalk cafés, opulent hotels, expensive shops, theaters and clubs, elaborate musical productions staged in sites of antique splendor, and the living presence of the Vatican's Sistine Chapel. The glory that was Rome at its greatest pinnacle of world power is still its glory today—and it is of the senses: sight, hearing, smell, taste, touch.

Stimulated and surfeited by the experience of Rome, we

made a journey, not far distant in miles but light-years distant in spirit, to the Umbrian hill towns. We came to Assisi.

Mount Subasio rises from a wide and fertile plain and as you approach it along the highway, you look up at the village of Assisi clinging to its slopes: pinkish stone houses, a large basilica, monastery with long and spacious arcade. The dwellings look like intricate mud daubers' nests built on a giant scale, beautifully constructed (one next to and atop the other) from the earth and water and stone at hand, tempered and proved by the weather of centuries. The whole scene is soft and mellow in the early afternoon sun, as if the materials used here, being nature's own stuff (unlike the steel and glass and chrome of larger, newer cities), absorbs all harshness and glare and gives back only a glow of warmth and harmony.

We drove across the plain and up the road which winds between olive groves and small farms, and then we came to the steep and narrow streets of the town itself. We found our rooms at a pleasant inn, which suddenly became magnificent when we opened French doors and found ourselves looking down on the valley from which we had just come. Across the plain was a patchwork quilt of golden grain fields, green gardens, and the blue-gray of olive groves. On the slope below us were small farms with tall haystacks, neat barnyards; a man with an ox plodded behind a load of hay in one of the fields. In a plot just below our window a farmer was digging onions, and the pungent smell of the fresh earth and the rank onions came up to where we stood. The whole wide landscape sweeping into the distance and the nearby intimate rural scenes all made one painting, alive there before us.

"This is my village," our Senior said. "You can have your fashionable Via Veneto in Rome. This is the most beautiful sight I've seen."

"You like the smell of the ground down there, and all the

flowers, don't you?" one of our Teens asked, revealing that he, too, had noticed.

His grandmother nodded. "No wonder St. Francis felt one with the birds and wind and woods."

It is the spirit of the gentle St. Francis that infuses Assisi —its steep, clean, cobbled streets with flower-decked shops and homes, its peaceful church with famous frescoes in which the master Giotto depicted the life of St. Francis, its plaza and fountain and many sanctuaries.

But to come close to the heart of Francis himself, you must make a five-mile pilgrimage deeper into the mountains, beyond Assisi. There, in a fold of the steep hills, surrounded by oak forests, is the Hermitage where St. Francis retreated with some of his followers for solitary contemplation and deeper communion with God and nature. The tiny church and monastery, of pink Assisi stone, are austere and simple and serene. The trails in the forest beyond lead deep into the ancient woods. Frequent beds of luxuriant green moss and fragile ferns made us feel quite at home. The plants and occasional ledges of stone were links with our own hill country.

We went to the Hermitage and into its woods in the morning. Sunlight filtered through the shade of thick leaves. Silence enveloped the mountains and the deep ravine beside the monastery and the whole green world around us. Even the birds were still.

In case we should be led astray by this present peace, however, into an oversimplification of the past and one of its most endearing figures, it seemed appropriate to remember what sort of youth and man Francesco di Bernadone had been.

Eight centuries before our own perplexing time he had undergone an identity crisis, rebelled against parental authority, and become what must have seemed to his neighbors and townsmen a troublesome beatnik. In fact, if we

Middlers see St. Francis today in any fuller perspective than that of the gentle figurines which are so popular in garden birdbaths and Christmas decorations, we are apt to be unnerved.

Yet we might, curiously enough, be comforted, too. In even this small example of the repetition of history (youth vs. age, the generation gap) we can hold up a mirror to ourselves—and perhaps relax a little. Maybe the young people whom we have so often thought are going to the dogs are really drawing closer to the gods than we suspect. How could Ser Pietro di Bernadone, a well-to-do linen draper, have known that his son was to become a saint?

Certainly he didn't start out as a saint. Born in 1182, Francis was a school dropout (languages were his chief attainment—Italian from his father, French from his mother, who had been born in Provence, and Latin from his parish priest). Being the wealthiest young man in Assisi he soon turned into what might be called today "a real swinger." He was tall, dark, and handsome, and he was a free spender. There were plenty of friends to help him drink and sing the minstrel songs that were so popular during the Middle Ages —and to let him pick up the tab for their revelries.

Since the songs of the troubadours which he sang so often exalted chivalry and conquest on the field of battle, the teenager began to have dreams of military glory. When Francis was twenty, Assisi was at war against its neighboring hill town of Perugia, and he joined the army. The engagement went poorly. Francis was captured by the enemy. During a year in prison in Perugia he had plenty of time for thought. During a second period of army service he was stricken with fever. It was then, as he lay ill, that he believed he received a summons from God to return home.

When he got home, however, his father had in mind a new agenda. The older man pointed out in vigorous terms that it was time his son gave some thought and support to the family business. But Francis' thoughts were ever more constantly turning to religious matters. He prayed often.

Then a moment of truth occurred in his life. He was approached by a leper on the street one day. Of all the afflicted wretches common to the Middle Ages, none were more pathetic or revolting than these emaciated, scarred, and rag-wrapped outcasts. Horrified, Francis turned away from the supplicant. But as his aversion to the dread contagion drove him away from the cripple, the love of God suddenly drove him back to the abject human being. He gave the leper all the money he had with him and he kissed the diseased hands. From that day on, Francis rejected no creature who needed his help.

But his father—with typical parental concern, perhaps wanting for his son a life more placid than inspired, more secure than spiritual—was outraged with embarrassment when Francis emerged from fasting in a poor chapel near Assisi looking so thin and unkempt that children in the streets called him a madman. At home, his father locked him in a closet. His mother released him.

This conflict simply drove Francis back to the chapel. His father followed him and ran one last gamut of appeals and commands, criticisms and entreaties. At last, in a scene of classic rejection, Francis appeared naked before the towns-people and church leaders and gave his father the little bundle of clothes and coins that were his only remaining possessions. Himself he gave to God, henceforth his Father.

The rest of his life was devoted to the ways of peace and humility and love he bequeathed his followers. For even as he had found those who would share his pleasures, now there were those who would share his passion and his work with the poor, the despised, the outcasts.

Is it legend or fact that he preached to the birds, and that the birds listened? Does it matter? The message is that life must be concerned with life.

Partially blind, suffering the chills and fevers and depletions of malaria, in October, 1226, Francis of Assisi died. He was forty-four years old. Two years later he was recognized as St. Francis.

After we had left Assisi, we found this passage in a tome of history: "Two other leaders dominated that dynamic age: Innocent III and Frederick II. Innocent raised the Church to its greatest height, from which in a century it fell. Frederick raised the Empire to its greatest height, from which in a decade it fell. Francis exaggerated the virtues of poverty and ignorance, but he reinvigorated Christianity by bringing back into it the spirit of Christ. Today only scholars know of the Pope and the Emperor, but the simple saint reaches into the hearts of millions of men."

There on the path in the oak woods that summer morning, looking across the deep ravine at the stone Hermitage, one of us said, "Kindness and joy were what he preached. Kindness to all living creatures. Joy in God."

After a while we went back down from the upper mountains to the village. Along the way were vistas of the golden plain in the distance.

We spent a night and two days in Assisi. None of us, I think, will forget it. The bare simplicity of the basilica alight with Giotto's frescoes, when human emotion was being released into painting; the small shops with handicrafts of weaving and pottery and ironworks that seem so appropriate here; the friendliness of an old man near Assisi's fountain; dinner in the waning evening light on an outdoor terrace hung above the olive trees and the wheat fields with that Brueghel canvas panorama in the distance. In the freshness of morning we watched the farmer bring out his ox again and the two of them make their slow deliberate passage down the winding road to the hay field.

Assisi seemed to have caught the fleeting essence of the simple life—tougher than it sounds, tough as the rough brown robes of the Franciscans themselves.

Kindness.
Joy.

A visitor to Italy may be a stranger when he arrives, but it will be impossible for him to remain a stranger long. For those of us of the Western world, Italy is one of our homes. Its artists, musicians, and writers have poured forth such treasures of our human heritage that the scenes, faces, harmonies, experiences they have rendered are part of our common memory. And the center of this creative exuberance and universality was/is the city of Florence.

Florence on the Arno, where Dante honed and perfected a language and wrought a masterpiece, where Brunelleschi set the crown on the age of the Renaissance with his immense dome for the Cathedral of Santa Maria del Fiore, and the creator of the world's two most famous paintings, The Last Supper and the Mona Lisa, Leonardo da Vinci, grew to manhood. Florence: heart and pulse and repository of the glory that was the Renaissance.

No individual has absorbed all the treasures that two centuries of the Renaissance bequeathed to Florence. Visitors today who have any time limitations at all must promptly become reconciled to this fact—which we soon did, and then we resolved to discover the large design rather than the minute detail of this magnificent city and its dynamic past.

It rained every day we were in Florence, excepting one afternoon. Heavy showers fell as we walked beside the shallow Arno in its rocky summer bed. A steady downpour curtained the bronze east door of the Baptistry, with its ten biblical panels of Ghiberti, which Michelangelo called worthy to be the Gate of Paradise, and discouraged the knots of students and clusters of tourists who hurried past us. Thin mist surrounded us on the Ponte Vecchio and cast a pale greenish light on the mold and moss of time along its arched supports and underpinnings. Rivulets ran down the statues and walks in the Pitti Palace gardens. But our enthusiasm, finding that of the city contagious, was not to be damped down or smothered.

In history's emphasis on the incredible artistic achievement of Florence, we often overlook a related fact which makes Renaissance Florence seem peculiarly modern, the fact of the city's financial arrangements and early industrialization. As long as six centuries ago Florence was a manufacturing and commercial center. By the mid-1300's there were eighty banking houses and some 200 textile factories employing 30,000 people in making famous Florentine cloth. Cargoes carried by Italian ships were insured. And rural-urban struggles for political power (between landowners and businessmen) were already under way, with the workers, too, seeking means by which they might have some muscle in shaping political policies.

One of the symbols which related Florentines to Americans is not found in the Uffizi Gallery or the Pitti Palace, but it is that of the pawnbroker's insignia, the three golden balls. For underwriting and nourishing the art which flowered in this city was the commercial genius which once made it a financial capital. Those de Medicis, whose family emblem was red balls on a field of gold, were forerunners of much of modern finance. When Giovanni de Medici was elected an official of Florence in 1421, it marked the beginning of a relationship between a family and a city that was to continue through three centuries. In numerous ways Florence became the lengthened shadow of the de Medicis.

That first Giovanni de Medici confronted a problem common to most states at various periods—a treasury depleted by costly wars. But he devised a solution radical for his time. Rather than following the custom, which placed the burden on the poor, he announced that taxes were to be levied according to each citizen's resources. The graduated income tax, enlarged and enforced by later de Medicis, became one of the achievements of that great commercial family—whose influence would reach down the centuries. Perhaps we should not, either, overlook the fact that the popularity of the de Medicis, always strongest among the poorest people, grew even larger and more potent after establishment of this more equitable tax.

Like so much else in Florence, the de Medicis are forceful enough and fascinating enough to consume months in making their full acquaintance. Lorenzo, called "the Magnificent,"—politician, poet, patron of the arts—is alone worth more time than we could give the whole city. But it is the legacy of this family and its abundant abilities that we encounter today; its native shrewdness and artistic appreciation, its financial realism and cultural idealism, its marriage of fiscal strength with civic and individual beauty.

This is the spirit which permeates Florence at present. It is compounded of exuberance and wit, self-assurance and serenity, which must surely be sustained by daily surroundings of a vital creative past and constant access to some of the world's finest galleries of art.

Florence was the nucleus of that flowering known as the Renaissance, when men emerged from the mud and mysticism of the Middle Ages, found sun and flowers and flesh, affirmed a faith in man as well as God, and fashioned cathedrals and filled canvases with the wonders of the sensual world as well as the mysteries of heaven. The exultation of their discovery, the freshness of their vision—ranging from Galileo to Cellini—is the gift of Florence today.

And if Savonarola was burned at the stake here in 1498 (the site marked today in the Piazza della Signoria, not far from the replica of Michelangelo's marvelous David and old

Cosimo de Medici forever astride his horse), he himself had kindled the flames on previous occasions when he lit bonfires of "vanities"—books and pictures and wigs (shades of 1967, the American year of the wig!)—on this same spot. He was a brave fanatic who saw more clearly than most exactly what was happening to his world; it was crumbling away. He tried to halt the tides of history and freeze them in the Middle Ages—and the Renaissance swept over him, destroyed him.

And if Machiavelli propounded here the cunning pragmatism of his early and elegant version of "politics is the art of the possible," why *The Prince*, published in 1513, may often seem too modern to be comfortable. It was not without reason that the Florentines were considered the first merchants of their time; and their politics reflected the qualities necessary to that pre-eminence.

We, too, delighted not only in the rich Botticellis, Raphaels, Titians, Andrea del Sartos, and numerous others who lend Florence luster today; we reveled also in the mercantile Florence which remains vigorous with a de Medici opulence. There was the mellow gold in the tiny jewelers' shops on the cream-colored Ponte Vecchio; the supple leathers in all manner of handsome men's and women's accessories; the fabrics hand-fashioned, and the frequently exquisite reproductions of museum masterpieces. We shattered our budget and crowded our bags and understood why the ascetic Savonarola had perished in Florence.

Onslaughts of neither man nor nature seem capable of destroying "Florence the Divine." The old Ponte Vecchio trembles and partly crumbles—and survives. The Cathedral and the palaces and the piazzas are despoiled—and survive. The chaste Madonnas and glowing Venuses, the innocent angels and suave aristocrats portrayed in profusion along the halls and vast rooms of the galleries—they survive. And the energy of the Florentines themselves—it survives.

Because it does, the vision of the Renaissance remains alive today. It is the ideal of the whole man: the philosopher-king, the merchant-artist; in the whole society: industrialization enlarging rather than obliterating the individual, technology rooted in culture, the physical-mental-spiritual harmony of each man and the total environment.

It would take longer than a lifetime to know the whole of Florence. But a few hours—days—weeks can impart an experience of centuries past, and renew identification with the creative spirit which is man's immortality.

One of our Teens made a friend on the scenic and historic bus trip from Florence to Venice. When we stopped at Bologna, with its miles of arcades and the oldest university in Europe and a great church we had to visit, our Teen asked his new friend where he would be going after Venice.

"Switzerland," was the quick reply. "And am I ever looking forward to it! I've seen about all the cathedrals and galleries and palaces I can digest. In Switzerland I'm going to take a vacation from my vacation!"

In the steep little village of Pieve di Cadore, in the dramatically beautiful Dolomite Mountains between Italy and Austria, we discovered a statue to the painter Titian. He was born here.

Looking at the rock-scarred slopes and the saw-toothed crests with which the Dolomites barricaded this town and its Piazza Tiziana, we thought of those paintings of its most famous son which we had seen in abundance during the weeks just past. And one of our Middlers wondered: Were the round women—the plump and soft and pink and eternally curvaceous females with which Titian filled canvas after canvas—were they possibly a contrast, an antidote, a negation to this sharp, angular, fierce landscape of his birth?

Whether he intended it or not, this was one of his achievements: absorbing the harshness of the natural scene in the warm landscape of the flesh.

"We want to go to Dachau."

Even as we uttered the words we realized their falseness, overheard their absurdity. We did not *want* to go to Dachau. We *had* to go there.

At this village in Bavaria—to be more exact, in the concentration camp located in the vicinity of this village—man had failed the test of civilization in the twentieth century. It was only one of some thirty major such hells which had come into being, flourished, and collapsed during the Walpurgisnacht of Nazi power.

Of the thirty, this was the oldest. It served as a proving ground for many of the abominations—leaders and atrocities alike—which reached their terrible pinnacle in Auschwitz, Belsen, Buchenwald, Lublin, Mauthausen, and those others whose names form a litany of horror for our time, a dirge beyond all conventional grief.

We were of that civilization, that century, and we had

need to know about its failure. By seeing the place did we hope to divine some secret, absorb some insight, penetrate some darkness of man's soul which had been revealed here?

"Yes," the blond young driver we were engaging for the afternoon said. "Just so. But first we will see Nymphenburg Palace. (He knew we did not want to see Dachau. He would help us evade it.) There are many beautiful things at Nymphenburg. A fine porcelain works one may visit. . . ." He nodded ever so slightly to the ladies.

"There is a carriage museum, royal coaches beyond description. . . ." With a glance at the boys.

"And a fine park to walk in. . . ." Offering this to the head of the family.

Something for everybody at Nymphenburg.

"Yes, we would like to see the Palace. After we have gone to Dachau."

Without the slightest movement or gesture, the driver's attitude switched from balmy warmth to rigid iciness. His appeal changed, too. No longer jovial, he informed us with brisk authority, "It is a distance to Dachau. Sometimes the roads are crowded and traffic costs time. You will not want to spend so much of your Munich visit in ———"

"We will go to Dachau!"

His capitulation was immediate and total. "Yes, sir." He refastened the top button on his navy blue blazer-style jacket. "It is twelve miles. We can depart at once."

The wind blows savagely across the plain which surrounds Dachau. In the distance are the Alps, but here only the level stretches which were once foggy swampland. Although it was a summer wind which blew through the barbed wire and the empty sentinel towers and the dry moats as we drove into the old prison grounds, once we left the luxury of our big black rented limousine the wind bit our faces with particles of gravel and tore at the folded umbrella we carried for protection against threatening skies. It bent the little blue wild flowers blooming in the green grass between the moat and the wire fence. It forced us to bend our heads as we crossed the yard toward the bleak buildings which are all that is left of "concentration camp Dachau."

"During the time of the prison, the ditch surrounding this place was full of water," our pink-cheeked driver explained carefully. Here and throughout our visit he became dedicated to patiently and precisely helping us know just how it had been at the camp.

"The barbed wire of the fence was charged with electricity along the top. At night the wall surrounding the whole was flooded with light. At any time a guard in one of the towers saw a prisoner step onto the grass strip eight meters in front of the ditch, he shot without warning. There was no way of escape from Dachau."

There is no greeting emblazoned over the entrance to the camp today. But those who entered as its victims, only a few brief decades (or is it a lifetime?) ago, were herded under a slogan which advised with ironic cruelty: *Arbeit macht frei.* ("Work makes one free.")

Inside the compound and inside its museum one of the things that strikes a visitor first is the fact that everything here is black or white. Gleaming white watchtowers capped with pointed black peaks, strung together by thorny strands of black wire. Long white frame buildings under black roofs. Black words printed large on white paper. Photographs blown up into a black-and-white life more huge than reality. No gray areas, no philosophic subtleties, no sophisticated nuances at Dachau. Hunted and hunter. Life and death. Good and evil.

The entrance hall contains a map pinpointing the Nazi web of concentration camps and their subsidiaries in central Europe, and a little farther along there is a curious small forest of posts. On these posts are emblazoned all the names of those nations who had citizens imprisoned in Dachau. America is one of the numerous nations represented. (Had our country's name not been there, would we have felt as Emerson did when he visited Thoreau in jail for not paying taxes to a government that permitted slavery? Emerson asked his individualistic friend, "Henry, what are you doing in there?" And the philosopher of Walden Pond, who had traveled widely—in Concord—replied, "Waldo, what are you doing out there?")

From the vestibule down through the long rooms, photographs and exhibits draw the viewer from one area to the next, from one year to the next, unfolding the power and rapacity of Nazism as it grew and flourished.

Enlargements of newspapers, handbills, posters chronicle the January 30, 1933, seizure of power by the Nazis.

Less than two months later, on March 22, the first German concentration camp was set up on the grounds of an old ammunition factory at Dachau in Bavaria.

Two months after that, in May, books by "undesirable authors" were publicly burned. And under that fantastic picture, which three of us remembered seeing in younger years—that picture recording the bonfire of books and, Nazism hoped, the destruction of ideas—are those prophetic lines of the poet Heinrich Heine: "Where books are burnt, humans will be burnt in the end."

The visitor is swept along as on a river. Only this is a river of time, of events, remorseless and destructive. As raindrops accumulate on mountain slopes, so the events of the troubled years following World War I multiplied, the rising tide of Hitler and his Third Reich gathered momentum, and finally the surge of devastation washed Western man to the brink of an abyss.

We moved, the five of us, rather strangely along this course. We did not, as we usually did, walk together. We went separately, as if each of us had to be on his own island, surrounded by a cushion of space and silence to comprehend and endure what we were learning there.

It was not crowded in the Dachau kitchen-laundry-storage-torture rooms which had been transformed into a museum. There were no conducted tours jostling through the passages. There were no eager groups of students massed before exhibits, listening to an expert's dissertation. There were no bored Beautiful People whiling away a few hours at a famous landmark they might find amusing to discuss at their next dinner party. Those few persons who plodded through the museum the day we were there were, in the main, Germans. They were plainly dressed, middle-class, attentive, undemonstrative. There were two other Americans. There were no children, no elderly people. The first were too young, perhaps, to remember what this name had once meant; and the latter too old to forget. There was an enormous quiet everywhere.

Our short, sturdy driver was helpful at every point. He condensed numbers of long German newspaper articles and memoirs for us. As the material focused with increasing sharpness on Dachau and on what happened here, he identified portraits, translated copies of official rules, memoranda, records. He explained details, pointed out significant facts we might have overlooked, told us what had happened when and where. He was accurate and detached.

We older ones had trouble remaining so poised. We stood beside the heavy wooden block (like a butcher's meat stand) and looked at the worn surface, at the idle leather whip lying across it. How many helpless men had been stretched here, feet and arms bound and dangling at each end, while an SS officer wielded this lash, its leather soaked in water, on bare back and buttocks until flesh was shredded and kidneys ruptured?

Who had worn the faded, torn prisoner's uniform now

exhibited in a neat glass case? And how many winter winds, sweeping down on this plateau from the surrounding Alps, had pierced the pitiful protection of this rough garment and chilled the emaciated body underneath?

There was evidence all along the way that Dachau was the first and remained one of the premier camps in the hierarchy of Nazi prisons. From its beginning Dachau demonstrated one purpose common to all subsequent camps, which was not only to subdue and punish and finally destroy the people within its walls but to subdue and terrorize (through dark hearsay, whispered reports, and an atmosphere of unrestrained evil) those who remained outside the walls. Thus everyone in the nation became a prisoner.

Totenkopfuerbaende—these were the Death's Head units of the SS, to whose care was given the guard duty of the concentration camps. Dachau's first commander, Theodor Eicke, was in charge of the first Death's Head unit in Germany. Eventually he became chief of all the concentration camps.

Many of the masters of brutality whose names and deeds were associated with Auschwitz, and the man who became known as the "Beast of Belsen," and numerous leaders at other sites received their early experience at Dachau.

Extermination equipment was proved here, too. A firm which manufactured crematorium materials solicited business at other camps, assuring its potential customers that four furnaces it had built for Dachau had "given full satisfaction in practice." In a burst of salesmanship and Third Reich fervor, near the close of one request for business, the managers of this firm suggested: "We advise you to make further inquiries to make sure that two ovens will be sufficient for your requirements."

Later, after we had returned home, we read again William L. Shirer's *The Rise and Fall of the Third Reich*, and we found this paragraph: "Before the postwar trials in Germany it had been generally believed that the mass killings were exclusively the work of a relatively few fanatical S.S. leaders. But the records of the courts leave no doubt of the complicity of a number of German businessmen, not only the Krupps and the directors of the I.G. Farben chemical trust but smaller entrepreneurs who outwardly must have seemed to be the most prosaic and decent of men, pillars— like good businessmen everywhere—of their communities."

Would that industrialist, we wondered, who built the ovens for Dachau, have shrunk from personally stuffing the bodies inside? Yet he had been proud of the full satisfaction his equipment had given in practice.

None of the Nazi horrors bypassed Dachau. As early as the spring of 1933, a city official of Munich protested the outright murder of four inmates, one by whipping, another by strangulation. Efficiency rather than compassion dictated that these means would not account for the majority of deaths, but the sadism which prompted such methods remained and grew in proportion to the number of its victims.

Collecting human skin for decorative uses, a hobby at several camps, became so popular at Dachau that it was hard to fill the demand. Whenever it was discovered that there were "not enough bodies with good skin," an accommodating doctor would furnish "twenty or thirty bodies of young people," because the skin "had to be from healthy prisoners and free from defects."

As a labor camp—using men in the gravel pit, on the plantation, harnessed like oxen to pull heavy road rollers or wagons—and as an extermination camp Dachau was eminent. But it has been suggested that medical experiments conducted here surpassed those at any other place in the Reich. For unremitting cruelty and utter callousness of conscience, anyone would have to look far to surpass the so-called scientific medical tests.

Some of the less harrowing of these tests involved patients who were infected with malaria and then left to suffer when the medicine under survey proved ineffective. Purulent sores were induced on a group of twenty priests. "Twelve died as a result of the test. Only eight survived after excruciating torments. Some of them had to have arms and legs amputated."

The experiments that were unique to Dachau were the diabolical Dr. Rascher's "high flight" researches. With Himmler's direct approval and encouragement, in the Air Force's decompression chamber which was moved from Munich to Dachau, victims were gradually deprived of air and oxygen so that bodily responses at certain simulated altitudes could be recorded. Among the Nuremberg documents was the recollection of one of the prisoners who had been forced to help in the doctor's office: "I have personally seen through the observation window of the decompression chamber when a prisoner inside would stand a vacuum until his lungs ruptured."

Then he described other reactions: "They would go mad and pull out their hair in an effort to relieve the pressure. They would tear their heads and faces with their fingers and nails in an attempt to maim themselves in their madness. They would beat the walls with their hands and head and scream in an effort to relieve pressure on their eardrums."

When altitude and oxygen tests began to pall, experiments were begun with "the extreme cold which an aviator faces at high altitudes." Their two-fold purpose was simple: to determine how much cold a human being could endure before freezing to death, and to discover the best way of warming up a body which had become nearly frozen.

Careful records were kept of the men who were immersed in ice water. At what point did consciousness leave them? How much distention of the heart and how much free blood in the cranial cavity was revealed by prompt autopsies? One medical orderly simply stated that the water-freezing test he witnessed "was the worst experiment ever made. Its victims lasted five hours before death relieved them. Even the guards were stirred to mercy by this prolonged misery and one would have chloroformed the dying men, but Dr. Rascher forbade it."

There were "dry-freezing" experiments, too. Men were placed naked on stretchers outside the barracks during the sub-freezing winter nights. Sometimes water was poured over them every hour during the long night. As they froze to death Dr. Rascher took their temperatures, recorded their pulse rates, noted their heartbeats and respiration.

To determine the best method of warming a person who had reached a near-frozen condition, several experiments were conducted with prisoners from the women's camps. The doctor's final conclusion? That hot baths were more effective than naked women in "warming" the frostbitten human guinea pigs.

The data was recorded in the most proficient way. Reproductions of some of the reports—neat, accurate ledgers of death—and photographs, made during the actual experiments, hang at Dachau today.

We stopped and looked at them. We saw the totals of certain figures. We saw the contorted face of a young man whose lungs were bursting for want of oxygen. But we could not comprehend what we saw.

What could we say? How should we feel? Reports cover savagery with a shroud of semantics. Statistics freeze bestiality into the convenience of symbols. The quivering flesh, the brittle bone, the living blood has long since gone.

Before the blown-up photograph of an old Jewish woman protecting two children in her embrace, the very walls of the prison around them exuding death's chill, the Senior member of our own family pauses—and the tears flow. She is not ashamed of her tears. Our Munich guide looks at her and she faces him with her moist eyes and wet cheeks.

"I have a small friend at home," she says, and her voice quivers but her chin is firm. "He looks just like that boy. . . ."

There were hundreds, thousands, millions. But it is the one who brings our tears.

Before the row of books telling about Dachau, at the very end of the museum, the man of our family stands and looks at the volumes of words that have vainly attempted to convey what happened here. Our young driver walks up and looks at the books, too.

"I bought this booklet by a former prisoner," James says, and shows him the eighty-page publication, "What Was It Like in the Concentration Camp at Dachau?" The driver nods, but he does not look at the book. He does not take it in his hands.

Inside its pages, a little later, we discover this passage: "No one person, even if he had been in Dachau from the day it opened to the day it was closed, could know the *whole* truth about it, nor give the complete answer to the question which is so often asked: 'What was it like in Dachau?' Still less could he answer such questions as: 'How many were imprisoned in Dachau?' Or 'Who died in Dachau?' Or 'Who were their torturers and executioners?'

"The answers to these and similar questions differ greatly. Thus, estimates of the number of deaths in Dachau vary enormously. Zauner, the retired mayor of Dachau, put it at 20,600, Pastor Niemoller (quoting an inscription written in Dachau in 1945) at 238,756.

"Why this great lack of certainty and the enormous differences between the estimates? Is it due to a lack of willingness to speak the truth, to feel and confess guilt, to be accurate and honest?

"I do not believe so. The root of the evil seems to me to lie much deeper: in the great secrecy which surrounded the concentration camp at Dachau from the very beginning to the end, as was the case with all concentration camps and all other such extermination centres of the Third Reich.

" 'Evil loves the darkness and hates the light.' Fog, impenetrable fog, lay upon the camp at Dachau during twelve years."

Thus the physical mire and marshes from which the land for Dachau had been rescued simply served as breeding place for a new miasmic wasteland, the swamp of man's own vileness.

And I—housewife, daughter, mother—return to the picture that has insinuated itself into my memory. I take one last look at the stark photograph—a pile of shoes. A great pyramid of shoes. All sizes, shapes, qualities, degrees of wear. But mostly they are sturdy, scuffed, tough leather, which has settled into the thousands of shapes of the thousands of feet which have worn them through hard daily routines, chores of farm or store or factory, and been removed at last only by force, at the gate of death. There is something intimately human about those mute, scarred, and eloquent shoes.

"At home in America," I try to explain to the driver as he unobtrusively passes nearby, "many people have their children's baby shoes 'bronzed.' It's a way to preserve something special, something very personal from their childhood. But this picture—how could we ever 'bronze' all those shoes in our memory, make sure that we will never forget?"

He looks at the picture and at me, his blue eyes very clear. He does not reply. I have the feeling that he would like to shrug, but does not dare.

The two young men of our family have left the museum. They have already walked down the long rows of poplars. These tall trees were saplings when the prisoners set them out thirty and more years ago to line the *Lagerstrasse*, or main road of the camp. Behind each of these two rows once stood the fifteen blocks, or barracks, where men were penned.

The young ones do not speak. They do not mention what they have seen or heard or thought. They are very sober.

There is now a memorial temple and chapel and church for those of three faiths who died at Dachau. Here, as at most of the camps, the overwhelming numbers were Jewish; but there were also many priests and pastors of other religious faiths. And there were numerous political prisoners from many countries. Memorials or statues are not sufficient, however. Somehow it is the very ground itself, soaked with blood and sweat, which is both contaminated and consecrated here.

We have already tried to take in too much. I feel nauseated with a deep, unrelieved sickness. My legs are suddenly weak.

Now, as we walk in the late afternoon light, the air is sweet. The wind smells of grass. Once, our memoir of Dachau says, "the prevailing wind was from the west, and, consequently, the smell of burning corpses filled the camp, reminding the prisoners of their approaching end."

Now there is silence. The rural roads and distant town do not intrude upon the compound of Dachau. At one time, as historians say, "The cries of the suffering [during Dr. Rascher's outdoor freezing experiments] often rent the night."

Our limousine for the afternoon, comfortable and powerful, receives us back into its cushions. We drive away from Dachau; its spiked and twisted barbed wire and gleaming white guard towers the last things we see fading in the distance.

"Now we shall see Nymphenburg Palace." The driver's words are both a statement and a question. "The porcelain, the park, the carriages?"

"Yes," we agree. Then, in one last effort, someone asks, "But you. You're twenty-four years old, you told us. What do you think of Dachau?"

His eyes are fixed on the road ahead. He answers immediately. "We younger ones say forget the concentration camps. Don't keep dwelling on them. There was a television program with photographs of the camps several months ago. Everyone was angry about the program. Why keep looking back?"

No one answered him as we drove to the great baroque structure where "good" and "bad" and even "mad" rulers of Bavaria once reigned. Here all is opulence and grace and pleasing vistas. Oddly, our guide's preoccupation with the dates and names of kings and royal splendors did not strike him as "looking back."

We found the answer to why we had gone to Dachau in a second personal reminiscence which we read late that night, when some of us could not go to sleep.

The Dutch Jewish prisoner who had survived to tell his story asked himself why he wrote of the horror of Dachau. And he answered, "The message of the former inmates of the concentration camp Dachau can be condensed into three words: Practice more humanity."

That reminder offered us a means of atonement wherever we might go, whatever we might undertake.

We stayed exactly the right length of time and at the right place in Freiburg. The time was a night and morning. The place was a small inn in the Old Town on Minster Square.

Freiburg was on our itinerary because we wanted to see the Black Forest of Germany. Our corner of the Southern mountains has a special link with the Black Forest, and that link affected the birth and development of forestry in the United States.

In 1898, the first classes in constructive forest practice in

America were taught near Asheville, North Carolina. George Vanderbilt, who had just completed his chateau, Biltmore House, modeled on the great French chateaux of the Loire Valley, especially Blois and its outside staircase, wanted to create a beautiful and well-managed woodland preserve of some 3,500 acres out of the 100,000-acre tract he owned. During travels abroad, Vanderbilt had admired the Black Forest and now he wanted to transport to the Southern mountains the vision and practices which had kept that German resource intact. For this purpose he brought to western North Carolina a German expert who had known the Black Forest as well as other areas of his native land, Dr. Carl Schenck. There was no tradition of forestry in the United States. There was little formal knowledge or material on the practices of cutting or preserving trees. Schenck and the young men he gathered on the Biltmore Estate began the first such studies and experiments, and they sowed good seed, bearing fruit across the country today.

On the way to Freiburg I thought of Dr. Schenck, the Prussian who had once come to Appalachia with an important commitment. We rode through a portion of the *Schwarzwald* or Black Forest. There were beech trees, broad-limbed and leafy, with low, sturdy, whitish trunks. Mixed among them were slim birches and tall magnificent white pines. But the profusion which brought the forest its name was in the dark-maned evergreens climbing up the gentle slopes and covering the rugged crests—spruce and fir and pine again. Numerous valleys of grassy pastureland and clear streams broke the expanses of the forest. It is not the poor soil but the ancient woods which are wealth here.

Since the forest must be kept intact, farmsteads may not be divided. And according to ancient customs and laws of inheritance, they are passed down from the father to the youngest son. We were told that the people of the Black

Forest are a silent folk who carry long grudges and feuds among themselves. What we could see for ourselves was that the venerable trees bear mute but eloquent testimony to the constancy with which they have been cherished. The residents of these farms and hamlets obviously have been aware of their special privilege as occupants of a proud and beautiful corner of Europe. Their yards and gardens were as neat as the works of the clocks for which they are famous.

"Why, why, *why*," our Senior said, as she stood up in her enthusiasm and leaned out the wide train window to let the pungent fresh woods air blow against her face, "can't we let our countryside at home look just a little like this—clean and cared for?"

One of our Juniors began to laugh. "What would they do if someone dumped an old refrigerator or a wrecked car here in the Black Forest?"

"I don't know exactly," his grandmother replied, "but one thing they wouldn't do, they wouldn't leave it there waiting for the next one to be piled up beside it!"

We saw only a portion of that Forest which stretches for some one hundred miles across the southwestern corner of Germany, but it was sufficient to let us know why George Vanderbilt had wanted to bring Dr. Schenck to America some seventy years ago, and why Thomas Wolfe, a native of Asheville, had celebrated this countryside so exultantly.

We came to Freiburg early in the evening and we had not done our homework very well this time. We were surprised and disappointed to discover that this was no picturesque village, as we had imagined. It was a hustling city of commerce, traffic, and more than 150,000 people. We thought we might locate some of the interesting points of the city as we drove from the railway station to our hotel, but we were lucky just to locate the hand straps in the two taxis which catapulted us there.

With demonic recklessness our drivers floorboarded it (as our mountain boys say) through crowded city streets, ignored traffic signs and laws of gravity and propulsion, and finally skidded to an abrupt halt.

"And what did you think of *that?*" asked our Junior, who had won his driver's permit just before we left home.

"They should be issued wings rather than licenses when they come of age to drive here," someone muttered.

Shaken (at least on the part of three of us), we climbed out of the taxis, and confronted the Freiburg we had expected to find. A small inn, with peaked roof and pointed gables and lights shedding a golden glow through the small-paned windows, faced onto a cobbled square, and directly across the square loomed the form of a huge cathedral. Somewhat revived, we went to find our rooms at the cozy inn.

Dinner was in the rustic dining room under a low-beamed ceiling with brass and copper gleaming along the walls, hunting trophies, flowers, and tables crowded in convivial closeness. There was much talk and bustle. The aromas which enveloped the room were heavy and rich. The trout we ate was delectable, as were the other dishes from hearty soup to ripe, juicy fruits.

When we made our way back up to the odd little third-floor corridor and our rooms, we were in a lethargic daze of too much food, too much forest, a long day. It seemed we might wake up at any moment and find that we were under gingerbread gables in the house of a "poor woodchopper. . . ." We slept soundly in this reincarnation of once-upon-a-time.

At dawn the next morning there were sounds beneath our windows. Two of us looked out. The square below us had blossomed. Rows of fruits and vegetables in small displays were stretched across it neatly. Men hurried busily between carts and trucks and the improvised stands. Women uncovered baskets and boxes, arranged their produce in attractive mounds or bunches, and laughed and talked with other women on either hand. It was market time in Freiburg.

We went down to the market. As we stepped into the square, the full size and beauty of the Minster rose before us. At night it had remained only a form, but now the Cathedral was a presence. Its sandstone was an unusual soft shade of red, and its sharp decorated tower seemed tall enough to puncture the sky, which was growing momentarily brighter and bluer above us. Its belfry boasted one of the oldest bells in Germany.

On the south side of the *Münsterplatz* was the Guildhall, with medieval arcades, and on every hand were steep roofs and needle-sharp spires, narrow streets and elaborately wrought signs and street lamps. The people filling the *Münsterplatz* with their improvised stalls and cheerful bustle seemed appropriate to the surroundings.

They were, for the most part, country people, not quite as round and plump as the people of Bavaria, whom we had just seen. Their hands were work-roughened; their complexions weathered; and they wore plain clothes. Many of the women and girls had tied scarves over their heads, and their faces were free of make-up. Their shoes were heavy and scuffed. They were proud of their produce.

Brittle orange-colored carrots spread their lacy green tops across a rough plank counter and were surrounded by immense red radishes still wet from their washing in cold water. Heads of crisp white cauliflower and lavish ripe tomatoes and plain brown-skinned potatoes were heaped in orderly array. Summer apples brightened scattered baskets.

Our Senior stopped and communicated haltingly, mostly by gesture, with a quiet middle-aged woman, whose manner was as reserved and old-fashioned as the long cotton dress she wore. When at last she understood that the American was trying to tell her that the small pink-cheeked apples on her stand were like those remembered from a long-past childhood in the United States, her face lighted with a smile. She chose a firm ripe one and offered it as a gift, while our Senior indicated she wished to buy a few of the apples. The exchange brought approval from nearby vendors, too, whose own pyramids of vegetables and fruits were beginning to dwindle as townsfolks arrived to do their morning shopping.

In front of the tall red Minster was the flower market: enormous black-eyed Susans, butter yellow and velvet brown; blazing spears of gladioli; tight buds of roses, ranging from pinks as pale as a blush to crimsons as dark as a blood clot; tall stalks of blue delphinium; and nosegays of tiny ordinary blossoms, the flowers-of-the-field arranged and bound into tight pretty patterns.

There in the shadow of the immense Minster, seven centuries old, bustled the life of these vendors for a brief spell each morning. The market and the Minster: one fragile, temporal, quick to wither and be consumed; the other impassive, enduring, alive only as it is used, consumed; together they were Freiburg as we shall remember it.

When our journey came to an end, we asked each other which country we had enjoyed the most. It is the question friends most frequently ask when you have returned home from any trip. And it is invariably difficult to answer. One place has beauty and another charm. One is alluring because of its past while another is exciting because of its future.

Without hesitation, however, the Teens in our family stated their favorite country: "Switzerland."

Their unanimity, which is not always so pronounced, and the promptness of their selection interested the other three of us. We knew that they had relished Paris and the countryside and cooking of France, that they had been awed and fascinated by Spain, that Italy had evoked streams of conversation and much exploration of byways, and that the corners of Austria and Germany we had seen had been of compelling interest.

Why, then, could they say so unhesitatingly that Switzerland had been most enjoyable? As I pondered the question on the way home and discovered not a few other travelers who had the same reactions that our sons had had, I came to a conclusion: Switzerland is most enjoyable in many ways to many travelers because it makes the fewest demands on visitors.

Switzerland's magnificent gift is, of course, its scenery. Snowcapped mountain ranges undulate along the horizon or thrust their pinnacles up to the sky in sharp outlines of majestic loneliness. Surely few have caught their first glimpse of that white remote empire called the Bernese Oberland and not felt the breath catch in their throats. The streams plunge pure and opaque with melting snow down the slopes, and rivers run swiftly to the deep blue lakes. Meadows are green with the succulence of summer grass and brilliant with wild flowers.

And everywhere the people have supplemented, rather than destroyed, the natural beauty of their country. Villages are so neat and sturdy that they dwell in harmony with hills and fields. Farms have adapted to the terrain, not distorted it. In the cities pride is evident in the well-kept streets and flower-filled parks, as well as in the immaculate hotels, excellent food, abundant goods.

To truly appreciate France, a traveler must have some sense of style, must have some acquaintance with the culture of the world. To find the deepest satisfaction in Italy, it is necessary to value the past, to know something about the roots of Western civilization. To understand Spain, an American must have flexibility of tastes and values, and he must make an effort of both humility and pride. To evaluate

Austria or Germany, some knowledge of history and music and mythology is required.

But in Switzerland it is only essential that we feast our eyes upon the scenery and our bodies upon the luxuries that are so abundant. There is no period of the history of art or philosophic achievement with which we must be especially familiar if we are to make our visit meaningful.

Is this an asset or a liability?

All we really need to enjoy Switzerland is a plentiful supply of money. The Swiss and Americans have this important characteristic in common: They respect money. And what better, more lasting basis for romance between people or nations than a healthy affection for gold reserves and cash in hand?

There are people who believe that beauty is the essential ingredient of love. Nonsense! Beauty helps, of course. The outer, highly visible assets that catch the wandering eye and make it want to return to gaze again, or the inner, less immediately apparent qualities of loveliness of character and experience that merit long acquaintance—these are naturally on the credit side of the ledger. But after that first affirmative appraisal, and after the pleasures of a lengthening acquaintance, there arrives that moment of truth; and then the more lasting allures begin to assume importance. At such times the solid attractions of the Swiss franc and the American dollar are not to be devalued.

Beauty fades. Character erodes. Vitality wanes. Money waits—in the cool vaults and the neat strongboxes and the quietly cumulative savings accounts.

American or Swiss—each knows the luster that cash resources can suddenly impart to a fading friendship or a diminishing romance. And the money-making ability of one and the money-keeping talent of the other has sparked a strong mutual admiration for generations.

In case all this should sound crass and commercial, as it is, we might try to understand why it should be so.

First, are Swiss and Americans any more mercenary in spirit and reality than other people—the French, for example? Well, folklore around the world seems to say so, and sometimes the way others see us becomes a part of what, indeed, we are. America is a new country. In moments of stress we have not had a medieval or Renaissance history, a cultural tradition, an unbroken lineage to fall back upon. So we have relied frequently on our distinctive resource: our know-how.

As for Switzerland, it did not have vast fertile fields for cultivation or tremendous underground resources for tapping or strategic ports around which much of the history of other countries was built. And its citizens learned that money was a reliable substitute for many other assets—while most other assets could be very unreliable substitutes for money. Thrifty Swiss took the lesson to heart, and then put their hands to it.

And if the Swiss are successful hotel managers and bankers, Americans can appreciate their talents. If American skills include a way with profit-and-loss, the Swiss can appreciate the results. Both respect the financial imperatives of life more than the artistic imponderables.

The Matterhorn and Jungfrau, cuckoo clocks, cheeses, and geraniums in window boxes—these flash across our mental screen at mention of Switzerland. But the stout adhesive binding Americans and Swiss is the romance, the mystery, the faithfulness of money.

The paper money in France is so pretty with its pastel colors and pictures of bewigged French monarchs, and the lire and the pesetas in Italy and Spain are so plentiful, and the German marks and Scandinavian krone and British pounds are so confusing that it is difficult for an American to take the money seriously—at first.

It is only when he sees his traveler's checks melting like thin ice in the noonday sun that he realizes this isn't play paper after all.

And no one, but no one, fails to take the hardest currency in the world today, the Swiss franc, as seriously as the natives themselves take it. After all, they have secured centuries of peace and prosperity with it, and perhaps that is as close as anyone can come on this earth to "buying happiness."

But one of the funniest moments of a long summer came one morning when we witnessed a real breakdown in the professional composure of a concierge in a Montreux hotel. He was quoting one of the guests the price of a car and driver for the day.

"Is that in your money or ours?" the lady asked.

"That, madam," he gravely replied, "is the cost in Swiss francs."

"Well," came the swift request, "don't quote me Swiss francs. Tell me what it would cost in *real* money, in American dollars!"

I can believe that the word "berserk" came from Scandinavia; to be more exact, from those ancient Norsemen called berserkers (bear-shirters), who were such wild warriors that when they rushed into battle, they howled and were reputed to assume the form of wolf or bear, and in their frenzy to become invulnerable to iron or fire. Ordinary survival in the land from which they sprang required extra-ordinary men, and the explorations and conquests they undertook demanded frenzy rather than rationality.

A journey up one of their fjords is enough to drive a writer berserk today. There are no words large enough or fresh enough to capture the largeness and the freshness of scene which unfolds not once but twice, a half-dozen—you lose count of the times.

Magnificent is a word for the mountains that slice down to the water in green and rocky masses, but it is not a precise one; it does not suggest the long white threads of streams that cascade down the perpendicular slopes from a glacier or pocket of snow high in the ranges to the waiting inlets of the sea. Nor does it capture the elusive blue atmosphere which surrounds the mountains as a traveler approaches their apparently impregnable barrier and gradually beholds a passage opening between two folds of land.

Superb might be for the waters that rest in the fjords in blue ebb and flow, but it is not an exact word; it does not convey the grandeur of their sweep or the sense of their depth, which is a source of serenity and terror.

None of the words is sufficient to communicate that awe aroused by the austere might and the subtle beauty of this bold north country. Little wonder that its early natives ran berserk in showing the dwellers of softer, sweeter lands how fiercely born and bred they were!

(And who could resist a land whose leaders are recorded in history by such descriptive names as Halfdan the Black, Svend Forked Beard, Magnus the Good, Olaf the Saint, Erik Priest-hater, and a flock of Harolds—Harold Bluetooth, Harold the Fair-haired, Harold the Stern. . . .)

Before we visited Scandinavia it was all one to us. But never again shall we think of lively European Denmark, bigger and richer and more industrialized Sweden, or rugged and individualistic Norway except as distinct, each unique unto itself.

The term "Scandinavia" used accurately includes only Norway and Sweden, but common acceptance adds Denmark, too. They are not identical triplets, as many tend to believe, but are as different as brothers and sisters of the same family may be and still boast common blood and heritage.

We were informed, for instance, after we had returned from a visit to the three: "Sweden is interested in its royalty, has a consciousness of class and status. Denmark is more relaxed, the gayest of the countries. Norway has deeply ingrained democratic spirit: every man both a commoner and king."

Or, as a friend of ours summed it up: "My travelogue of Scandinavia is brief: no illiteracy in Denmark, no slums in Sweden, no conformists in Norway."

We encountered proof of each of her statements. A plainly dressed country girl with whom we shared a compartment on a train in Denmark spoke such excellent English that we asked her if she had studied in England or America. She told us that she had finished the equivalent of our high school and she spoke two languages in addition to her native tongue. We wondered how well her counterparts in America could speak Danish and French.

And our first trip by boat along the waterways of Stockholm almost shocked us by the consistency of the city's modern face. Glass and steel thrust up into light and air, unblemished by patches of dilapidated, warrenlike shelters and decaying neighborhoods. Extremes of luxury and need were not readily apparent.

We smiled when we read the observation a Norwegian set down almost a century ago about his fellow countrymen: "The national character is oppositional."

During World War II there were many people around the earth who thanked God for Norway's "oppositional character," which called upon deep reserves of courage and resourcefulness in negating the Nazi occupation.

There are smaller differences, too, by which Scandinavia breaks the mold of our preconceived notions. Daily schedules may vary widely among the countries. In Sweden long lunches are accepted business and social custom, while Norwegians pay scant attention to lunch and often skip it altogether. (After one breakfast in the fjord country—our choice of egg dishes, herring, tongue, ham, meat salads, goat cheese, and sour cream, among many other items—we could understand why lunch might seem superfluous.) Of course, dinner hour in Norway, any time from five o'clock in the afternoon on, is earlier than in any other European country.

There is also the business axiom which suggests some of the various traits, as well as natural resources, of the countries: "Get a Swede to make the product, a Dane to sell it, and a Norwegian to ship it."

And the fact that Sweden has 172 cars for every 1,000 people, while Denmark has 100 and Norway only 69, may reflect not only the higher per capita income of Sweden but the more precipitous terrain of Norway as well.

Geography and the ways of life are so clearly linked in these lands. Glaciers moving through the Ice Age sculpted the coasts and carried away much of the top soil. Today only 9 per cent of Sweden is arable and only 3 per cent of Norway is cultivated. As a visitor discovers the expanses of forest and the heights of the peaks, there is little room for wonder that the sea has dominated much of the life of Scandinavia, and that its people were early on the prowl. France, Russia, Iceland, and Greenland—all felt the force of their onslaughts. Ireland, Scotland, and England still bear mementos of their conquests. And maps of their early voyages to America are a source of contemporary controversy and astonishment.

The prayer of their neighbors was simple and universal: "From the fury of the Norsemen may the good God deliver us!" Nothing could seem further from their present hospitality.

Who can travel here and not recall fragments of the ancient legends of these lands? In the Norse mythology, second only to the Greek for its variety and vigor, gods were men magnified a hundred times in their strength, weakness, love and lust, sacrifice and revenge. During long winter nights, enclosed by the frozen mountains and howling winds and bitter darkness, the imaginations and hungers of men created another, larger world. As we crossed bleak and beautiful barriers and penetrated only a corner of the awesome fjord country, "The Ride of the Valkyries" (although composed by the German Wagner, its spirit is still that of the Norse myths on which it is based) did not seem so much romantic exaggeration as the echoing ring of ancient shouts that once reverberated through this blue stillness.

Copenhagen, the first of the Scandinavian cities to which we came, was flowers and food and friendliness. We did not pry beneath the surface for any reasons for a high rate of suicide or the problems of trade or any matters of survival. It simply seemed that here everyone should want to survive.

Perhaps this is as appropriate a spot as I am likely to find for including one of my favorite tidbits about Denmark. One historical account recorded the delightful paradox that "Gorm the Old, the first King of all Denmark, was a devout heathen."

Apparently no one in Copenhagen had heard of cholesterol. Butter, eggs, and milk saturated everything, and that delicious Danish bacon, grown on scientifically fattened pigs, appeared with regularity.

The Little Mermaid in the harbor—her bronze body and fins appearing as slippery as if she dripped water fresh from the sea—proved once more that fiction may be stronger than fact. Hans Christian Andersen is more alive in Denmark than the name or achievement of a whole roster of kings, financiers, or statesmen.

At Elsinore we discovered that the name is really Helsingör, and that neither is the name of the castle, as in Shakespeare's play about the "melancholy Dane," Hamlet. Elsinore-Helsingör is the name of the little town some twenty-four miles from Copenhagen and Kronborg is the name of the castle. Melody of language, not geographic authenticity, dictated the playwright's choice of names. The castle is interesting (an immense stork's nest built on a barn roof ridge along the way was just as arresting), and provides no more penetration to the heart of Hamlet than a visit to that thatch-roofed cottage at Stratford yields the genius of Shakespeare.

Of course, the chief attraction of Copenhagen since 1843 has been Tivoli. In this enormous, sprawling park (whose flourishing beds of brilliant tuberous begonias especially attracted our Senior's attention) there are trees, grass, flowers, water—and space. There are twenty-three restaurants, ranging in design from Moorish palaces and Chinese pagodas to French terraces and informal cafés. The range of entertainment is equally wide. There are halls for music, theater, ballet. There are roller coaster and Ferris wheel and boat rides. Embracing the youthful amusements and the lasting satisfactions of cultural events, Tivoli is a presence in itself. It seems almost an embodiment of the happy and hospitable spirit of the people who built it and have maintained it in the heart of their capital for a century and a quarter.

I could not forget, either, during our visit to this country, an incident which occurred during World War II. The Nazi occupation chiefs issued an order demanding that all Jewish residents of Copenhagen must wear an arm band bearing the Star of David. The morning this decree went into effect King Christian X appeared in public wearing on his arm a band with the Star. Immediately, many non-Jewish Danes followed their King's example. The symbol that was supposed to be, by Nazi standards, a stigma inviting separation became a badge of brotherhood and valor.

Sweden seemed an idyl of green woods and water. Figures may say that one half of Sweden is covered by forest, or that there are 100,000 lakes, but to see those living trees and to behold the great harvests of logs floating down the rivers like matchsticks, to pass the fields of hay drying in the summer sun, to watch the jewels of inland water reflecting woods and light is to witness the statistics brought alive.

Stockholm was the green copper of old pointed towers and roofs, and the glistening glass of new apartments and offices. The twelve islands on which the city is built are connected by 42 bridges and a subway, and nowhere were we far from the sight and smell of water.

In the third largest country of Europe (France and Spain are larger than Sweden), in its capital dripping with flower-decked balconies and busy with industry, the old and new meet creatively. In that "Swedish modern" which has transformed so many of our homes in the Western world, the old handcrafts and sense of utilitarian beauty have played their part toward design and production.

Of all the man-made attractions in Scandinavia, my own favorites were the remains of the Viking ships in Bygdønes, at Oslo, and the stave churches of Norway. In Norway, nature seems to reach a grand culmination, and so did man's early responses to her challenges and discipline. The Viking ships, with their sturdy construction, powerful oars, and fierce dragon's-head prows, carried their builders through many a conquest. Chiefs were buried in their boats, which were then set afire and floated out to sea. Looking at the Viking remains at Bygdønes, it is fascinating to visualize what the scene might have been when these vessels were still plowing the waves, propelling their horrific dragon's heads toward new horizons.

The stave churches seem at first sight to be landlocked

Viking vessels on green slopes, in a narrow valley, or in an outdoor museum. They are dark brown and their wooden-shingle construction gives them a scaly appearance as they rise in narrowing tiers until the steep roofs thin out to one small sharp tower. Jutting from the ends of the roof ridges at each successive level—somewhat like the gargoyles of Notre Dame—are dragon's heads. It is these which give the buildings the aspect of a Viking ship. Indoors, the stave churches are dark and cramped. They seem to suggest that man is small when set in this grand environment, but that he can endure.

There was a morning in Norway when we walked along a country road above one of the deep, still fjords that penetrate the majestic mountains.

Tiny farms sat snugly on green benchlands and rivulets of melting snow coursed down the hillsides. On the sod roofs of some of the barns grass grew green and tender and clumps of long-stemmed violets were in bloom. It was the first time I had ever reached up to pick a violet!

Steep pastures were soggy underfoot. The air itself was drenched with moisture and smelled of a deep undersea wetness. Below us lay the cold dark waters of the fjord; above us steep mountains thrust their jagged pinnacles; and all around us was the damp, green, growing world of summer in this Far North country.

The lines of the poet, Gerard Manley Hopkins, seemed appropriate to the stillness, the chill, the sponge-soaked vitality of the world around us:

What would the world be,
once bereft
Of wet and of wildness?
Let them be left,
O let them be left, wildness
and wet;
Long live the weeds and
the wildness yet.

Norway is not yet bereft of the wet and the wildness. It is a good land.

Oslo is one of the half-dozen largest cities in the world, in acreage if not in population. There are not many capitals with so few people and so many trees. But it does have Frogner Park, and that accounts for a few hundred additional people—all in stone.

Gustav Vigeland worked here for thirty years sculpting the human form in every shape, contortion, and frenzy of which it is capable. In addition, muscular men and women with flying hair and children with bodies as sturdy as fire hydrants depict family groups in various ferments of stress or delight. Everywhere there is action carried to its extreme.

The park is climaxed by the Monolith. This is a round pillar 56 feet high, consisting of 121 figures writhing like caterpillars, entangled with each other in their struggle upward, toward the top, reaching. Frogner Park does not suit everyone's taste. But it is the only exhibition I know which celebrates the size 44 figure solely and in all its diversity.

Mountain people seem to have in common certain characteristics, or characters, no matter where their mountains may happen to be located. We discovered that similarity in Norway's second largest city, Bergen, on the western coast, where the joke circulates about old-timers who used to say, "I'm not from Norway. I'm from Bergen."

Since we had made the spectacular journey across that unyielding country from Oslo to Bergen, we could understand how residents of the latter city might consider themselves closer in many respects to Hamburg or Amsterdam or London than to their own capital.

And we were reminded of certain Tennesseans who, when asked which state they were from, invariably replied, "East Tennessee." They, too, for many years felt that intervening mountains cut them off from their capital and they were closer in some respects to Washington than to Nashville.

The people of both Bergen and East Tennessee are mountaineers. The sharp difference between them is that the natives of Bergen are also a seafaring people, while most of our mountaineers have never glimpsed the sea.

Thus, while there is a kindred lack of sophistication, an open friendliness, and a highly developed sense of personal freedom (it has been said that "freedom comes from the mountains"), which seemed to make us feel at home in Bergen, there was also the influence and background of ships and the salt sea which marked the difference in our experiences.

The fish market at the east end of the Vaagen (smaller of two harbors and two lakes almost completely surrounding Bergen) was a revelation to any hill dweller from another niche of the world. It seemed incredible to us that every week-day morning there could be such a variety and quantity of fish offered for sale.

Ruddy-faced men with strong hands, wearing large loose aprons and rubber boots or tough high work shoes, presided over tanks and trays and tables of fish fresh from the ocean within a matter of hours. The smell was overwhelming: rank fish oils and sea water and salt. Underfoot some of the walkways were wet and slippery.

The sound was raucous, lively: fishmongers shouting and trading, chopping generous hunks of steaks from slithery white and pink specimens, wrapping small individual fish in rough paper, doling out mackerel—strong-smelling, strong-tasting, endless mackerel.

Surrounded by steep pinnacles and forbidding mountain ranges leading inland, we could stand among the counters and carts and boatloads of fish and understand why these stout people turned their gaze outward to the horizons of the ocean. We also realized more clearly what men mean when they talk of farming the seas, harvesting the oceans, living from the waters of the earth.

Bergen, then, pulled our gaze in two directions: to its mountains, behind which lies the rest of Norway, and to its harbors, beyond which lies the world. And as our boat left that long broken coast, heading for the British Isles, we tried to look in both directions at the same time.

The god Odin, in the *Edda*, sets forth the wisdom he gleaned through long travels and meeting many sorts of men. One of his observations: "Much too early I came to many places, or too late; the beer was not yet ready, or was already drunk."

It was good to feel that we had come to Norway, Sweden, Denmark neither too early nor too late. The full measure of this land of the white nights could not be drunk at a single feast, but we had tasted deeply.

We remembered Edvard Grieg's *Peer Gynt Suite* as we walked down the leaf-shaded woods path in Bergen to the little clapboard cabin-study where he composed. Deep in the mountains beside one of the fjords we had felt some kinship with the past of this hard chill land, because a woman named Sigrid Undset once wrote novels as massive and memorable as her native place. I should hate to visit Norway or any of its distinctive northern neighbors without having read at least one of Undset's novels, having known at least one of Ibsen's plays, or having listened to Grieg's music. Each provided us with those memories which a traveler must bring with him to a country if he is to take rich memories away.

For most Americans going to the British Isles is like going back home. If we have not visited there in person, we have been there in history, in the poetry and plays and novels we have read, in the children's games we played, in our folklore and ballads, our collective memory and inherited allegiances.

And when we view that gentle green landscape materializing out of a restless ocean, something stirs in us. It is a mixture of the anticipation and apprehension we experience when we are going to meet relatives for the first time, relatives we want to like but are not sure we can, whom we hope to find interesting and witty and warm, though we fear they may be only dull and self-centered.

For many travelers that first glimpse arouses memories of the real and legendary figures, notions, half-truths of a lifetime: a worthy Arthur releasing the sword Excalibur from its rocky prison; Sir Walter Raleigh, resplendent in plumes and velvet, spreading his cape and smoking the tobacco weed from the New World; the lucid madness of the poet William Blake, stripped, seeing angels in his garden and cruelty on city streets; civil servants from "Out There" returning home with tropical fevers, stiff upper lips, and emeralds worth a rajah's ransom; old Bedlam and the playing fields of Eton and village pubs, where smooth ale and rude wisdom is dispensed in equal parts.

A visitor grows suddenly glib with remembered fragments of Shakespeare: "This blessed plot, this earth, this realm, this England"; and Dr. Samuel Johnson: "When a man is tired of London, he is tired of life; for there is in London all that life can afford"; and Robert Browning: "Oh, to be in England/Now that April's there. . . ." Then the boat docks or the plane lands, and you begin your own discovery.

This marriage of memory and reality may endure throughout a visit to the British Isles, lending a rich double vision to each new scene and impromptu friendship. When, for instance, I looked up one foggy afternoon and saw the sign "Baker Street," I saw more than the name of a street and its rather ordinary surroundings; I saw Sherlock Holmes greeting a mysterious new client and explaining to Dr. Watson the easy deductions by which the newcomer's occupation, home county, and income could be ascertained at a glance. I saw Holmes departing for those lonely moors where he would solve the sinister riddle of the great hound of the Baskervilles. And when, later on, I stood on the moors myself, not only Holmes stood with me, but the wild troubled spirits of Emily Brontë's Heathcliffe and Catherine Earnshaw seemed present, too.

Or when, on a peaceful, pleasant afternoon we paused to peer at Blenheim Castle, I could not see stout walls and tiers of windows and acres of rooftops only, for there were the face and voice of its famous son who had once rallied his people to superb courage and victory. "We shall fight them on the beaches . . . blood, sweat and tears . . . this was their finest hour."

Or when we stopped on the road to Canterbury, and the man of whom we asked directions volunteered to go with us and show us the way, and told us as we went along together about his experiences in World War II with American soldiers, how could we help but recollect Chaucer's "A knight there was, and he a worthy man . . ."?

There were scores of sites, names, sounds to rake the memory: the meadow of Runnymede, which appeared so small and even unimportant until we recalled the confrontation which had taken place here between the arrogant king and some restless, resolute barons; the lonely glens and hills of Scotland, which we knew had once rung with the war cries of chieftains slaughtering each other for glory—or for God; the thatched farmhouses and bits of Irish farms, where a terrible potato famine had once driven families by the thousands to a new world across the Atlantic; the labyrinths of London where Oliver Twist, Mr. Micawber, and Pickwick seemed more alive than fictional.

So memory of that past about which we know and reality of the present about which we learn merges into one heady experience. Of course, it may also dissolve into rage the first time an Englishman fixes his gaze precisely six inches above your head and remarks, "American. Um-m-m," in a falling tone whose full message is impossible to reproduce on paper. It is the ultimate in polite withdrawal and dismissal.

While we were in England, we reminded ourselves several times that people speak through their homes and gardens, through their public character and laws, as well as by lips and tongues and words; and then, if we had been momentarily alienated, we promptly felt at home again. Or more so. For where we have wealth and poverty, England has a past empire's opulence and industrial wretchedness; where we have garden clubs scattered sporadically through our towns, England has gardens in every village and cottage plot; where we have laws, England has Law; where we have characteristics, England has Character (especially the character to be intensely individualistic).

Oddly enough, it seems to be this individualism which sometimes separates us from these distant cousins. Discovering the difficulties of communicating in the same language can be a hard blow. For when most of us arrive in England, especially after visiting other countries in Europe, we may think how easy it will be to know the people *here*. We all speak the mother tongue, or one of its woods'-colt offspring. It does not take long to learn that the same language does not always assure friendliness any more than lack of a common language guarantees hostility. British are by nature, custom, and folklore simply more reserved than Americans. Or Italians. Or most Scandinavians, for that matter. And this is difficult for most Americans to understand.

I have come to the conclusion that the big difference between America and Britain is not in any balance of trade or diplomatic rift or cultural lag; it is the privacy gap. Too many Americans hardly know what privacy is—nor do they care. Most Britishers cling to it as one of their oldest virtues and dearest rights. The contrast in size between our countries has undoubtedly influenced our contrasting attitudes. Until quite recently, most Americans lived in a geographic spaciousness that often bordered on loneliness; the people on these islands, however, had to cultivate privacy to keep from being overwhelmed simply by the numbers of their neighbors. A smattering of picture windows, an outcropping of gossip-type publications and well-packed discotheques—none of these tremors of jet-age, mod-set revolution have yet completely canceled out the inherent British instinct for privacy. And once a visitor realizes that it *is* an instinct and not an insult, both he and his host can be more congenial.

For the British Isles are a congenial land. Their smallness is, at first, astonishing. England is only 600 miles long and, at its broadest, only 300 miles wide. But their diversity lends enchantment. There must be few places in the world today where the complexities of our Western civilization are more pressing, yet where the meaning of the simple life is better understood or appreciated.

The simple life seems always to have been possible in

Great Britain, not only possible but probable. Anything associated with the out of doors could be assured of faithful partisans: shooting grouse or defending a sanctuary for sedge warblers, picking mushrooms or playing soccer, mountain climbing or spading up a flower bed. The essence of the activity was simplicity, that simplicity born of steadfast self-confidence, a lifetime habit of unostentatious discipline and tenacious achievement. Not only villagers and farmers and fishermen are rural, insisting on the attendant elementals of life, but political and industrial and social and intellectual leaders are frequently partially country people, too, in a way largely unknown in the United States.

Consider the matter of walking, for instance. England, Scotland, Ireland, Wales, city or countryside—each is made for walking. Whether you stroll around some square in London (which may have an atmosphere quite distinctly its own and different from that of another square not far away), or along the lake at Windermere, or undertake a hike into the wild Scottish highlands, you will be following a national tradition.

Chances are that you will meet fellow strollers or hikers wherever you are. Nothing will discourage them. We encountered a flock of schoolboys at Bettws-y-Coed in Wales one midday, hiking in *lederhosen* and high good humor under a cold downpour of rain. This was no atmospherical mist suggesting tales of mystery, no poetic shower conjuring up visions of daffodils and apple blossoms to come, but a hard persistent day-long rain, which its victims heeded only long enough to don some slickers.

I wonder, did the British as walkers come first and develop their cities and leave their countryside undeveloped as places for proper walking? Or did the landscape, man's and nature's, come first and demand that those who would know it should walk?

Many people (all in America, never in England) asked us

how our Senior managed with this walking. Our answer was that, like Abou ben Adhem's name, she led all the rest, in high gear—especially after one glimpse of fuschia in full bloom along a roadway, of heather covering a hillside with soft lavender bloom, of a brilliant plot of geraniums or begonias or dahlias in some city square or circle. Or especially if there were some rumored cottages, people, shops just around the next bend.

"English folks aren't as reticent and unfriendly as all that," she announced one day after a foray into a village and some of the nearby countryside of Devon. "I've just been talking with several. All that you need to find is something that interests them, ask a few questions, and then listen."

Well! Hasn't that always been the formula for social success: *their* interests and *your* interest?

Despite the stylish mode of the Mayfair set and the mod fashion of Carnaby Street and the angry young men (who were young a few years ago anyway) of the Midlands and the gray industrial complexes, despite change and apparent contradiction, the exquisite flower beds flourish like many-colored jewels before modest homes as well as in perfectly manicured parks and sprawling estates. The countryside itself is more than the familiar storybook land of green patchwork fields and meadows and rolling hills; it is a reflection of those who have tended it. And that is a reflection largely of patience quiet as grass, forethought as enduring as oaks, and a sense of beauty elegant as hybrid roses and wild fuschia.

Memorable days and places stretch across these Isles: Ullapool on Loc Broom in northern Scotland, wrapped under lowering clouds when the weather was "dampening on" and the lake repeated the dark turbulence of the sky; the jutting headlands and jagged coves of Tintagel, roaring with the rhythm of waves breaking relentlessly on the Cornish coast of England, a wild and legend-ridden corner; Glengarriff and Killarney and a dozen other Irish towns surrounded by a countryside cross-stitched with stone walls enclosing tiny fields, dotted with brown turf diggings, lively in the easy conversation of anyone with whom the stranger seeks to strike up conversation.

The big ones, the Required Seeing list, we searched out: London's British Museum (with its enormous quiet befitting the world's greatest library, boasting also the magnificent Elgin Marbles, and a host of treasures), Westminster Abbey, Parliament, Tate Gallery; Edinburgh's dark and forbidding castle, and its fantastic Albert Memorial looking like something out of Walt Disney; Sir Walter Scott's estate at pastoral Abbottsford; the timeless towers and enclosures of Oxford; the camera-wise charm of Stratford-on-Avon under thatch, and medieval Chester embraced by its ancient wall; Dublin's streets wide and narrow, its celebrated university, and cubbyhole pubs and wise-faced children equally plentiful; royal castles, cathedrals, and stately homes scattered thick as mushrooms across the countryside. All these a visitor would have to see and contemplate, but he must find more, if he is to arrive at understanding.

For rooted deep within the crannies, as well as in the landmarks, is a cardinal simplicity. It seemed to us that it was a simplicity which could only be won by a rare and complex people.

One of the most satisfying features of returning from a long trip is unpacking suitcases. Those clothes that have been folded and shaken out, refolded and reshaken, laundered or pressed and repacked with relentless regularity may now be put to rest for a while.

Souvenirs and trinkets that have been accumulated along the way from persuasive salesmen, talented craftsmen, enticing shops emerge from unlikely corners—the toes of shoes, an empty powder box. Folders, maps, and leaflets long forgotten flutter out of luggage pockets and other hiding places.

All the memorabilia collects in one heap until it can be sorted out and re-evaluated. Each bit was brought home for a special reason and it will illuminate a specific memory.

So, too, we "unpack" our minds on arrival home. And it is often the little souvenir of a recollected incident, the trinket of a scene perceived with heightened clarity, the pattern of a conversation or an insight which emerges with unexpected force. Its value does not have to be declared at customs— fortunately, for it is inestimable.

A summer provides time to gather a wide assortment of moments, impressions, people, and places, none of which will shake the political foundations of the world, but each of which promotes our understanding of a full life.

From our collection, a random sampling:

A wise British traveler, an experienced woman, once said after a visit in Italy: "When it comes to knowing, the senses are more honest than the intelligence."

And Jean Renoir, son of the Impressionist painter who flooded his canvases with sunlight and air and wrapped his exquisite subjects in atmosphere, observed: "A child is being continually astonished by things."

Perhaps a child's astonishment and delight are made possible because he is living by the honesty of his senses. He hears everything for the first time, sees it through his own eyes rather than the interpretations or prejudices of others, and tastes, smells, feels by his own unblunted perceptions.

So, too, the traveler must scrape the barnacles off his senses before he searches out new experiences. He must become as a child again, trusting his own wisdom, unashamed of the freedom to be astonished.

Our Southern mountains still boast many men and women who follow the old ways of craftsmanship. Throughout our summer's journey we were reminded of the kinship between handicrafts everywhere. In this country or another, despite differences of language or history, country people who have had to meet the pressures of necessity by their own ingenuity have created objects of art and utility.

Hand-woven wool stoles in Assisi, wood carvings in Madrid or Interlaken, ceramics of Scandinavia, these and a host of other items fashioned by hand made us feel akin to strangers.

On board ship some of the lesser devices which people have contrived in an effort to banish or diminish boredom are turned into a way of life.

Our Senior remarked in midpassage, "I've never been so exhausted in my life—doing nothing."

Continuous and enforced leisure does not come easily to someone whose chief pleasure in the spring and summertime is planting and tending flower and vegetable gardens; whose satisfaction in winter may be found in building and tending log fires in her spacious fireplace because she likes the glow of living flames and the murmur of crackling wood and the smell of pine or apple or hickory smoke.

Our Juniors made the ship their planet, for extensive exploration and intensive enjoyment. They swam in both swimming pools (their sense of class consciousness is definitely underdeveloped), entered numerous competitions (from ping-pong to bingo), and struck up some light romances and sturdy friendships which pursued us across Europe.

Our Middlers? We reached one tentative conclusion, bundled in our deck chairs looking out over the Atlantic, which seemed both boundless and fathomless. There are mountain people and ocean people, those who relate to land and those who relate to water. We are of the former group. The eternal restlessness of the sea is not so meaningful to us as is the stillness of the mountains. Both oceans and mountains are in constant change; both harbor their own dark treacheries and dangers. But we feel that the varieties and perils of the land are comprehensible in a way that will never be true (for us) of the watery deeps.

A stranger, interested in our family-style travel, asked, "With no prearranged schedule of sight-seeing or activity, how did the five of you agree on what to do each day?"

The answer was, of course, that we didn't. Not each day. And so sometimes we went our separate ways: to bookstalls or museums, Le Drugstore or antique shops, sidewalk café or beach, or simply private exploration. This proved to be therapeutic, relieving us of each other's constant presence yet reuniting us in a special sort of comradeship when we came back together and pooled our various experiences or impressions.

Inevitably there were times—the majority of the days, in fact—when it seemed that all of us should be acting more or less in concert, for mutual profit of experience and thrift of purse.

Such times often demonstrated the weaknesses, and strengths, of democracy. We had agreed to abide by the simple majority vote in most such decisions. Sometimes we used up an hour—or more—deciding. (Democracy is often costly in time.) Sometimes we discovered that reluctant explorers can be restless companions. (The administration of democracy is often demanding.) We found that a benevolent dictatorship may be at least one solution to the anarchy of five widely divergent opinions and tastes (all strongly held). But what such dictatorship saves in time it sacrifices in enthusiasm. Since enthusiasm is one of the priceless gifts a traveler must have, we tried to grant a maximum autonomy to each of the five states which made up our one world.

It is instructive to watch tourists (including ourselves) at a favorite pastime: shopping.

If maps suddenly disappeared and other usual means of orientation failed, it would still be possible to determine where you are on a journey by the accessories newly adorning a majority of visitors. In Scotland, plaid scarves and skirts and hand-knit sweaters suddenly blossom in fresh brightness on visiting bodies. In Florence, uninitiated leather handbags decorate countless arms. In Switzerland, new watches gleam on men's, women's, and tots' wrists. In Paris, scents of heady perfume suddenly waft across the atmosphere in steady gusts.

Shopping brings out the timid and the bold in our natures. It accentuates all that is acquisitive and greedy. It feeds on the herd instinct. I sometimes wonder if more harm is not done to international good will across the shopping counters than across military barriers.

Our awareness of shoppers and their habits abroad reached its climax during our return voyage home aboard the *France*. The Galeries Lafayette, a Paris department store, has a shop on the *France*.

The first morning out of Le Havre we were passing the shop when we suddenly became aware that this was where the action was. It was action resembling the running of the bulls at Pamplona or the Oktoberfest in Munich. We paused to ask what it was all about.

A woman with three bottles of Caron cologne and three packages of Patou perfume and two sweaters and one scarf informed us quickly enough. "Think of what these would cost at home! And this will be our last chance to *buy*."

Apparently a continent of passengers had discovered that perfume cost a few cents less than in Paris and a few dollars less than in New York or Idaho. And they had made the horrendous discovery that they were returning home with a few unspent dollars. Frantically, even grimly, they were grabbing, buying, holding, and then buying more.

Lines of them pushed toward the two girls at the counters, and even these stalwart clerks finally lost their French chic under the assault; by the time the shop closed in the late afternoon they presented a disheveled picture of disarranged hair and distracted countenance, which was only exceeded by the sadly demolished appearance of the small shop itself.

Each day, however, the doors were reopened. (By rough calculation I estimated that the hold of the *France* carried almost as many bottles of perfume as it did of wine, rouge *and* blanc, and twice as large a quantity of either perfume or wine as of water.) Each day the stampede was repeated. The appetite for things seemed insatiable.

During my last foray into the struggle, I watched for a moment as two women mauled a rack of designer neckties. Then the larger, sun-tanned, carefully coifed shopper said to her friend, as she draped three of the ties across her braceleted arm, "I don't really like any of them, but we have to buy something!"

Perspective is a valuable by-product of travel. It may also be a source of acute discomfort.

Late one night, as we wound our way through some of the narrower back streets of Madrid, one of our family stopped and said, "Do you realize we would be afraid to walk around at two o'clock in the morning on side streets of New York or Washington or Chicago or Los Angeles?"

We walked at all hours in dozens of villages and towns, hamlets and cities, in numerous countries; and it never occurred to us at any point to be worried about our safety. In how many of their American counterparts would this same spirit of relaxed enjoyment be possible?

In each of the places we visited we read the local newspapers, in the native language where possible and in the English editions otherwise. We watched newsreels. We talked with many different types of people. And one of the strongest impressions which emerged from this effort, as we looked at our own country from this distance and followed its news through strangers' eyes, was that Americans are a violent people.

The assassination of a young President had revived abroad memories of previous Presidents killed or wounded. Our massive involvement in an ambiguous and frustrating war in the Far East had caused deep concern even among our friends. News of group murders, several of a peculiarly bizarre nature, and city riots of brutal intensity had deepened the conviction of our violence.

Re-enforcing this reality is the stream of popular American movies we export. There are the old standbys, the Westerns, Good Guys vs. Bad, in which the atmosphere of violence and the ultimate reliance on guns is as basic as bread and water (or bread and butter). In addition, now, are the slick sophisticated films where sadism permeates the plot and purpose until meaningless suffering and unmotivated cruelty become the *raison d'être* for the so-called entertainment.

Thus, both fact and fiction seem to be joined in presenting Americans as a people of tempestuous nature, flaring

temper, little discipline, hoping to achieve by force and up-
heaval what cannot be secured by rational effort.

To glimpse such a view of ourselves and our fellow citizens, and to understand the basis for its existence, is an unsettling experience.

Why is it that we Americans so often become defensive
when we travel outside our own country?

As soon as we set foot on foreign soil we seem smitten
with the urge to pin our hearts on our sleeves, set those
slippery chips on our shoulders, and with all reserves mus-
tered at the ready launch forth hoping for friends but expecting foes. It is an unproductive way to begin a visit.

Our defensiveness takes one of two forms: We are either
obnoxious in our superiority or insufferable in our inferiority.

In the beginning, without being hampered by any first-
hand observations or facts, some of us enjoy citing the superiority of America's newer buildings, numerous bathrooms,
and innumerable hamburgers.

On the other hand, some arrive in Europe cringing with
inferiority because America is in such short supply on
medieval castles, Romanesque churches, titled aristocracy—
and truffles.

We seem to alternate between boast and apology—and
both for the wrong reasons. At either extreme the natives of
our host countries gain a false impression of us.

Cartoons to the contrary, not every U.S. tourist arrives at
Southampton, Le Havre, or Naples weighed down with a
costly camera and cheap manners, a big bankroll and narrow

background. Some arrive with a simple wish to see and hear and know, to play a little, learn a little, enlarge the dimensions of daily routine.

Yet we often betray ourselves along the way, assertive over what does not need assertion, oddly defensive about what needs no defending.

One day during the summer a member of our family, watching the rest of us emerge from the Prado in Madrid, greeted us with the accusation, "We look just like Americans."

Came the prompt reply, "And what else should we look like?"

I suppose it was the combination of drip-dry shirts, catch-all purses, dog-eared guidebooks, and expressions of earnest vulnerability that made us so conspicuously identifiable. But those clothes were practical. The books were packed with bright informativeness. And if our countenances had lost their cool—well—they simply reflected the excitement a new experience could arouse. There was no reason other than the most ridiculous snobbery for us to try to look like suave art dealers from Parke-Bernet Galleries or bored jet-setters with no visible roots in any national allegiance. We did not try.

There is no reason for Americans to feel inferior. There is no need to feel superior. Countries, even as individuals, have their unique assets and their characteristic liabilities. One may be beautiful—and boring. Another may be rich—and hostile. The secret is to see the whole.

An old New England master once informed a friend that a writer would rather be understood than liked. Nations may have the same hope. They long for understanding as well as underwriting. They want us to look beneath the surface, to view deficiencies with sympathy and assets with appreciation.

Perhaps we should all relax a little more. "We" won't

boast about our plumbing and our DiMaggios if "they" won't remind us too often of their palaces and their Michelangelos.

Americans are supposed to be preoccupied with size. We are said to be impressed by anything that is the highest, longest, widest, deepest—or largest.

Perhaps this is true, and if it is, part of the reason may be found in our own geography. A visit to the countries of Western Europe sharpens awareness of the size of these United States. No wonder we have CinemaScope vision. Most of our forefathers came from countries so much smaller than their new homeland that at first it was often difficult for them to grasp the scope of this continent.

Today it is difficult for those who live in Europe to understand just how large the U.S.A. is. It is an even greater problem for them to understand how this physical reality influences our economics, politics, religion, social life, and our relationships with the rest of the world and even with each other.

The whole country of Switzerland is about the size of two of our small New England states combined, Massachusetts and New Hampshire. France, one of the largest countries in Europe, even including Corsica in its land area, still lacks 50,000 square miles of being as large as Texas.

A French lady with whom we were having tea one afternoon in her tiny apartment near Notre Dame smiled as she recounted an experience she had had on her visit to "our" country. She was spending some time with friends in South Carolina, she explained.

"Oh, your distances!" she gasped lightly, making a quick

gesture with her hands. "I cannot forget how surprised my hostess was when I asked her one day if I could run up to Maine for tea some afternoon.

"You see, I had friends in Maine also, and I had understood it, too, was on the Atlantic Coast, and I thought perhaps I could go very easily in an afternoon. Oh, no, no, no!"

Then there was a Swiss man who told us a story about a Texan who visited in Switzerland. A farmer in the district where they produced Gruyere cheese showed the visitor around the boundaries of his farm. There were a few hills and slopes and it took about two hours to drive all around the fields.

As they finished the Texan said, "That's a nice spread, but at home it takes me two days to drive around my farm."

The Swiss host looked at him and shook his head. "I used to have such an old car, too," he said.

An Englishman asked us what part of the United States we lived in. As our explanations about Southern mountains brought no light of comprehension to his face, we finally said, "Just seven hundred miles south of New York City."

"Just seven hundred miles!" he exclaimed. "Ah, you Americans. Who else could estimate such distances in such a casual manner?"

If all the surveys and surmises, statistics and hogwash written about "the American woman" were placed end to end, the accumulation would probably have reached to the moon long before our first Surveyor satellite.

Mr. Sigmund Freud discovered that Oedipus had a

mother; Mr. Philip Wylie discovered that Americans had Moms; Mr. Alfred Kinsey discovered that men had women; and in 1920 the male population of the United States discovered that women had the vote. To listen to some of the laments littering the air today, it would seem that most of our current problems would be nonexistent if it were not for the truths expounded by Messrs. Freud, Wylie, Kinsey, and some six or eight million other masculine voices.

The American woman emerges from under the scrutiny of the sex-behavior pollsters, the slick-article writers, assorted counselors and clinics as a creature at once pampered and aggressive, a household tabby or a manicured tigress, doomed if she stays in the home and damned if she participates in a larger world.

Compared with her European sisters she lacks femininity, style, tolerance. She is portrayed as a coldhearted gold digger with the instincts of a black widow spider and the power of a latter-day Amazon. She is selfish and materialistic, as revealed by the number of automatic dishwashers she buys each year and the number of heart attacks her husbands have each decade.

Ten minutes in any country in Europe (twenty minutes if your faculties of observation are slightly retarded) should help to put some of this mythology in the deep freeze, where it belongs. One encounter with a female concierge in the capital of France, one skirmish with a female Italian café owner, one brush with a little old lady fruit vendor in Germany will make her American counterpart seem an awkward novice in the art of self-protection and domination.

For sheer verbal bludgeoning power I defy any shrew in the states of Iowa, Maine, or Arizona to compare with the ladies of Naples. For stubborn smoldering resistance at the local and household level I doubt if the wives in U.S. hinterland or city could match the subtle effectiveness of their Spanish sisters.

As for greed, the amateur American female can't even enter the contest with the Parisiennes. Those French girls have been playing for the high stakes—châteaus and kingdoms and little old palaces—for so long that our mundane accounts involving an occasional mink coat or white convertible seem decidedly paltry.

In the area of romance there is more sentiment and romanticism per square inch of any American suburb than in all of France or Italy combined. The operatic versions of these great romantic countries are strictly for the songbirds. The great realists of all times are the French and Italian peasant women. They acknowledge with the politicians and philosophers (all men) that this is a man's world; then they proceed to rule their little corner of it with zest and efficiency.

Even a comparison of divorce rates may suggest (contrary to many opinions) how romantic the American woman still is. She believes, in her naïveté, that the perfect husband may exist—somewhere. But European wives, indeed more tolerant of infidelities and assorted peccadillos, hold on to their imperfect husbands. And their homes. Better give up a heart than a hearth.

Compared with others of her sex around the world, the American woman may not be as unattractive an ogre as some of the fashionable playwrights, dress designers, and nearsighted psychiatrists would have us believe. After all, who else could survive all those surveys and surmises, statistics and hogwash, and still be attractive enough to find her own All-American husband?

A small canticle of praise to the breads of Europe. The rolls, the sticks, the croissants, but, above all, the long loaves of the bread of France. Ah-h, simply to name it is to re-create a memory which awakens all the senses.

None of our three generations was able to resist the bread on the Continent. From the moment we set foot aboard the French liner and found delectable dinner rolls at our place for each meal until our departure down the same gangplank a season later, we left a trail of crumbs scattered across the villages and cities and countryside through which we passed like nonvegetarian locusts devouring all the bread in sight.

One morning in the little town of Ax-les-Thermes in the Ariège valley, I could no longer resist the lure of the bakery, so I slipped inside and from a tall basket on the counter selected a loaf which seemed at least four feet long. I laid my coins on the counter, tucked the unwrapped bread under my arm (bread in Europe is innocent of cellophane or bags), and marched out as matter-of-factly as any good local housewife doing her daily shopping. My family were a little astonished when they saw me approaching with my appetiz-ing trophy, but their astonishment soon turned to hunger. In our car we each broke off a nibble of the still-warm bread. Like piranha fish at their first taste of flesh, we tore into the rest of the loaf until all that was left of my staff of life was a collection of scattered crumbs.

As I say, it's a matter of the senses. . . .

There is the sight. The loaves are baked fresh each morn-ing for restaurants or shops. Their crusts are golden brown and so crisp they flake off unless they are deftly sliced. (In one incomparable little country restaurant in France we watched the waitress chop off chunks from the long loaves with quick sharp strokes of a meat cleaver. Each basket of bread was cut fresh for each new customer. With bowls of thick soup, a subsequent omelet of tender consistency, and a delectable fish, we managed to keep that sturdy maid busy at her cleaver and bread block during a long lunch hour.) Each morning housewives attend to the day's marketing, and stick the day's supply of bread in their ever-present net shopping bags as they finish their rounds. It is a goodly sight.

The touch is equally distinctive. While the crust is hard, the inside is tender. But it also has texture. Perhaps this texture is the secret of flavor, for it indicates flour that has not had all its body and richness refined away. The best way to eat such bread is to break it apart with your fingers and not slice it at all, for the touch is at once crisp and soft in subtle harmony.

And the smell? Precious above the perfumes of Chanel or Balmain. Full-bodied, nutlike, born of the earth's ripeness, promising in its aromatic reassurance of hunger to be satisfied. It transforms the most common denominator of each meal into an experience of daily delight.

Can bread have a sound? Oh, yes—the delicate noise of its crust crumbling and its chunks or slices yielding to knives or fingers. It is the sound of flakes whispering of goodness yet to be relished.

The taste—the flavor of wheat in all the fullness of grain, flour in all its nourishment, yeast and salt, milk and butter in all their health. Give others the champagne and caviar; I'll take the bread of Europe.

Is it unfashionable to speak of the lady in New York harbor? I shall run the risk. Tall and lonely, she stands apart from the mainland. The waters of river and ocean wash at her feet, yet her strength is not eroded; the winds blow from east and west, north and south, yet she remains steadfast. At noon and midnight, in our awareness or our heedlessness, she abides.

Fashions do not alter her, for she is pre-eminent in the permanence of her own style. Fluctuations of markets, wranglings of governments, pressures of popularity do not alarm her, for her mere presence bespeaks permission of all these lesser shifts and changes. Assaults do not diminish her, for her toughness is born of a universal longing for the freedom she represents and her tenderness is bred in the justice she promises.

Like mother, wife, irreplaceable friend, she endures. The meaning of her presence is the measure of our lives. When we are leaving her behind, she seems to wave farewell, God-speed, go in health and return in peace. Her upraised arm reflects the glow of early afternoon sunlight; and the longer we look at her the smaller she grows, until she is a hazy ghost behind us.

When we are returning to her the torch she lifts catches the glint of early morning sunshine; and the longer we look, the larger she becomes until she is a sharp reality before us—charging, reminding, revitalizing us.

Everyone who travels from or to our country should go sometime by boat. This was the way many Americans came to their land—under sail or steam, in fetid hold or lofty cabin, through tortuous months or a few swift days, by wish or force or hungers more ravaging than fear of death. To approach America aboard a ship is to become part of an immense and unique happening.

The land emerges on the horizon. There is a quickening of the pulse, a straining of the eyes, and, yes—why should we cower admitting it?—a yearning of the mind.

For the lady arises out of the water and suddenly—through the perspective of our absence and our experience of other places—we know why the Statue of Liberty is there. She speaks through every hour and in each successive season. Yet after we have been away her face grows clearer and her voice is more distinct.

She welcomes us—not only the privileged and the beautiful, but all of us—bequeathing us this spacious and fragile
land which may be ours if we make it so by dream and
responsibility, by courage of our heart and hand.

She promises us not an easy way, not instant wealth or
perfect justice or democracy achieved but fresh hope of
possibility. The pledge is of freedom to make all things
possible.

The ships move slowly past her. The lady in the harbor
stands, one with the sky and water and morning sun. And
there wells up within a wanderer the gentlest grief a person
can endure—nostalgia; and the brightest anticipation a person can enjoy—homecoming.

On our way from ship to home we asked the same question that we had posed at the beginning of our trip: What
do you think is the most important thing we could have
taken with us on this trip?

Again, we had five different answers. Two of them were
the same that had been given the first time—with a little
elaboration.

"Enough money, with sense enough to realize that the
memories you buy will be more important than the things
you collect."

"A sense of humor—and good feet."

"A little advance knowledge of the places you'll be visiting. A lot of knowledge would be even better."

"Imagination. If you have imagination, geography comes
alive, history relates itself to today, populations become
people."

And finally the answer which devastated all the others: "Our family."

William Hazlitt, an English critic, once observed, "I should like to spend the whole of my life in traveling . . . if I could anywhere borrow another life to spend afterwards at home."

There is my biography in brief, my dilemma summarized in a sentence. Perhaps I shall never resolve the conflict, and I am not sure I should like to. To seek out that which is strange, or be content with the familiar; to yearn for the unique, or accept satisfaction in the commonplace; to find the rare and the exotic or become accustomed to the easy and the conventional—that is the quandary.

As we return home it seems to me now that I and the others of my family would be content to spend the rest of our lives here. Our dog, our neighbors, even the birds at their bath and feeder in our yard seem glad that we have come. The rooms—some larger, some smaller than we remembered them—are comfortable to us. Even the distinctive smell of the house is good, and makes us welcome.

But I know, too, than when tomorrow comes—or perhaps it will be next week—there will arrive a moment, and in that moment the splash of the fountains in the gardens of the Alhambra in Granada or the sunshine mellowing the ancient walls of the Colosseum in Rome, the medieval canals of Amsterdam and Bruges or the green hay fields and forests of Sweden will flash across my memory. Then I shall want to go again. I shall feel homesick, if that is possible, for a distant corner of the world that has never been my home.

Then the tension will be revived, that healthy, pleasant, exciting tension between "the whole of my life in traveling" and "another life to spend afterwards at home."

It is healthy; it is exciting; because each choice supplements the other. Genuine appreciation of the familiar often makes possible a larger appreciation of that which is strange. We live by two dimensions—depth *and* breadth.

We go so that we may return. And we return so that eventually we may leave again. It is a cycle which makes up for the fact that since we cannot live two lives, cannot "anywhere borrow another life," we must therefore live this one with double vision, double intensity. Perhaps three generations at a time?

So—we are ready for another period at home. But I shall drape the "Bon Voyage" ribbon across my kitchen mirror. And we have never yet at this house filed a map farther away than at arm's reach.

"Now you Can Have a Miracle Garden in One Hundred Days or Less!"

Those were the words that leaped up at me from the smudged paper in the drawer I was cleaning out on our back porch. I picked it up gingerly. Bits of dried earth and water stains attested to its past use.

I took the leaflet to the screen door and gazed from its glowing words to the scrawny plants it supposedly described in my flower bed nearby. The gap between hope and fulfillment, daydream and reality was never wider!

I had first heard about these Rainbow-Hued Cushion Mums on a television program. A man of sincere and open countenance had stood before a row of plants which were so loaded with blooms that stems and even leaves were almost invisible. He floundered for words to describe adequately the various brilliant colors of each cluster of blossoms and then he pointed out that these did not bloom only during one short period, but on and on, and on—till frost. All autumn long the garden of one who planted these chrysanthemums would be an extravaganza of color.

Furthermore, there would be "little or no" work involved in achieving this miracle.

Choice of a proper location ("Chrysanthemum plants prefer all the sun they can get, although they will grow in partial shade"), and correct planting ("12-15 inches apart as the mums will form dense plants like mound-shaped cushions") would assure "a riot of color" and a spectacular effect of continuous blossoming for months.

Who could resist such a possibility?

Certainly not I, especially since I would be away most of the summer and would be unable to make my flower beds a riot of color in any other way. I sat down promptly and ordered a helping of Rainbow-Hued Cushion Mums.

When the package arrived, I felt my first misgivings. It was little more than a paper folder stapled together. Inside were what appeared to be bits of twig with hairlike roots and dried-up beginnings of leaves. The attached folders anticipated my apprehension, however, and reassured me with firm instructions to "divide and plant." It was difficult to divide anything as spindly and solitary as those seedlings, but I tried. In a "sunny location" I laid them gently to rest, and hopefully to root.

We returned from our long summer's absence. I rushed to view the spectacular effect fulfilled by miracle plants. Three puny stems, one struggling to produce a single faded bloom, stood twelve to fifteen inches apart. The intervening gaps looked more like twelve to fifteen feet.

Chrysanthemums, books, boys, whatever—strong roots and successful flowering come by work, not miracle.

On an autumn afternoon I was walking on the bluff in front of our house. The sun was warm and gold, but the shadows were cool and deep and there was no doubt that it was September.

Some little animal, hidden by the undergrowth, broke from his cover in front of me and dashed to another hiding place at a safer distance. A blue jay called its high shrill cry from a towering oak tree above my head.

And I remembered that only a few weeks before, on this same day of the week, I had been at the Salzburg Festival in Austria. Surrounding me and my family were music lovers from all parts of the world who come to this city in the Alps each year to enjoy a feast of concert and opera.

This was the town where Mozart was born and ignored, where much of his genius flowered, and where he was buried in a pauper's grave. Today no man knows just where he was laid away in death. But everyone at this festival in his honor knows where he lives: in the melody and elegance that are the essential spirit of his music.

The opera we attended was written almost two hundred years ago. Mozart was only eighteen years old when he gave it birth. It is light and witty and beautiful, its music at once as limpid and strong as when it was first composed.

The setting for this presentation was appropriate: the "Residenz." This palace was the residence of the former Prince-Archbishops, and it is as elaborate of design and well-proportioned as the word "palace" would suggest, especially the great hall where the opera was performed. The summer evening was cooled by brisk mountain breezes, and stoles, capes, light wraps were welcome. The charming city with its long, often intolerant past, and its hospitable present seemed to guard the Residenz like a jewel in its bosom. The splendor of the music warmed the evening, rose above all the surroundings, and finally became as large and enduring as the pinnacles surrounding Salzburg.

What do an afternoon on the bluff and an evening at the Salzburg Festival have in common? My appreciation of them.

I can imagine many of the beautifully dressed people at the festival scorning the rough woods I like in September. And I suspect that many of those who might share my enthusiasm for the blue jays and the unknown scurrying creatures in the leaves would dismiss Mozart and Salzburg with a shrug of misunderstanding and bewilderment. How much each misses!

How tragic that we limit ourselves to one type or style or kind of pleasure. As we look to each day, rich with variety, we may achieve the only true sophistication, the only genuine affluence: the wholeness of experience.

"Your tickets. You do have your tickets with you?"

Your sons—one now taller than you, one almost as tall— reach again into the inner pockets of their coats, each feeling the edge of the envelope safely lodged there. It is approximately the seventh time you have asked this same question and they have made the same gesture. They nod for the seventh time.

"We still have our tickets," one of them says.

"Your baggage checks. What about your baggage checks?"

They nod again. "They're stapled onto the tickets. We have them."

There is a little pause. The sound of an approaching plane fills the air around you. Your throat tightens.

"Wouldn't you like a magazine? Couldn't I get you something to take on—"

They hold up the papers and magazines you bought only a few minutes ago. But they are not laughing or even smiling at your thoughtlessness. They know it is born of a deeper thoughtfulness, a need to say something, to fill this moment.

The plane you heard approaching is roaring to a standstill. There is a flurry of activity in the waiting room. People come outside and form a casual line. Your two are now part of that line.

"You will call us? Call tonight and tell us how the trip was. Tell us about your rooms for this year and the classes you'll be having—and how the weather is there. . . ."

"We'll call."

The plane has disgorged its incoming passengers. Now it is ready for a fresh lot. The line edges forward.

"It was a good summer. It really was." The boys extend their hands, fearful of a sudden public display of emotion.

"It was a wonderful summer." You do not let your hand cling too long.

They walk to the plane and climb the steps, and although they have to duck at the door, they do not seem very tall to you. Suddenly, in fact, they seem quite small. Smaller, more vulnerable than anyone can realize.

All the little talk that filled the void before they left—you realize how words disguise as well as disclose what you would say.

The plane taxis down the runway, ascends into the sky. Good-by. Good-by. And hurry home.

With mounting stridency we are assured each day of the generation gap and the communication gulf which marks the seal-off between those human beings smart enough to be twenty-one and under and those luckless enough to be thirty and over.

But I have been listening as well as I can and seriously trying to hear what it is the drums (and other noises) are trying to tell those of us who were born in another time and went through our own style of dissent and conformity. I haven't broken the code completely yet, but I believe that we (thirtyish and more) are making both too much and too little of what they (twentyish and less) are trying to say.

Perhaps I should explain that nowhere am I speaking of the LSD-turned-on and the dropped-out. As a matter of fact, I believe that the acid-head and the escapist exemplify just the opposite of what most of the young dissenters of our decade want.

They, I think, are admonishing us and themselves to be more sensitively "turned-on" to all of life: to the ugliness we spawn as well as the beauty we ignore, to the immoralities we practice as well as the pieties we profess, to the fullness of each day rather than the fractions which fragment our hours and lives.

They are seeking ways by which they may honorably and honestly "drop into" a world racked by brutal war, murderous greed, and tyranny wearing a variety of overt and subtle guises.

They are even asking that we, too, drop into this, our own world, more completely. They are shaking us to comprehend that there are other routes than the LSD trip by which we may "drop out," and many of us have followed those routes. They consist of any business, profession, recreation, legislation, or other activity which places things above people, ends above means, success above service.

Man, they would have us realize, is more creator than consumer. He is more intangible spirit than regulated automation. And where we have subordinated the greater to the lesser of these capacities, we have diminished a person, made him mean, weary, suspicious, death-ridden.

Perhaps, then, the gap and gulf about which we hear so much and deplore with such anguish, is not altogether inter-generation communications. It may be intra-generation, too.

Within myself, for instance, can I deny that there is a hostile gulf between the old acquisitive consumer who wants more and more of every *thing* (frequently with less and less satisfaction) and a younger creative self dedicated to understanding torn and wasted humanity everywhere? Within myself can I deny breakdown of communications between the need I see and the deed I do, the hope I cherish and the reality I support?

Beyond the differences in our outer trappings—ages (their freshly minted impatience and my weather-beaten enthusiasm), costumes (their miniskirts and my shirtwaists), dialect (their far-out, way-in jargon and my square antiquated language)—I suspect that the young dissenters are also saying, "Look to this day!"

They mean it, too.

I mean it. And I admire them—when they follow their own advice and look critically, listen sharply, think deeply, feel strongly. If they—if we all—turned on all the creative powers within us and dropped into real awareness of the wonder of our world, why then we should not have time or need to talk so much of gulfs and gaps. We could fulfill a vision.

Mists hang low over lawns and gardens, fields and pastures and watercourses in the early morning and again in the late evenings. The noonday sun burns, but shadows grow chilly. Insects hidden among leaves and limbs of trees and dry grasses cry with shrill insistence. Orange buses, like huge brilliant beetles, crawl along country roads and city streets once more. It's that time of year again. Autumn.

Autumn is thought of as the season of harvests and ripeness. Its atmosphere is that of nostalgia for summer past, preparation for winter to come.

Yet this is a season of fresh beginnings too. For children, the fall of the year, more than spring, marks a turning point in their lives. When they embark on the adventure of kindergarten, first grade, high school, college, exploring the vast kingdom of formal knowledge for the first time or in fresh surroundings, they are at a threshold. For parents, teachers, students—from the most sluggish second-grader to the most dedicated graduate scholar—this is the moment when daily schedules quicken to a new tempo.

There is a different rhythm along city streets. In the emporiums of fashion fresh clothes hang bulky on the racks, welcoming a new cycle of weather. In studios and stations across the country there are schedules of new programs for another television and radio year. Along Broadway there are tremors of anticipation and apprehension, as talent and money in quantity are once more channeled into the small area which dominates so much of our cultural life. Business offices and industry and even Wall Street, being run by mortal men and therefore sensitive to the moods of men, seem aware of a subtly altered world, as another season dominates the calendar.

Why do we sometimes insist on clinging to summer when the riches of autumn open around us? (Why do some of us clutch frantically at adolescence when maturity and middle age bring new rewards we may neglect?) Let the faded swimming suit hang in the closet. Retire the sandals to storage. Put aside the suitcases and travel folders. Summer had its pleasures.

Fall brings its wealth, its own distinctive happiness. It is a time for new beginnings.

ABOUT THE AUTHOR

WILMA DYKEMAN, whose two earlier novels, *The Tall Woman* and *The Far Family*, have been rewarded with critical acclaim and continuing sales, writes a newspaper column for the Knoxville *News-Sentinel*, which served as an inspiration for *Look to This Day*. Hal Borland in the New York *Times Book Review* comments on *The Tall Woman*, "The novel is rich with detail and atmosphere . . . at times the story has the flavor of old ballads. At times it almost sings . . . Wilma Dykeman is thoroughly at home with both her setting and her characters. She has given us a warm, well realized account of a strong woman, of her family and neighbors." And of her second novel, Lillian Smith in the Chicago *Tribune Books Today* has said, "You feel compelled to find out what happens next . . . there are vivid and complex flesh-and-blood characters in a heart-shaking crisis out of which grow plot and story. But it is much more: for this mountain family lives in the nuclear age and knows it; its members participate in varying degrees in the anguish and terror of their changing world . . . Miss Dykeman tells her story well."

Also the author of the earlier nonfiction book, *The French Broad*, a notable volume in the Rivers of America Series, and of *Neither Black Nor White* and *Seeds of Southern Change*, which she wrote with her husband, James R. Stokely, Miss Dykeman has also written *Prophet of Plenty* for the University of Tennessee Press. A native of Asheville, North Carolina, Miss Dykeman is a nationally-known reviewer and lecturer.